Love and the
Fighting Female

Love and the Fighting Female

A Critical Study of Onscreen Depictions

ALLISON P. PALUMBO

McFarland & Company, Inc., Publishers
Jefferson, North Carolina

This book has undergone peer review.

LIBRARY OF CONGRESS CATALOGUING-IN-PUBLICATION DATA

Names: Palumbo, Allison P., 1976– author.
Title: Love and the fighting female : a critical study of onscreen depictions / Allison P. Palumbo.
Description: Jefferson : McFarland & Company, Inc., Publishers, 2020. | Includes bibliographical references and index.
Identifiers: LCCN 2020024289 | ISBN 9781476677392 (paperback : acid free paper) ∞
ISBN 9781476639772 (ebook)
Subjects: LCSH: Women heroes in motion pictures. | Women heroes on television. | Motion pictures—United States—History. | Television programs—United States—History.
Classification: LCC PN1995.9.W6 P35 2020 | DDC 791.43/6522—dc23
LC record available at https://lccn.loc.gov/2020024289

BRITISH LIBRARY CATALOGUING DATA ARE AVAILABLE

**ISBN (print) 978-1-4766-7739-2
ISBN (ebook) 978-1-4766-3977-2**

© 2020 Allison P. Palumbo. All rights reserved

No part of this book may be reproduced or transmitted in any form or by any means, electronic or mechanical, including photocopying or recording, or by any information storage and retrieval system, without permission in writing from the publisher.

Front cover image © 2020 G-Stock Studio/Shutterstock

Printed in the United States of America

*McFarland & Company, Inc., Publishers
Box 611, Jefferson, North Carolina 28640
www.mcfarlandpub.com*

To my partner
Scott Woodham,
for always standing beside me

Acknowledgments

Every project takes a village, from those who offer support and encouragement to those who help whip the lumps out of the ideas, and I have been fortunate enough to have a wonderful village. Special thanks to Susan Bordo for being a phenomenal inspiration, critic, and guide as well as to Virginia Blum for the encouragement and for leading an excellent class that led to the paper that would become THE BOOK. I would also like to thank Roxanne Mountford and Karen Tice for their professionalism, enthusiasm, and input into the process. I will always appreciate my cohort from the University of Kentucky and my friends and colleagues at Big Bend Community College for being my cheerleaders. For sending lifelines across the miles, I thank Heather Chacon, Julie Naviaux, Leah Toth, Andrea Holliger, and Ashley Bourgeois. And I never would have made it without the people who shaped me into the passionate critic and determined humanitarian I am today—Mom, Dad, and Eric. And Jeanne Becker, I can't ever put into words how grateful I am for all you did to help me launch this book and my career. Finally, I would like to thank McFarland for making my dream come true, including Mark Durr, Dré Person, David Alff, Beth Cox, and Kristal Hamby. I am especially grateful for the enthusiastic support of Charlie Perdue.

Table of Contents

Acknowledgments	vi
Introduction	1
ONE. To Love, Honor and Be Oppressed: The Problem Hetero-Romance Poses for Feminism	21
TWO. Mixing Business with Pleasure: Love-Buddy Fighting Females and the Politics of Romance in the Workplace	32
THREE. The Struggling Romaction Genre: Love-Warrior Fighting Females and the Politics of Romance on the Homefront	81
FOUR. What Doesn't Kill Her Makes Her Stronger: The Fighting Female as a Survivor	123
FIVE. Women Leaders and the Men Who Love Them	175
Conclusion	202
Epilogue: Evolving Pleasures	216
Chapter Notes	219
Bibliography	225
Index	233

Introduction

Like many children in the 1970s, I worshipped superheroes. One of my favorite childhood pictures shows me standing next to my older brother as we wear matching Superman Halloween costumes. But the first hero to capture my attention was Wonder Woman. Accessories as weapons, a fun costume, superpowers—what more could a child ask of their favorite hero? First, I had the Underoos, then the makeshift costume—with sweatbands for bracelets and a jump-rope lasso. I wanted to fight for good as Wonder Woman did. I wanted to do things that no other human could do, and because of her, I thought both were possible. As one who was raised as a female, in a time where roles for women on-screen allowed little room for heroism, Wonder Woman provided a unique inspiration for me. The 2017 reboot on the big screen only further reinforced this perception for me as I watched Diana Prince fight once again to save the world while totally owning the DC Comics film world, as Captain Marvel arguably did for the Marvel film franchise only two years later.

The "Strong, Independent Woman" Archetype

More than just an inspiration, characters like Captain Marvel and Wonder Woman are examples of what I will henceforth refer to as the "strong, independent woman" archetype, which is exemplified by an empowered female-identified character whose behavior stands in striking contrast to dominant historical views of women as "the weaker sex," both mentally and physically. That's not to say women have always been presumed to lack any strengths. Maternal instincts, nurturing capacities, domestic abilities, and moral integrity have all been considered important traits in womanhood within the past two centuries. These traits not only set women apart from men but also gave them an important platform for asserting their worth: for education, for political franchise, for economic independence, etc. But physical force and vigor, aggression and the exuberant exercise of power, pleasure in competition and defiance, competent authority, and autonomy have been largely absent from cultural notions of women's "strengths." The archetype of the "strong, independent woman" arises precisely in response to that absence.

Feminist scholars analyzing film as far back as the early 1900s have identified variations of the "strong, independent woman" archetype on-screen. Ben Singer provides a thorough and compelling overview of "serial queens" who fit the strong, independent identity. These early "intrepid young heroine[s]" featured in more than 60 serial melodramas between 1912 and 1920 (91). Maria DiBattista identifies another version in the "fast-talking dames in romantic comedies from the 1930s." Phillipa Gates refers to them as "hard-boiled" and "independent" girl reporters of early female detective films from the same period. Lori Landay's version is the "female trickster," whom she describes as exercising "covert power" during the über-traditional postwar years. Yvonne Tasker's conception of the "'independent heroine' as stereotype" comes the closest to mine; however, her examples are limited to only a few characters from the 1970s, and the stereotype she describes emerges from "stories of women who are independent of men, who are sexually free and who, to an extent, determine their own lives" (18).

Today, there are more examples of the "strong, independent woman" archetype than ever in America, not only as fictional characters but also as real women: women running Fortune 500 companies, acting as whistleblowers and participating in combat, reigning on billboards and primetime, crushing Olympic records and dominating championships, and winning the popular vote for president. In the 2020 election, several women vied for the Democratic Party nomination for president, more than had ever run at the same time. These women are role models whose presence in popular culture makes the concept of empowered women seem like a norm for Americans. They also show us that being tough, autonomous, intelligent, aggressive, and rational no longer means being a man. In fact, those traits don't even mean being masculine, at least not in the sense of being incompatible with or the opposite of feminine. Strength and independence are now part of what many women learn, through mass media, about being a woman, in narrative after narrative.

At least, it's what I learned as I continued to watch strong, independent female characters on screen. I sought them throughout my childhood in my Saturday cartoons, religiously waking myself up at 5:30 in the morning, so I could watch the latest exploits of Jem and She-Ra or the kick-ass Scarlett and Lady Jaye keeping up with the boys on *G.I. Joe*. My favorite game for pretend was to play spy, creating an amalgam of whatever James Bond woman happened to be popular at the time (though Grace Jones was always my favorite)—and Bond, too, because I wanted to run the show. One of my dreams was to be Joan Wilder from *Romancing the Stone* (1984) and *Jewel of the Nile* (1985). She had exciting international exploits, found love, faced death, and used it all as fodder for another best-selling novel. To me, Joan combined the most interesting aspects of some of my favorite stories: heroic adventures, important careers, and romance. For at the same time that I sought stories of kick-ass ladies, I sought stories of love for characters that achieved success in their careers. I watched movies like *When Harry Met Sally* (1989) and *Baby Boom* (1987) over and over. I was devoted to television characters like Laura Holt, Maddie Hayes, and Clair Huxtable: model career women who followed their dreams and their hearts on the burgeoning path to having it all.

By my early twenties, I was still devoted to heroic woman stories, but the love narratives had started to lose some of their appeal. The release of a new Meg Ryan/Tom Hanks vehicle seemed far less interesting to me than the latest installment of the *Alien* movie franchise. Had I lost interest in romance? Far from it. In fact, this was at the time in my life when I was very serious about finding a great love. However, I was also struggling to be my own person, to understand my identity, to follow my own dreams, and to start down my chosen career path. I had plans to travel the world and to attend graduate school. I was coming into—and exercising—my own forms of strength and independence. But I was tired of the one-sided representations of male-identified characters doing this, of feeling that only one version of this kind of empowerment existed. I wanted balance and social justice. I wanted to see more evidence of women on screen doing the same, women making a difference, doing something amazing, and being the heroes of their own lives and stories. Unfortunately, there weren't very many female-bodied characters who did that who also got to find love. In fact, the more romance a woman enjoyed in a narrative, the less strength or independence of any kind she expressed in the story, especially before the last two decades.

An example is *You've Got Mail* (1998), that quaint story about finding romance in unexpected circumstances with an unexpected person, as a fierce business competition leads to love. Meg Ryan's character, Kathleen, starts out as an independent business owner, but by the end of the story, she's lost her business. Furthermore, she loses it to the man she ends up loving! *You've Got Mail* tells us that gaining love is enough for a woman to make up for losing a career, a legacy. How depressing is that trade-off? Trades-offs for women are typical in romance narratives. Another Meg Ryan character, Kate from *French Kiss* (1995), gives up her citizenship, a teaching job, and *all* of her hard-earned savings to a man with questionable ethics and a surly demeanor in exchange for his eventual devotion and life on a vineyard in a country where she doesn't even speak the language. If women on screen aren't giving something up for love, then their obsession with, and neuroses about, love defines them more than their career ambitions, like Bridget Jones, who does have success at work, but it always seems like an accident. Or, the female characters rely on love to save them in some way, as in *Pretty Woman* (1990) or its lesser counterpart *Milk Money* (1994), in which a female prostitute with a heart of gold is rescued from her terrible life by a generous man. (In both movies there is a good dose of *Pygmalion* thrown in, as the woman transforms into a proper leading lady.) Then, of course, there are the numerous films adopting the classic *Taming of the Shrew* storyline, movies in which a woman with a very driven or hard-ass personality is softened just the right amount to be palatable thanks to the love of the right man, as happens in *Ten Things I Hate About You* (1999) and *The Proposal* (2009). Giving up or changing a career to make a relationship work or even for bettering one's self isn't necessarily degrading or sexist. It's the fact that we don't see stories about men doing the same thing amid the repetition of stories about female sacrifice and improvement that is the problem behind these fantasy "choices."

But what about the action and excitement? What about the fantasies in which women characters dare to tread on and undermine the false gender binary demarcating heroism and protection firmly on the male side? It has often seemed that the more explosions, the bigger the fight between good and evil, and the more driven the woman, the more she can take care of herself, the less likely she was to enjoy the fruits of romance. There are plenty of characters I watched growing up who illustrate this. A few of the more iconic ones include Lt. Ripley (Sigourney Weaver) in the *Alien* franchise, Sarah Connor (Linda Hamilton) in the *Terminator* movies (1984 and 1991), Clarice Starling (Jodie Foster) in *Silence of the Lambs* (1991), Thelma and Louise (Geena Davis and Susan Sarandon, respectively), the amazing Alice (Milla Jovovich) in the seemingly endless *Resident Evil* franchise, or all of the female heroes I watched in my early youth, like Wonder Woman (Linda Carter), the Bionic Woman (Lindsay Wagner), and the ever-changing cast of *Charlie's Angels*. Little can detract from the positive impact they had on my own imagination, their feeding of my own rebellious, ambitious, aggressive tendencies—even taking into consideration the sexism that still often lurks behind their portrayals. I appreciated their stories and seeing sisters "doing it for themselves." But while they could take down the bad guys, back then, they never got a good guy (much less the good girl)—not for very long anyway.

As a viewer, I was left torn: I wanted the women to have it all, not to seem to be excluded if they dared to transgress traditional female gender roles, but I found myself presented with heroines who never did, heroines who seemingly had to choose between heroic accomplishment and romance, and who made it more complicated to see these options as possible for other than the male-identified. This representational "either/or" is one more symptom of the so-called war between the sexes that continues to confound feminists about the roles romantic relationships play in our lives and even the idea of romance itself: how are we to be dedicated to empowering ourselves and others but also to find a real romantic connections if that interests us?

In the Introduction of *To Be Real: Telling the Truth and Changing the Face of Feminism*, Rebecca Walker reflects on a similar confusion about being confronted with "contradictions" in her desires, interests, and relationships that she "had no idea how to reconcile" with her attempt to "make sense of how to make feminist revolution" (xxx). Walker's concerns reflect those of many young women from my so-called Generation X who have been grappling with a feminist perspective that has influenced their lives but doesn't always seem to fit their lives, one in which they feel their desires conflict with what they have learned about fighting patriarchy from earlier feminist generations. One of the contradictions Walker describes facing includes feeling that "I would never be able to maintain my independence and artistic strength as a woman" (xxix). She was conflicted by both her "attraction to stable domestic partnership" and her "desire to start a business and pursue traditional, individual power" (xxx).

I bought Walker's book around 1996 when my own journey toward feminism was beginning, and I remember reading her words with a sense of connection and a touch of depression that she didn't have the answers. The more reading I did, the fewer answers I found, whether in the fiction of my favorite authors, like Erica Jong, Zora Neale Hurston, Louise Erdrich, and Colette; in the essays and autobiographies of Anaïs Nin, Alice Walker, and Adrienne Rich; or in the philosophies by people who recognized the problem romance poses in a patriarchal society, like Simone de Beauvoir, John Stuart Mill, or Mary Wollstonecraft. Even Emma Goldman—who so bravely and radically committed herself to political and social change—sought a partner in the cause and in love, even as she very thoroughly rejected institutionalized ideals of marriage and womanhood. Writing over 70 years before Rebecca Walker, Goldman mentions similar fears, only with far more hopelessness. Her extensive writings, both personal and political, reveal her struggle to accommodate her "yearning for a personal life and the need to giving all to my ideal" (Goldman, *Living My Life* 153). She believed that "[w]e all need love and affection and understanding," and she felt "consumed by longing ... for some human being of my own" (Goldman, *Nowhere at Home* 128).

This problem—the reconciliation of feminist goals and activism with romance and its ties to narrow conceptions of womanhood—has been far from solved for feminists growing up in the 21st century, whether on screen or in real life. This problem is at the heart of my own yearnings and my attempts to find assurance and even decent blueprints in the unsatisfactory on-screen fantasies about the strong, independent woman, and it has long raised many questions for me, three of which are central to my investigation: Why, entering the third decade of the 21st century, is it still somewhat rare to find portrayals of a complex, empowered woman in love who doesn't sacrifice her strength and independence to enable a successful romance narrative that doesn't reinforce traditional notions of gender that assert male domination and female subordination? What kind of romance would make this possible, and how would it complicate our understanding of heterosexual norms, gender identities, and women's agency? Would such a romance be considered feminist, or at least feminist-friendly?

Because there has been a lack, though, doesn't mean such portrayals didn't or don't exist. There have been glimpses of alternative romance narratives—not only in niche genres or in programs with small but dedicated followings, but also in Hollywood blockbusters and primetime television—that represent an empowered version of womanhood that still finds room for intimacy, even if it is a struggle. These alternative romance narratives offer sites of potential resistance, transformation, and agency. They show us examples where feminist-friendly heterosexual intimacies are being advanced and even celebrated, where pockets of popular culture are replacing the feminist man-hating stereotype with a feminist man-loving ideal—whether the love is romantic or not—that portrays female relationships with men in ways that avoid or question the old caricatures. My purpose with this study is to pick one such pocket of transformation: the fighting female romance narrative.

The Fighting Female Character

The fighting female character is one version of the "strong, independent woman" archetype. She differs from other versions noted previously, however, because her strength is represented visually as well as internally, exhibited when she uses her body and other weapons in violent combat. Moreover, fighting female narratives rely heavily on her exercising violence to protect herself and others. In other words, she poses a physical threat, maintains elements of self-reliance, and performs in ways most typically reserved for male heroes. Fighting female characters in a variety of genres and types have multiplied on-screen over the last few decades. Yvonne Sims, Stephane Dunn, and Gates characterize the Blaxploitation heroines of the early 1970s as the original fighting females on-screen who "not only paved the way for other action heroines but *redefined* the ways in which women in general were represented in film by portraying a new character that could hold her own among men and women equally" (Sims, emphasis in the original, 26). As these critics argue, the Blaxploitation heroine was a crucial character who created the mold for the "tough action women" of the last 40 years (Gates 220): they were the first American film versions and the first crime-fighting females to be the full-fledged protagonists. Previously, women who killed on-screen were relegated firmly to villain territory, like the unruly *femmes fatales* of film noir and rampaging vixens in Russ Meyer B movies.

Introduction 7

Other contenders for the first fighting females on screen were imports: the iconic Mrs. Emma Peel (from *The Avengers* television show 1961-9 and the Kung Fu movie fighting female characters Golden Swallow (Cheng Pei-pei) from *Come Drink with Me* (1966) and the women of the avenging Wang family in *14 Amazons* (1972).[1]

Other fighting female protagonists include the aforementioned superheroes like Wonder Woman, Captain Marvel, and the increasing number of heroines emerging from *The Avengers* film and TV universe (providing some much-needed companions for the previous token Black Widow character). To name a few: the awesome and brilliant warrior, spy, and genius women of *Black Panther* (2018) and the kick-ass, alien-fighting females in *Guardians of the Galaxy 1* (2014) and *2* (2017); Brunnhilde, the Valkyrie (Tessa Thompson) in *Thor: Ragnarok* (2017) and *Avengers: Endgame* (2019); *Jessica Jones* (2015-19); the brief-lived *Agent Carter* (2015-6), and the multiple dazzling female stars in *Agents of S.H.I.E.L.D.* (2013-present). Even the DC universe is expanding its small screen representation of female superheroes, like *Supergirl* (2015-present); the powered daughters of *Black Lightning* (2018-present); the varied fighting female villains and heroes in *Arrow* (2012-present), *The Flash* (2014-present), and *Legends of Tomorrow* (2016-present).

Beyond that, fighting females have entered just about every genre on film and television. There are babes like the ballerina-cum-spy Dominika Egorova (from *Red Sparrow* 2018), Charlie's Angels, the Bionic Woman, the varied feisty women of James Bond films, and Lorraine Broughton, the Bond-like female super-sexy spy in *Atomic Blonde* (2017); alien fighters like Dana Scully (*The X-Files* TV series 1993-2016 and films) and Cassie Sullivan (Chloë Grace Moretz) from *The 5th Wave* (2016); the titular fledgling assassins *Violet & Daisy* (2013); the demon-slaying high school heroines in *Buffy the Vampire Slayer* (1997-2003) and their British 21st-century counterparts in the short-lived *Crazyhead* (2016). There are the warrior women of the 1980s like *Red Sonja* (1985); the 1990s, like *Xena: Warrior Princess* (1995-2001); and the more recent *Game of Thrones* (2011-19), *Vikings* (2013-present), and *Norsemen* (2016-present). There are the wushu flying female fighters in *Crouching Tiger, Hidden Dragon* (2000) and the Kung Fu masters in *Kill Bill 1* (2003) and *2* (2004). There are military officers like Jordan O'Neil (*G.I. Jane* 1997) and the female Navy crew members in *The Last Ship* (2014-18). Daughters have taken up the fighting of their fathers, as in *Wynonna Earp* (2016-present) and *Van Helsing* (2016-present). There are the domestic violence avengers from *Sleeping with the Enemy* (1991) and *Enough* (2002). And there are sci-fi heroines like the awesome Jedi Rey from the latest additions to the *Star Wars* franchise, Olivia Dunham (*Fringe* 2008-13), Sarah Manning (*Orphan Black* 2013-17), Kiera Cameron (*Continuum* 2012-15). There are even two zombies—one who fights crime (Liv Moore from *iZombie* 2015-19) and one who eats bad men

(Sheila Hammond on *Santa Clarita Diet* 2017–19). Last to mention, but not least, are also the crime-fighting female duos like those featured in *The Heat* (2013), *Spy* (2015), and *Rizzoli and Isles* (2010–16). There are also the varied lead or co-lead female fighters I will address in this book, who range from private detectives like Laura Holt (*Remington Steele* 1982–7) to cops like Cagney and Lacey or Kate Beckett (*Castle* 2009–16) to spies like Sydney Bristow (*Alias* 2001–16) and Evelyn Salt (*Salt* 2010). Finally, there are the dystopian revolutionaries like Katniss Everdeen (*The Hunger Games* franchise) and Tris Prior (*Divergent* franchise).[2]

Fighting Female Romance Narratives— Considering the Audience

In the 1980s and early 1990s, excessively violent fighting females whose characters exhibited the same kind of firepower and "musculinity," to borrow Tasker's description, as male action heroes were generally more controversial for audiences unused to seeing women taking the lead in action. Take the response to *Thelma and Louise* and what some viewers took as a "revenge killing" when Louise shot Thelma's would-be rapist after he had stopped his attempt. Hilary Neroni, briefly summing up the reactions, notes that "[s]uch revenge killing gets little notice when committed by a male character," but Louise's transgression received extreme attention, including in major magazines like *Newsweek* and *Time* (77). Critics referred to the film as everything from "fascist" to "a butt-kicking feminist manifesto" (Levy). Tiina Vares' article on "Action Heroines and Female Viewers" points to a similar discrepancy of views articulated by women she interviews after watching *Thelma and Louise*. Some of the women felt that female violence means women simply "imitate male standards of force" (223) in an anti-feminist way. Others thought that film depicted "a wonderful fantasy" (235) and a liberating version of "real women's violence, not just action violence" (231). In fact, before 1991, there was rarely a fighting female who enacted excessive, explosive action violence who lived to tell about it, much less one who found a potentially egalitarian romance. For the most part, the ones who lived existed in niche film genres like the "final girls" of horror, avenging victims in rape-revenge, and Blaxploitation heroines, or the rare early first leading-lady versions of lone-wolf traditional male movie genres (like the aforementioned Lt. Ripley).

However, by the beginning of the 21st century, the fighting female capable of spectacular violence had gained a firm ground; there were more versions of them than ever before on the big and small screens, and the number only continues to increase. Audiences growing up in the '70s, '80s, and '90s, male and female, have been raised on depictions of women on screen who could more than hold their own and didn't need to be protected, at least no more than a man did. They had the fighting female forerunners mentioned above. Within the first five years of the 21st century, there had even been four blockbuster family films that showcased a professional and heroic fighting female mother, *The Incredibles* (2004)[3] and *Spy Kids* (2001) with its two sequels in 2002 and 2003.

Today, some viewers who seek or expect constructions of female identity that cohere with expectations for a strong, independent woman who can take care of herself and save others have less patience with uncomplicated stereotypical representations of the utterly helpless female, no matter the genre. Philip Green, author of *Cracks in the Pedestal: Ideology and Gender in Hollywood*, argues that there's an "audience of 'new women,' alerted by feminism to the new possibilities of spectatorship," who are comfortable with seeing more women on screen and in leading roles, an audience that tends to reject a more "traditional female protagonist who is passive or hysterical in the face of attack, or who embraces her victimization rather than striking back against it" (158–9). As part of this change in female audiences, I would add that more women find the fighting female exhilarating to watch, that they have come to see the spectacle of action as compatible with female heroics and simply enjoy identifying with female characters who take charge in the kinds of plots that men have dominated for the past few decades. As of 2018, this change in female audiences has been confirmed by a survey Fandango completed that included over 3,000 female moviegoers: "the most popular genre for women was action movies, at 22%. Coming in last was romance/romantic comedies, at 9%" (Wittmer). This survey confirms a similar finding in a smaller study of 1,000 television watchers done by Adobe Digital Insights in 2017 that found that women, moms, in particular, watch crime and action films more than any other genre, including romance: at 40 percent, 36 percent, and 27 percent respectively ("What Are Women's Favorite Movie Genres?").

In addition to the "new women" Green notes, there's an audience of new men who are more comfortable not only with these new fighting female characters but also with the concomitant changes in male characters whom these women love and with whom they live and work. Young men today grew up watching movies starring violent women, with male characters who get saved by women, and with male characters dealing with women who no longer need their protection—who can save themselves. More importantly, they grew up watching what Elizabeth Abele refers to as the "homefront hero," a more sensitive, family-oriented male character in the action film genre, one that values personal relationships and rejects the lone-wolf or the alienated action hero. As she points out, "the last decades of the 20th century saw more and more frequent constructions of a heroic figure equally capable of romance, commitment, and family ties" with actors like Bruce Willis in the *Die Hard* films "bridg[ing] the classical American divisions between the frontier and the hearth, between movie viewing for 'guys' and 'chicks'" (6). Additionally, just as more recent statistics show that many women tend to prefer action genres, they also show that romance is a fairly popular genre for men, romantic comedies, in particular, as we see in a 2018 study from Statista that surveyed 2,200 men and women. Sixty-seven percent of men responded that they are romantic comedy fans, and 55 percent are fans of the romance genre. While this number isn't as high as the 90 percent who favor action or adventure genres, the numbers still reflect a majority of men (Watson).

In other words, a large enough number of contemporary men seem to accept a fighting female protagonist of equal stature in a story with a male protagonist in addition to a plot with as much romance as action. On the one hand, this allowance could be attributed to the "more fluid definition of American heroism and masculinity" that the homefront hero represented and the large number of films portraying love "as the primary value" in films throughout the late 1980s and early 1990s (Abele 55). When romance takes a larger part in the action, it makes sense that the object of affection would as well. On the other hand, the allowance and the emergence of the homefront hero himself could also be a result of the way female characters gained more traction in the action. As Abele also points out, "When women and minorities are portrayed as less dependent on the male protagonist than in previous movies, the duties and the justifications for the white male protagonist must also change" (11). And, as Abele's analysis reveals, these protagonists have changed in ways that make room for others' strength and independence.

No matter which way the influence runs, the fact remains that even back in the 1980s, some men sought examples of female characters who could hold their own in the action. Take, for example, Roger Ebert's point in his review of *Romancing the Stone* from 1984.

> Movies like this have a tendency to turn into a long series of scenes where the man grabs the woman by the hand and leads her away from danger at a desperate run. I always hate scenes like that. Why can't the woman run by herself? Don't they both have a better chance if the guy doesn't have to always be dragging her? What we're really seeing is leftover sexism from the days when women were portrayed as hapless victims. "Romancing the Stone" doesn't have too many scenes like that. It begins by being entirely about the woman, and although Douglas takes charge after they meet, that's basically because he knows the local territory. Their relationship is on an equal footing, and so is their love affair. We get the feeling they really care about each other, and so the romance isn't just a distraction from the action.

Do all audiences respond to the fighting female's appeal? Certainly not—just look at the controversy caused by Charlize Theron's character in *Mad Max: Fury Road* (2015). As one disappointed, anti-feminist viewer notes,

"Fury Road was not going to be a movie made for men. It was going to be a feminist piece of propaganda posing as a guy flick" (Clarey). Plenty of viewers agree with the comments Mr. Clarey makes in his blog. But judging by the number of articles written for websites like *The New York Post*, *The Guardian*, *Salon*, and *Slate* that praised the feminist impulses of the *Fury Road* (in spite of problematic aspects) because of Theron's character and the fact that the film earned over $300 million in its four months, there are plenty of viewers who were happy to see a woman take charge in the über-masculine franchise film. Do all audiences respond positively to non-normative depictions of gender in romance narratives? Again, the answer is no: even outside of the action genre, there are plenty of plots involving hetero-intimacy that still incline toward traditionally conservative depictions of love and romance and that maintain gender divides and power imbalances, proving that gender conformity remains the dominant cultural narrative. My point is that it's not the only narrative and that gender-flexible portrayals of both heroism and intimacy between men and women are gaining more influence that should be recognized.

The increase in the number of kick-ass women on-screen, particularly in the last thirty years, has occurred in part because they so fully embody an empowered-woman identity—a woman who can take care of herself (or at least can appear to), who can be independent and forceful in pursuing her goals, and who can still be the hero. Such an empowered woman appeals for various reasons, depending on the audience. For some who might find the character troubling or threatening to their ideals of or expectations about proper femininity, the appeal might be in clues that she's not so independent or capable, as those viewers look for ways the narrative punishes her for her strength and independence or attenuates those characteristics. For others, it might be the titillation of the fighting female, who is often still scantily clad and whose (typically) lithe fighting form is enhanced by the spectacle of combat. Objectification is still a pervasive problem for women on screen in any genre and continues to undermine even the most feminist-friendly female characters. For others still, the appeal might lie in seeing a woman do for herself what male characters have always done—be a protector, seek justice, or maybe just beat the crap out of bad people—instead of being forced to watch on the sidelines or, as is often the case, be excluded completely. This latter view is more feminist-friendly and reflects the assumption that critics like Martha McCaughey and Neale King and Charlene Tung share: fighting females can be empowering and function as "possible tools in the liberation of women" (McCaughey and King 20) as well as "offer the possibility of an alternative embodiment for women" that can "embolden" them (Tung 96–7). This is all accomplished through the power of fantasy.

Fighting Female Romance Narratives— Considering the Critics

This symbolic position reflecting potential empowerment makes the fighting female character a useful lens through which to view the relationship between romance and power and to understand the way narratives and norms revolving around hetero-intimacy both reflect and contribute to broader assumptions about that relationship. Until now, there have been few in-depth feminist analyses of the relationships depicted in these narratives, and there have been none that attempt to explore cultural perceptions of heterosexual-intimacy through these characters, as I shall do in this study. Feminist critics who focus on various fighting females—like Jeffrey A. Brown, Philippa Gates, Sherrie A. Inness, Hilary Neroni, Rikki Schubart, and Yvonne Tasker—have done exceptional work concentrating on the fighting character's function as variants of the strong, independent woman archetype, exploring specifically the parameters of her self-determination, self-reliance, and all-around autonomy in relation to her gender. Their work helped prove that fighting females have important cultural significance and play out the confusions, rationalizations, exclusions or contradictions about what such a strong woman in a culture that continues to struggle with, much less make room for, women's rights. They have addressed both the problematic and transgressive gender dynamics orienting around fighting females, yet when they refer to her relationships with men, any romantic aspects of the narrative tend to fall almost entirely on the problematic side. Perhaps such critics have tended to favor interrogations of the former elements over the latter because they defy typical representations of females and femininity and do not intuitively connect with the interdependent and attachment-oriented traits of intimacy, for as Brown claims, "The dynamics of working with others is more complicated for action heroines than it is for their iconic male counterparts" (54). These critics have done this for laudable reasons, and I do not mean to criticize their work or even their exclusion of the romance. In many cases, the problems they note do still exist when a male partner—romantic or not—enters the picture: the fighting female is reduced to a token exception, or she is overly sexualized, or her strength is underemphasized or lessened, or she still needs to be saved by the man, or the man is reduced to a feminine stereotype, or the relationship seems tacked on, a cheap trick or an easy resolution.

Thirty-odd years ago, when feminist critics started analyzing varied kick-ass women on the screen, to speak of the romance-only elements as I do was irrelevant to their projects because there were very few even remotely progressive representations. When these critics did begin analyzing the relationships, they made some useful observations about the gender politics behind limitations that often occur for fighting females because of their relationships with men. Now that there has been such an extensive inclusion of various forms of violent women on-screen, and such thorough work on the characters themselves, there is room to consider evidence of potentially feminist-friendly love fantasies offered by some fighting female character's relationships with men, which imagine independence and romance or intimacy not in conflict but in concert.

The representational partnership between independence and intimacy is not without its tensions. Still, interrogating these fantasies as old stories of love portrayed in new settings with new character types offers insight into the way the romantic genre has been appropriated in service of proving a liberated vision of female empowerment and the way old conventions and expectations appropriate those visions. Examining several different versions—from "buddy" partnerships to successful sexual/marital unions to "fraught" relationships—will show how the fighting female romance genre is "a site of simultaneous complicity in and resistance to patriarchal structures" (Jowett 30).[4] As such, these narratives, fantastical as some of them are, "offer a recognition of how women negotiate the problems of romance in a postfeminist era" (30). Both Lorna Jowett and I use the term "postfeminist" not as a theoretical identifier or standpoint but as a historical marker to reflect society following the 1960s and 1970s when varied feminisms—and feminist issues/activism—were introduced to the public on a large scale.[5] In this budding postfeminist era, challenges to gender roles and the acknowledgment of the personal as political have had lasting—and often highly contradictory—impacts on both female and male identity, on hetero-relations, and on the way these are portrayed in the popular media (Jowett 30). This is the standpoint for the analysis of fighting females' hetero-romances and intimacies in this study, which will address the way combining intimacy and independence in fighting females' on-screen lives increases the level of viewing pleasure and in the past decade has led to female characters who portray the kind of human complexity and depth that many feminist media critics have been demanding since the 1970s.

Defining Feminist-Friendly Love

Before I move onto my discussion of the cultural importance of fighting female fantasies and their stories involving hetero-relations, I need to define some important terms that occur throughout this project. The term "romance" refers to the story of love—its development or the related courtship and sex relations. "Intimacy" regards the nature of the knowledge and private actions between individuals, which may not necessarily be romantic; thus, it applies to a wider range of relationships. The term "feminist-friendly" characterizes the kind of content that might appeal to feminist-identified viewers or to feminist-influenced viewers who may not openly identify as feminist (most often because of confusion about the term's connotations) but who do promote and support goals for equality and even some explicit feminist agendas. "Feminist-friendly" refers to what some might call "progressive" aspects of an on-screen female's characterization that defy both stereotypes that limit women's identities and caricatures that degrade femininity. It's a diffuse notion because feminist influence on the media is tricky and diffuse and can be applied without intention and instead as a reflection of feminist influences on society over time. That's why I am not calling these fantasies necessarily feminist, but they aren't necessarily anti-feminist, either.

In short, "feminist-friendly" media attempts to advance women's agency or highlights women's issues and/or the viewpoints that have long been sidelined, which is in keeping with some broad-ranging feminist goals. Some aspects emphasize women's capability as equal to that of men; some problematize traditional gender roles by blending masculinity and femininity in male and female characters, by showing women in positions of power, leadership, or equal partnership with men. Some argue against sexist comments/characters/plot, either implicitly or explicitly. Some seek greater representation of and respect for women's diversity, not just in gender but also in race, sexuality, sexual orientation, ability, age, ethnicity, and other forms of historically marginalized identities. In other words, feminist-friendly media projects a fairly expansive notion of what it means to be an empowered woman in American society, at least in terms of recognizing there are many ways the media can express feminist-related principles.

The "love" part of "feminist-friendly love" refers to portrayals of romance and/or intimacy in keeping with progressive feminist assumptions—meaning it's a relationship that emphasizes equality as integral to the intimacy and fosters trust and support between the individuals. In other words, "feminist-friendly love" is a liberating love that empowers women. It rejects portrayals of gender roles that maintain masculine or male superiority or that limit either of the partners to static personalities or characteristics based on sex difference. Feminist-friendly love allows for both partners to enter the relationship freely and to be desiring subjects while enjoying the pleasures of being an object of affection. It also allows both partners to express and explore their identities, to be successful in multiple roles, or at least not to be limited in emotional or intellectual ways (even if they might be limited in physical/material ways, including economically). Feminist-friendly love can take the form of a romance-based relationship, a friendship-based intimacy, or both. Ultimately, it's a love wherein the strong, independent woman can trust she will be able to retain her identity as such.

Granted, the versions of empowered women in this study will not fit every version of feminism that exists, and this study is not unified with any specific feminist wave or type of feminism. That being said, the majority of the fighting females in this analysis are white and easily identifiable as middle class and heterosexual—for reasons that will soon become clear— and they reflect privileges that shape both the opportunities and experiences they have. This is because I want to understand why, beginning in the 1980s, there was an increase in fighting female romance narratives that has continued steadily since then, how those narratives contribute to and reflect new norms for female-identified behavior and identity, and what those norms imply about American culture's affirmation of the "strong, independent woman" ideal. I focus on fighting female narratives where the character is a lead or co-lead only—not a supporting sidekick to a leading man but a character with development and equal billing—roles in which she is not a villain or criminal. Obviously, there must also be a romance present at some point in her story.

My focus also primarily includes characters who live in a more "realistic" world that is relevant to the type of romance fantasies they portray, ones in which there aren't superheroes or people with magical powers who exist in worlds with possibilities and conflicts that are far removed from everyday reality. (There are a couple of notable deviations I'll address in Chapters Four and Five). After all, a romance that takes place on a spaceship or that includes an indestructible woman may be an exciting and inspiring story, but it's a fantasy that no woman can ever attain, and that alters the impact of the dynamics of the relationship and the woman's role within it. The field is further reduced by the numbers of fighting female narratives with romance in more popular, mainstream narratives from film and television that have larger audience bases, which I use here to stress both the broadening appeal of the strong, independent woman ideal (important for assuring a fantasy's cultural impact) and also to support my argument about the way certain feminist-friendly conceptions of womanhood and hetero-relations have begun to inform stories even in one of the most conservative-leaning arenas, the action genre.

There are few options of fighting female narratives on screen within these parameters that feature much diversity—when one considers age, ability, race, ethnicity, sexuality or sexual orientation. These exclusions certainly reduce the feminist populations the characters in this analysis inhabit or reflect, and these limitations increase the potential for claims that this study advances a heteronormative perspective. I know very well, as one who is neither heterosexual nor cisgender, the frustrations caused by watching the mass media's skewed vision of the world through a heterosexual filter and being expected to make sense of my own experiences, desires, and thoughts in spite of this.[6] The white and primarily heterosexual identity of the fighting females that determine this new norm plays an important role specifically because of the historical and cultural role white women have been expected to play in a white-male-dominated patriarchy. In other words, the narratives offer a character whose race specifically invokes sexist outdated and/or degraded notions of fragile, passive femininity undergirding common white-woman stereotypes in violent narratives: the damsel in distress or, rather, the object-to-be-protected-or-avenged by a man.

Yet, the complications, repercussions, and limitations that emerge from accepting the idea of a war between the sexes that is central to heterosexual dynamics—which I will address through my case studies—apply to any woman who has a relationship with a man, including women who aren't white, middle-class, or heterosexual. The power imbalances engendered through a hierarchical hetero-divide is one reason many women who were abolitionists in the 1800s, racial uplift advocates in the late 1800s and early 1900s, and civil rights or socialist activists of the mid–20th century splintered from the male-dominated groups that excluded or degraded them, either through hostile or benevolent sexism. Based upon this fact, I believe we benefit from taking opportunities to see ourselves seeing through any filter, even the dominant filter of heteronormative relationships, and doing the consciousness-raising work that such opportunities offer, as part of our necessary project to dissolve this filter. Working within these exclusions, I plan to render visible the principle mechanisms of white, cis-gendered heterosexuality and their deep ties to women's subordination—and to use them to critique regressive, traditional representations of heterosexual romances and intimacies that marginalize or counteract women's agency and varied needs and identities. Furthermore, interrogating these attempts at empowering hetero-romance fantasies does not challenge compulsory heterosexuality, but it will make it possible to complicate the idea of a heteronorm and show that there is not a single, dominant, one-size-hetero-romance-fits-all ideal and that some versions of this "norm" are more inclusive and progressive than others in ways that encourage more diversity.

Through my analysis, I hope to provide a starting point for further exploration that contributes to what bell hooks calls "a new ideological meeting ground for the sexes, a space for criticism, struggle, and transformation" and that shows readers there are already places within the overdetermined spaces of the mass media that are reframing relationships in ways that fit the kinds of feminist movement hooks envisions—relationships in which "the alienation, competition, and dehumanization that characterizes human interaction can be replaced with feelings of intimacy, mutuality, and camaraderie" (35). Ultimately, my goal is to argue that some fighting female relationship narratives merit our attention because they reveal a new cache of plausible empowered female identities that women negotiate *through* their intimacies and romances with men—however currently limiting they are. These negotiations, in turn, enable innovative representations of male-female relationships that challenge long-standing cultural scripts about the nature of dominance and subordination in such relationships. Combining cultural analysis with close readings of key popular American film and television texts since the 1980s, my study asserts that certain fighting female relationship themes question regressive conventions in male-female intimacies and reveal potentially progressive ideologies regarding women's agency in mass culture. In essence, certain fighting female relationship narratives project feminist-friendly love fantasies that reassure audiences of the appeal of certain forms of empowered women while also imagining egalitarian intimacies that might further empower women.

Chapter Overview

Chapter One explores the difficulties heterosexual love poses for feminist goals because of its relationship to women's oppression. Because the fighting female characters in this analysis exemplify one version of a "strong, independent woman" archetype, they combine to offer a useful lens through which to interrogate the problems that romance poses for the feminist critic in terms of representing female empowerment. The central problem is that mass media often employ romance and hetero-relations to undercut signs of female strength or independence and excuse any sign of gender transgression. As a response, feminist media critics have tended to be skeptical of fighting females who are partners or who function under male mentorship. They are also inclined to privilege narratives of lone-wolf heroines and eschew romance-based storylines. This chapter will contextualize this tendency in terms of feminist (or proto-feminist) thought ranging from Mary Wollstonecraft to Wendy Langford on the thorny relationship between love, romance, and women's liberation.

Each remaining chapter focuses on one rendering of a fighting female identity that aligns with the strong, independent woman archetype where the character navigates and negotiates her empowerment through her intimacies and romances with a man or men. Chapters Two and Three examine two distinct fantasies where the fighting female unites with a male co-lead as a partner in romance and combat:

Chapter Two highlights television shows like *Remington Steele, Moonlighting* (1985-9), *Bones* (2005-12), *Castle,* and *Chuck* (2007-12), all of which combine a crime-fighting business partnership with an intimate relationship in ways that assign the fighting female a co-protector "love-buddy" identity. This identity assumes that her empowered role as a liberated career woman makes her an ideal partner for men and attempts to conjure a feminist-friendly love fantasy that constructs an egalitarian workplace meant to foster cooperative hetero-relationships.

Chapter Three continues to concentrate on the hetero-partner-couple in the struggling Romaction film subgenre, which combines a romantic comedy narrative with an action plot. Romaction fighting female narratives like *Mr. and Mrs. Smith* (2005), *Date Night* (2010), *Killers* (2010), and *Knight & Day* (2010) attempt to critique regressive domestic gender roles and portray a feminist-friendly love fantasy of egalitarian romance by partnering the couple to fight threats to their home and family life. These movies rely heavily on assertions that women are empowered by male domesticity and nurturing even as they endeavor to construct an empowered identity for the female as a "love-warrior" character.

Chapter Four moves beyond the love-buddy and love-warrior pairing to tackle the fighting female in film and television productions where she is the primary hero and not a co-lead, including television and film texts like *Cagney & Lacey* (1981–88), *Prime Suspect* (1991–2006 and 2011), *The Closer* (2005–12), *Alias, Murder by Numbers* (2002), *The Girl with the Dragon Tattoo* (2009 Swedish and 2011 American release), the four versions of the Nikita story, and *Salt,* among others. In these narratives, battling male domination—portrayed through sexism, gender-based violence, or paternalism—empowers the fighting female as a "survivor." Because this character's relations with men often force her to negotiate a position as both a victim and an agent, the stories project conflicting messages about the possibility of feminist-friendly love for the empowered heterosexual woman.

This study concludes with Chapter Five, which revisits texts like *Prime Suspect* and *The Closer,* discussed in earlier chapters, and includes newer texts like the *Divergent* and *The Hunger Games* film franchises, as well as the films *Snow White and the Huntsman* (2012), *Maleficent* (2014), *Alice in Wonderland* (2010) and its 2016 sequel, *Alice Through the Looking Glass.* This analysis will demonstrate how fighting female fantasies are key to an evolving mass-media representation, not only of the feminist-friendly female but also of male identities that depend on and reinforce the empowered woman ideal and alternative narratives of hetero-relations. The chapter concludes by exploring ways that an empowering male character who is both supportive of and subordinate to a female hero character functions in narratives that construct a fighting female as leader identity.

While these narratives' progressive female identities and resistant hetero-relationships foster female empowerment, they cannot always resist the persistent and problematic framing of male-female relationships as an inevitable source of antagonisms at best or a continuing battle of the sexes at worst, conflicts in which women remain on the losing side. The fighting females discussed throughout this study are not uncontestable role models, but those don't exist in life or on-screen. Their romances can also be challenging, just like love today can be challenging for anyone, heterosexual or not. But now, there are many more narratives of love to consider. As Renata Grossi observes, "[R]omantic love can be understood in myriad ways. Love can be both liberating and progressive. On the other hand, it can be oppressive." There are clear ties to oppression, at worst, or something to question or critique, at best, in each fighting female romance narrative I address. Beyond the previous limitations I've mentioned, these females do exist predominantly in fantasy worlds where almost all of the women are young and conventionally attractive and many of the men are enlightened (or at least teachable). These are also worlds where heterosexuality and monogamy are the uncontested choices for romance, where the pairing of a woman and man on-screen almost always leads to inevitable union.

The stories tread a narrow path being affiliated with romance, one that overlooks a lot of potential pitfalls. Still, as Jowett notes, "while compulsory heterosexuality is a way of maintaining control over women, and the myths of romance make this palatable, this does not necessarily negate the desire for a(n equal) sexual and companionate relationship" and the pleasures in seeing examples of these relationships (35). In interesting and recognizable ways, all of these fighting female fantasies indicate ambivalence about egalitarian hetero-relationships and reveal the lingering problems patriarchal social and political structures pose for fostering male/female parity. In the end, fighting female narratives afford contradictory viewing pleasures that reveal both new expectations for and remaining anxieties about the "strong, independent woman" ideal that have emerged in American popular culture postfeminism.

ONE

To Love, Honor and Be Oppressed

The Problem Hetero-Romance Poses for Feminism

In 2015, Michelle Obama spoke on a panel at *Glamour* magazine's "The Power of an Educated Girl" event. One line of Obama's remarks was picked up by a variety of outlets reporting on the event. Obama encouraged girls to "Compete with the boys. Beat the boys," and she stated, "There is no boy, at this age, that is cute enough or interesting enough to stop you from getting your education. If I had worried about who liked me and who thought I was cute when I was your age, I wouldn't be married to the president of the United States." One report on Amy Poehler's *Smart Girls* website had the headline, "Michelle Obama Says Books Are Better Than Boys" (McKenzie). MSN.com posted a video of Obama speaking with the headline "Michelle Obama: Books Before Boys, Girls," and *New York Magazine* posted a similar headline stating, "Michelle Obama urges girls to forget boys and focus on education" (Roy). In reality, Obama never says to "forget boys." Rather, she advises that an interest in romance with boys should not interfere with girls' intellectual development. Her point is laudable, and it's important to encourage young women to be their best and not feel forced to focus on romance at a young age. There is no doubt a problem with young girls denying their academic abilities, especially as they enter their teen years, and there is a problem with girl culture that makes boys seem more important than education and career goals.

Nevertheless, there are some unfortunate assumptions behind Obama's statement: first, that homosexual romance for girls doesn't pose the same problems as heterosexual romance; second, that girls should seek an education to attract the right kind of man and marry up, which implies that, ultimately, her relationship status rather than her career remains the primary (or at least preferred) indicator of female success. Finally, her statement implies an opposition between heterosexual relationships and success for women. This opposition lies at the heart of the divide between the strong, independent woman and romance that we so often see in popular culture.

This opposition mirrors and emerges from the deeply embedded tensions between autonomy and heterosexual love in American women's lives. The very nature of the ideals of romance and intimacy with men has been problematic for centuries of women seeking self-determination and/or liberation, as Wendy Langford reminds us in *Revolutions of the Heart*. She provides a compelling overview of key feminist arguments detailing the ways that romantic love, marital unions, or heterosexuality have been used to create and maintain structural inequality between men and women.[1] Additionally, Langford argues that the idea of love hurts more than it helps, and for her, there is little possibility for a liberating love. In explaining *Why Love Hurts*, sociologist Eva Illouz has also noted that "romantic pain" (3) and "the failures of our private lives [...] are shaped by institutional arrangements" that organize "our emotional life" (4). Because of this, love plays out in a "marketplace of unequal competing actors" where "some people command greater capacity to define the terms in which they are loved than others" (6). Additionally, Illouz notes how feminists have routinely questioned the "popular mythology" that love conquers all and see it rather as a rift between women and men and an obstacle to women's liberation (4–5).

Love and/or romance as a basis for women's subordination has been critiqued by many of the most well-known proto-feminist thinkers and feminist theorists. Over two hundred years ago, Mary Wollstonecraft noted that both women's misconceptions about love, cultivated by a society that refused to recognize their rationality, and men's insistence on relating to women as objects subjected women to the curse of frivolity and prevented them from meeting their potential. In the early twentieth century, Emma Goldman wrote an essay about "marriage and love" that argued the liberating potential of love was not possible because society uses love to hide the social and economic function of marriage. Mid-twentieth century, Simone de Beauvoir interpreted a woman's devotion to ideas of love and romance—again, encouraged by men who would "lead her into temptation"—as proof of "bad faith" or a form of false consciousness that confines a woman to a limited feminine life and prevents her from "taking charge of her own existence" and overcoming her oppression (721). More radical feminists emerging in the 1960s and 1970s, like Shulamith Firestone, characterized love as "the pivot of women's oppression" (121) and claimed that romance is one of several "artificial institutions" that serves "male supremacy" (139). Germaine Greer makes a similar claim about romantic fiction in her chapter titled "Romance" from *The Female Eunuch*. In a succinct overview of how critics like these "were unambiguously critical of romantic love," Stevi Jackson explains:

It was the bait in the marriage trap; it served to justify our subordination to men and rendered us complicit in that subordination; it involved an unequal emotional exchange in which women gave more than they received; its exclusivity was taken as indicative of the emotional impoverishment in our lives; it diverted women's energies from more worthwhile pursuits [114].

The work of these critics and other feminist thinkers from the 1960s to the early 1980s—figures like Andrea Dworkin, Mary Daly, Kate Millett, Adrienne Rich, and Gayle Rubin—addresses institutions surrounding ideals of love, romance, and intimacy and has influenced the way Americans understand love, not only in relation feminism but also in relation to female empowerment in general. They spawned important academic debates about compulsory heterosexuality and heteronormativity and the sex/gender divide. They also contributed to the debates about feminism and intimacy of other feminist critics, discussions that the mass media have taken up. Examples are Arlie Hochschild's ideas on the working woman's "second shift,"[2] the concept of the "mommy wars,"[3] and Anthony Giddens' ideas on the "democratization of intimacy,"[4] to name a few that are particularly relevant to ideas about contemporary love postfeminism.

Most of these critics and feminists, and those who have continued to follow their critical paths, have not argued that feminism is against or incompatible with love; they rightly sought to show that our ideas about love itself are cultural constructs that have taken many restrictive forms for women. In other words, their aim was to show that "love is not itself necessarily oppressive, but it becomes so because of the social context in which it is constructed" (Grossi). The primary source of reluctance to address the feminist potential or value in representing empowered females in love is the notion that women need to extract themselves from the heteronormative circle of male influence/patriarchy that is now more clearly understood to circumscribe female existence. In a culture where women are only relatively recently being imagined on a large scale to possess more than a wholly passive, weak, emotional, or nurturing personality, there's been an understandable rationale behind feminist media criticism that seeks alternative images outside of romance. For in pop culture depictions of women, as Jennifer K. Stuller points out,

love has often been the motivating impetus for women. And it is perhaps because of this that female heroes are often shown in tandem, either as a team or as the sidekick to the professionally superior male [...]. This could easily be interpreted as a way of containing women's power by only depicting them in more traditional roles [...]. It could also be suggested that a solo woman warrior is still too outrageous to be taken seriously and therefore requires assistance in her heroic adventures [8].

Based on this logic, seeking a lone-wolf heroine as a more ideal candidate to represent a feminist-friendly character makes sense. The goal of many feminist media and culture critics is to find role models of women—whether real or imagined—who defy negative assumptions, who are self-sufficient, strong and capable, aggressive, rational, power-seeking, and successful—as well as to unveil the heteronormative assumptions behind continually positioning women in relation to men. Such alternatives are absolutely necessary to bring women's issues and experiences into the cultural narrative, to recognize women as subjects and citizens—or, as the feminist adage states, to accept the radical notion that women are people, too. Such role models have been part of the important goal to change the way women are subject to oppressive and restrictive assumptions, policies, and practices.

Desperately Seeking New Stories

In 2015, the "Bechdel Test"—also known as the Bechdel-Wallace Test (Garber) from Alison Bechdel's comic strip *Dykes to Watch Out For*—celebrated its 30th birthday. From its inception in 1985, this test immediately gained favor in feminist media criticism, and its assumptions still resonate for many contemporary critics analyzing women in popular film. There is a website, *Bechdeltest.com*, dedicated to maintaining an up-to-date database rating whether a movie fits the criteria. Numerous media websites mention it, including a Tumblr blog titled "Does This Pass the Bechdel Test?" and the websites *TV Tropes, Film School Rejects,* and *Feminist Frequency*. The test has even been referenced by characters in the film *Seven Psychopaths* ("Useful Notes"). Reflecting the test's global impact, in November 2013, several theaters in Sweden began to include ratings that indicate how well a film meets the Bechdel Test criteria, sparking new interest in and debates about the media test. By 2016, the practice had expanded to 30 theaters around the country. Theaters run a brief trailer before the film that explains its rating. In 2013, 30 percent of Swedish films passed, a number that doubled to 60 percent by 2015 (Kang).

The "Bechdel Test" helps characterize what many believe is required of on-screen characters to represent feminist-friendly models: a television show or movie must have at least two female characters who talk to each other about something other than men. The assumption is that this requires new stories of female experience and provides stronger proof of women's empowerment. Contributors to *The Washington Post, The Guardian,* NPR, and *The Huffington Post* regularly refer to the test in commentary when discussing popular media, including new film releases like *Solo: A Star Wars Story* and *Deadpool 2* (which fail the test) and television series like *Orange Is the New Black* (which passes with flying colors).

Essentially, the premise behind this "test" is that women are not merely underrepresented in media (hence the criteria for at least two women)—a fact that has been documented recently by several media research groups (Siede)—but that their representation tends to be anchored to a male's presence and that they are represented as having no lives or interests outside of their relationship with the male (hence the criteria for the women to talk to each other about other aspects of their lives). This model rejects representations of male domination and privileges representations of female community over heterosexual relations or romance because of the way the latter has been overly represented by popular media and because it often seems incompatible with enlightened thinking about sex and gender equality.

The importance of female community to feminist thought stems from the idea that patriarchy discourages female bonding that would encourage women to recognize their shared subordination and unite to fight against it (Langford *Revolutions* 6).[5] Additionally, patriarchy excludes queer and/or non-cis-gendered women and denies the validity of non-heterosexual orientations. The idea of female community, whether for heterosexual or queer women, also offers an ideal egalitarian intimacy that doesn't have to negotiate the dominant/subordinate sex divide that affects representations of hetero-intimacies. Inness provides a useful example of this assumption about the power of female bonding for media analysis when she distinguishes between homosocial and heterosexual intimacies in her analysis of Xena from *Xena: Princess Warrior* as an exceptionally tough woman character. Though Inness doesn't refer specifically to Bechdel's test or to specific theories about feminist female bonding, she points out how Xena's close friendship with Gabrielle doesn't "detract from her tough image" because "toughness in women does not have to be antithetical to friendship. The result is a new vision of the tough woman hero that emphasizes both her physical toughness and her connection to other women" (*Tough* 168).

Quite a few feminist media analyses assert that progressive love/intimacy can really only be shown within female homosocial/homosexual relations because it's assumed that when a man becomes involved, as Inness points out in her analysis on tough women in popular culture, "heterosexual desirability in a woman often signifies submissiveness to a dominant man" (Inness *Tough* 43). Emphasizing even the strongest women's heterosexuality, from Inness's perspective, renders them "sexual objects" reined in by the male gaze (69); is used "to reduce her toughness and broaden her appeal" (48); indicates "that they are still at the beck and call of a man to whom they are sexually attracted" (82); and keeps the female's narrative constrained within the realm of "traditional women's concerns" (125) or "primarily feminine issues, such as heterosexual romance" (152). Granted, there are those who question the basic tenets of the original Bechdel Test (usually offering ways to improve the test that will maintain its original spirit). Aymar Jean Christian points out, "the test really only measures one thing. It gauges male dominance not necessarily female empowerment." Blogger Anna Waletzko notes the test "does not measure the artistry or gender equality within a film, but rather represents a superficial measure of the value of a film. The measures used to gauge gender equality with the Bechdel Test are too two-dimensional to accurately measure the message of female empowerment in movies."

Moreover, the test doesn't take into consideration power dynamics between women based on ethnic, racial, economic, or sexual orientation, though there are new versions of the test that are specifically aimed toward racial diversity, like the Chavez Perez Test, which determines whether two characters from a historically marginalized race and/or ethnicity in a movie speak about something other than crime. Also, relevant to my work, the test partakes in the assumption that heterosexual romance or intimacy automatically alienates viewers looking for empowered women because romance, as we have seen, doesn't fit well in stories of female success or power.

Overall, however, there remains some critical consensus today with the assumptions Inness voiced almost twenty years ago about heterosexuality downgrading strong women characters' feminist-friendly appeal. In 2004, describing Laura Holt (Stephanie Zimbalist) from *Remington Steele*, Linda Mizejewski argues that Laura's potential was "tempered by her position within the classic screwball courting couple." Despite Mizejewski's concession that "Laura Holt proved that the game of the detective genre can be played with a ready-for-primetime woman investigator who is smart, attractive, heterosexual—and not glamorized," Mizejewski ultimately sees the romance as a mitigating factor rather than an aspect of the series to be viewed with feminist implications (*Hardboiled* 77). Additionally, although she sees feminist implications in *Moonlighting*, what troubles Mizejewski is that the position of Maddie Hayes (Cybill Shepherd) as a female investigator was not interrogated in the way her relationship with David was. The "imposition of a romantic subplot" and the "heterosexual partnership" are, for her, attempts to settle the "problem" the female detective presents as a woman in a man's role ("Picturing the Female Dick" 6–7). That's why, for Mizejewski, a show like *Cagney & Lacey*, with a female partnership at the forefront, one often lauded by feminist media critics, is not necessarily better but certainly a stronger reflection of feminist viewing interests; it "evoked the very anxiety that screwball quells—the question of loyalty to men," the screwballs, in this case, being *Remington Steele* and *Moonlighting* (*Hardboiled* 80). So, love assures the audience of a woman's desirability—an important marker for women—and hence lessens the threat of her supposed masculinity and other gender role reversals.

Both Lisa M. Dresner and Hilary Neroni make similar assertions in 2007 and 2005, respectively. Dresner identifies ways that a female investigator's abilities are "bracketed" by the inclusion of male partners whose presence implies her incompetence (68). Neroni, one of a few critics to advance a chapter-long interrogation into a female hero's hetero-intimacies rather than avoid such texts in favor of single female hero plots, still ultimately sees the use of romance as a way to attenuate the "trauma" the violent woman on-screen presents in terms of her threat to established gendered behaviors. Gates' 2011 book *Detecting Women* likewise addresses how "[t]he 'problem' of the female detective is more often worked out along the lines of, borrowing Andrea Walsh's term, the 'femininity-achievement conflict'" (139). In other words, the female detective's 'feminine' success is determined through her ability to acquire a proposal of marriage, while her 'masculine' success is determined by her ability to discover 'whodunit'" (33). Gates excuses the marriage resolution that tended to wrap up the plots of the feminist-friendly female detective films she analyzes from the 1930s by explaining that they are just "tacked-on" (132). However, she is less willing to overlook the way female detectives who followed Clarice Starling's "unqualified success as a detective" returned to having their success qualified by their "acceptance of a heteronormative relationship, (most often with a male colleague) at the end of the film" (276). This qualification reflects the way that the capable woman's gender remains a "problem" so long as she remains unattached, making her more of a threat to the status quo. This assumption also informed her reading of the main character in the film *Untraceable* (2008), who is "allowed the success in both her personal and professional lives that was denied her predecessors of the last two decades—without the former being defined by a heteronormative relationship" (295). Rather, what determines the "success" in the character's personal life is that "she has a happy family life defined by female companionship" with her daughter and mother (297). In terms of offering a counter-position for women, I wholeheartedly agree that, in terms of new stories, this is a refreshing offering and, until recently, has few parallels. On the other hand, romance is once again assumed to qualify a heroine's success, just as when the female detective "is expected to give up her independence and work as part of a team—with a partner (both professionally and personally)" (Gates 289), a point Dresner also makes in her analysis of female investigators in popular culture (69). The partner in this scenario is always a man. Like Inness, the one example Gates provides of an enlightened partnership is one between two women, the FBI agents Gracie Hart (Sandra Bullock) and Sam Fuller (Regina King) in *Miss Congeniality 2: Armed and Fabulous* (2005).

Brown, who published his second comprehensive analysis of action heroines in 2015, gives more credit to some of the hetero-oriented partnerships on-screen in his chapter on "Teams, Partners, Romance, and Action Heroines," where he analyzes shows like *Burn Notice*, *Castle*, and *Bones*. Brown argues that the fighting females in these narratives break free from the constraints of the problematic token female and honey trap tropes that occur when women are aligned with men on-screen, mainly because of the women's extreme fighting capabilities. He even sees progressive potential in some of these pairings for the way "the women are able to achieve the relatively equal status of buddy-partner" (54), a partnership that has replaced the "buddy-cop" genre and that merges the conventions of romantic-comedies with action storylines.[6] In Chapters Two and Three, I will also explore romance-based partnerships in more detail. Even so, Brown aligns with other critics' assumptions about fighting female hetero-romances. He concludes this chapter by identifying how the fact "that the equality of a professional relationship must be accompanied by a romantic relationship is troubling" because "[t]he implication that men and women working together as equals must result in a romantic attraction undermines the possibility that women can merely be incredibly good at their heroic jobs and find enough satisfaction on a professional level" (77). Again, the two steps toward on-screen equity these "buddy-partner" action heroines take end up being diminished by a step back toward of the romance narrative.

The problem romance poses in popular-culture representations of empowered heterosexual women can be seen in online discussions about the latest *Mad Max* installment, *Fury Road* (2015). The film prompted intense debates about whether or not it's a feminist movie. One viewer's perspective on why it's not asserts, "A feminist agenda would have said screw the love interest and focus on the roundhouse kicks. But, since no such feminist agenda actually existed, the production team solved the problem with a last-minute save—the budding romance between Capable (one of the wives) and repentant War Boy Nux" (Depares). The romance in the movie didn't even involve the protagonists—these two are side characters. The mere fact that romance was integrated into the narrative was assumed to reduce the film's potential feminist implications for Ramona Depares, a view that coheres with what many of these critics think: making a relationship primary to a female character's story simply places her back in the sphere of intimacy that has always been expected of women and therefore limits her transgressive potential. After all, hasn't finding love and getting married—rather than getting the bad guy or making the world a safer, better place—been the preferred happy ending for women since Shakespeare?

Romancing the Feminist and the Feminism-Influenced

The excerpts given above offer neither unusual nor exhaustive examples of feminist critiques of heterosexual romance that occur in narratives that feature some of the strongest, most independent versions of female characters, like detectives (private and public), violent women, action heroines, and warrior women. Unfortunately, feminist critiques of heterosexual relations in narratives and/or feminist calls for female community stories have been commonly misunderstood or misrepresented to mean that feminism is anti-love (at least anti-hetero love) and that all feminists hate men. The people who subscribe to this misapprehension, though, completely miss the point. Interrogating love and re-envisioning love does not mean destroying it, or as Jackson explains, "It is not necessary to deny the pleasures of romance or the euphoria of falling in love in order to be sceptical about romantic ideals and wary of their consequences" (114). That's the fear, though: that love and feminism can't coincide because feminism critiques love.

Author and blogger Sara Dobie Bauer characterizes this fear perfectly in a post where she writes, "I'm not a feminist. I share certain feminist ideologies, but [...] I'm not always tough, and sometimes, I want to be saved." Admittedly, Dobie Bauer writes this post in service of supporting the strong male lead. It's her implication about feminism and romance that interests me here. On the one hand, she equates being unrelentingly tough with a feminist view that purports no need for men. On the other hand, she equates being somewhat tough but also wanting to depend on a man in a relationship with not being a feminist. Her belief brings us back to the assumption of feminist critics who champion the lone-wolf female hero—women doing it all on their own or only with other women is "feminist" and truly tough, and women who do it with the help of a man are "pseudo-tough" (14), as Inness put it.

Misapprehensions like Dobie Bauer's reflect one of, if not the, most difficult obstacles for feminist movements to overcome—the source of many women's reluctance to call themselves feminists even when they believe in feminist principles (the so-called "I'm not a feminist, but..." phenomenon). Often the reasons women give are based on their desires for relationships with men, or more specifically, their fear of appearing anti-male. Take actress Shailene Woodley's quote from a May 5, 2014, *Time* magazine article. She's dedicated to presenting strong women on-screen, yet when she was asked, "Do you consider yourself a feminist?" she replied, "No, because I love men" (Dockterman). Her statement was very close to one Lady Gaga made during a video interview in 2009: "I'm not a feminist. I hail men, I love men" ("10 Celebrities").[7] The misapprehensions of both the Dobie Bauers of the world and anyone who oversimplifies the relationship between feminism and heterosexual relationships expose the difficulties associated with imagining women who find a happy medium that combines empowerment and successful romance between women and men.

Many women's lingering fears of alienating men are easy to identify as further proof of subordination of women's interests to compulsory coupling and, because of this, just how deeply entrenched women's lives are in romance fantasies and how necessary it is to focus on the non-romantic aspects of their lives and identities. After all, there are many routes to personal satisfaction that men have been allowed to pursue, and women should be able to find that same satisfaction outside of romance. There are also many kinds of fulfilling relationships to pursue outside of "the couple." And as Brown warns, including romances on screen may be based on audience expectations for the typical "happily ever after," but "taken as a repeated convention this romantic trope may only be reinforcing or shaping cultural perceptions of romance as the ultimate end game [sic] for women" (77). Romance, whether heterosexual or not, as women's *raison d'être* is a problem because it reflects a denial of both their potential as individuals and for potential satisfaction in other relationships. Still, we do well to remember that the desire for close human companionship isn't the same as a fantasy, even though those fantasies do shape desire. Imagining a world without men isn't the answer, and I know of no feminist who thinks it is, but neither is imagining a world where women aren't concerned about their relationships with men, whether those women are heterosexual or not and whether those relationships are intimate or not.

Some feminist critics see the progressive potential in romance storylines. In the 1980s and 1990s, feminist media critics like Ien Ang, Janice Radway, and Lynne Pearce with Jackie Stacey began to reconsider so-called women's genres—romance novels, soap operas, and melodramas—and the role they play in women's lives by addressing their subversive potential for expressing female agency. Feminist critic bell hooks has made her own arguments for love as a practice with radical potential, particularly for groups who continue to be excluded by the myopic agendas promoted by feminisms that only serve the needs, or reflect the perspectives, of bourgeois and predominantly white women. In *Feminist Theory: From Margin to Center*, hooks thoroughly depicts the way that "their devaluation of family life alienated many women from feminist movement," while also noting that "[i]ronically, feminism is the one radical political movement that focuses on transforming family relationships" (39). This potential is particularly important to note for women of color, for as hooks explains, "black women find the family the least oppressive institution. Despite sexism in the context of family, we may experience dignity, self-worth, and a humanization that is not experienced in the outside world" (38). Of course, family doesn't only or even necessarily include a primary romance-based relationship, as I will show in Chapter Two, and romance doesn't need to be monogamous or couple-based.[8] When there is a hetero-couple portrayed on-screen, there is a likelihood that the subordinating aspects of romance will play out in the man's favor, but that is no longer a complete given. Not all on-screen relationships are created equally unequal.

That's why Michelle Obama's well-intentioned advice that young girls shouldn't worry about young romance so they can focus on getting smart is slightly problematic in terms of reflecting the nuances of female identity and experience. Yes, girls need to see that being smart—as part of being capable—and being strong and independent are good things, and they should put in the efforts that will lead to their success. Yes, American society needs to continue to develop educational infrastructure and promote cultural values that will encourage girls to succeed. And yes, it is important that girls grow up with a confidence that allows them to determine their own worth and not fall victim to the limited/limiting idea that their whole being should revolve around romance. More than that, I will say yes, many people's expectations for and assumptions about love do cause problems today for women, and these need a wide-scale reimagining. However, Obama's advice and some critical dismissals of heterosexual love on-screen or off imply a damaging either/or perspective: *either* girls can be smart and educated, *or* they can enjoy the titterings of early crushes and the hormone-induced pursuits of young romance. What I'm attempting to provide is a little nuance in the ways we address hetero-relations in connection with female empowerment, referring to the fighting female narratives that provide some of that nuance. They don't always manage a happy medium, but some certainly try, and these attempts need to be more deeply interrogated.

Two

Mixing Business with Pleasure

Love-Buddy Fighting Females and the Politics of Romance in the Workplace

Once upon a time, there were Nick and Nora Charles, the darling movie couple of *The Thin Man* (1934). They were, and still remain, loved by critics and fans, and their popularity spawned five movie sequels over the next thirteen years (and a short-lived television series from 1957 to 1959). In Nick and Nora's sparring, flirtatious dialogue and penchant for encountering intrigue, mass media encountered a basic blueprint for a crime-fighting couple narrative that cleverly combined screwball chemistry and mystery drama, a formula that has had a particularly lasting effect. Outlines of Nick and Nora remain visible decades years later in character couples like Laura Holt and Remington Steele from *Remington Steele* (1982–1987), Maddie Hayes and David Addison from *Moonlighting* (1985–1989), Temperance Brennan and Seeley Booth from *Bones* (2005–17), Kate Beckett and Richard Castle from *Castle* (2009–16), and Sarah Walker and Chuck Bartowski from *Chuck* (2007–12).[1]

One similarity between these couples and Nick and Nora—the clever banter and exchange of barbs—remains an important element of their relationships, as does the way solving crimes together provides an opportunity for innuendo and romance. There are, however, a few crucial differences between the characters then and now. These more recent protagonists don't start off the story married—we get to see them meet, fall in love, and (sometimes) marry. There is no graphic violence in *The Thin Man* series and relatively little fighting. Nick is comfortable wielding a gun or throwing a punch when necessary, but there is no blood. The depiction of crime, including murder, in today's series exhibit much more gore, more shooting and hand-to-hand combat, and even the occasional explosion. Probably the biggest difference, however, between Nick and Nora and these other couples is that the more contemporary ones include a fighting female, whether an amateur like Maddie Hayes (Cybill Shepherd) or a full-on professional fighter like Sara Walker

(Yvonne Strahovski). Nora, while spunky and always up to solve a crime, never fights. She points a gun once, playfully, at Nick in *The Thin Man*, but she only takes one punch and never throws one of her own. (The punch comes from her husband Nick, who knocks her out to keep her from following him as he pursues a possible dangerous lead.) The introduction of a fighting female into the dynamic—a woman capable of protecting herself and others and who can fight both physically and intellectually—in today's on-screen couples made possible the construction of "love-buddies," a dual-protagonist male/female relationship that partners a woman and a man in romance and combat.[2]

The love-buddy fighting female has been one of the more popular and consistently replicated versions of the empowered, strong, independent woman to hit the small screen. Like other fighting females, she exudes self-reliance and strength in the pursuit of justice. But the love-buddy narrative differs from other fighting female narratives in that the dramatic tension is characterized as much by the question of whether or not the male and female co-stars will get together and stay together as by the question of whether or not they will catch the criminal (both of which they almost always do). This question plays through the love-buddy program as the narrative interrogates the possibility of romance obsessively—will they or won't they? Should they or shouldn't they? Why or why not? What will happen? Etc. In other words, the negotiations around coupling are integral to the series as a whole.

This chapter focuses on fighting female romance narratives where the hetero-intimacies take place in the workplace where the women occupy the position of both crime-fighting business and romance partners. The fantasies of feminist-friendly love that emerge within these narratives both expose and endeavor to resolve male/female antagonisms assumed to have emerged due to both women's participation in the workforce and their entrance into careers generally denied them. These conflicts have long impacted hetero-relations, most particularly in the last forty years, when women's contributions have been more public. To accomplish this resolution, the fantasies require audiences not only to question the traditional heterosexual contract but also to question assumptions about heterosexual compatibility, which are based on the traditional contract. The term "heterosexual contract" here is loosely based on Monique Wittig's definition of it as a "political category that founds society as heterosexual." It is a contract that defines women as a sex in relation to men and marginalizes their position within a larger social contract that establishes rights, responsibilities, privileges, and the exercise of authority in the public sphere (*The Straight Mind and Other Essays* 44). The heterosexual contract is a personal and political relationship that determines, on the surface, divided but complementary gender roles for men and women that, underneath, maintain a hierarchy based on that difference that justifies male domination and patriarchy.

The traditional heterosexual contract delegates the role of protector and/or breadwinner to the male (whose duties situate him traditionally in the public sphere) and the role of the protected and/or dependent person to the female (whose duties situate her traditionally in the private, domestic sphere). The empowered woman's access to the workplace and her associated potential to unravel the traditional heterosexual contract raises a lot of questions: How do women in the workplace affect notions of male/female compatibility? Can a woman successfully pursue a career and a romance? What does such a love entail? Would such an intimacy be feminist-friendly?

This analysis of the love-buddy fighting female begins with the emergence of the character, focusing predominantly on the last thirty years when narratives began combining a crime-fighting business partnership with a romance fantasy that addresses male/female relationship antagonisms in the work sphere in both problematic and progressive ways. On the one hand, the combination either presumes the dubious nature of female authority, a problem for women attempting to enter traditionally male careers (as seen in the early love-buddy series), or it overemphasizes the presence of enlightened workplaces and distracts from remaining gender inequities (as seen in more recent love-buddy series). On the other hand, the way the narratives address male/female relationship antagonisms in the work sphere reflects the emergence of an empowered female co-protector identity that assumes a woman can be an ideal partner and relies on the construction of an egalitarian workplace that can be seen to foster cooperative hetero-relationships. This egalitarian workspace then becomes a progressive ideological space that celebrates the end of the traditional heterosexual contract and the beginning of heterosexual feminist-friendly love.

Love Buddies Emerge: Romancing the Fighting Female Partner

While the love-buddy narrative has some historical antecedents, the formula didn't really solidify until the 1980s. Love buddies before this period were either flirtatiously platonic as in *The Avengers* (1965–69),[3] or married as in *Get Smart* (1965–70), *McMillan & Wife* (1971–77),[4] and *Hart to Hart* (1979–84). None of these versions included the couple discussing their feelings, detailing their attraction, or encountering any kind of relationship tension over getting and staying together. There was definitely some sexual innuendo in *The Avengers* between John Steed (Patrick McNee) and his partners Emma Peel (Diana Riggs) and Tara King (Linda Thorson), but this served for only brief titillation rather than actual narrative tension. Additionally, with the exception of Steed's female partners, the female characters in these other shows exist generally to be saved and fretted over and thus at best would be considered pseudo-fighting females: women who are embroiled in the drama, like Nora Charles, who have moxie but are helpless to protect themselves or others.

The female co-stars of the love-buddy narratives that began after 1980 not only have true fighting females in them—women who fight with fists, guns, and intelligence—but there's that necessary relationship tension between her and her male partner. Those two elements are absolutely central to the fantasy presented by the love-buddy and also explain why these popular love buddies are all crime-fighting narratives. The police precinct and detective agency—arenas of justice and violence that long discouraged female participation and even in the 21st century are heavily male-dominated—become the ultimate imaginative territory to examine women's ability to succeed in the workforce.[5] She needs to have some level of aggression, some ability to face challenges, and some confidence to accept the responsibilities of her professional position and rely on herself. These capacities signify a woman who can do more than fulfill a traditional role of nurturing and looking after the family—a woman who was once thought only to be able to succeed in traditionally female positions like nursing, teaching, or administrative work. Just as importantly, her fighting capacities represent a woman who can be more than a subordinate to a man, for, through the performance of strength and independence in her fighting capacities, she challenges the traditional dominance/subordination sex relational pattern. The challenge sets her apart from other noteworthy strong female characters on-screen: Mary Richards from *The Mary Tyler Moore Show* (1970–77), Maude Findlay from *Maude* (1972–78), or Alice Hyatt from *Alice* (1976–85). They had sassy and independent personalities and challenged authority but either had little of the authority that the fighting female's prowess conveys or posed less of an ideological threat to gender divides.

With her physical, emotional, and intellectual strength, the fighting female embodies the necessary characteristics of a woman who could symbolically be accepted as a colleague of and collaborator with a man. She also enacts a feminist-allied character, even when she doesn't identify herself as such, because of her implicit—through a look or act—or explicit verbal rejection of chauvinistic or sexist standards or characters. Because of these associations, the fighting female presence on-screen complicates representations of the heterosexual contract that presumes female dependence on male protection and control. This complication is the basis of the love-buddy fantasy, which creates a male/female work partnership determined by and deeply invested in the empowered woman model relevant to certain feminist ideals. This fantasy relies on the assumption of an equal-opportunity workforce that makes the work partnership seem possible, and as the work partnership turns toward an intimate relationship, it also has the effect of promoting the desirability of strength and independence in women. Basing the fighting female's allure not only on the spunky traits of the intelligent and quick-witted woman—who has been popular on-screen since the 1910s, as Singer and other critics remind us—but also on the autonomy and courageousness of a fighter goes a long way toward counteracting what critics have argued restricts fighting females in the romance plot.

The 1980s were the ideal period for the love-buddy to emerge because it was a period when the fighting female had gained acceptance on the small screen and had thus proved to be something of an audience-pleaser. The popularity of television shows like *The Avengers*, *Policewoman* (1974–78), *Charlie's Angels* (1976–81), *The Bionic Woman* (1976–78), and *Wonder Woman* (1975–79) demonstrated not only that women could hold their own as crime-fighters but also carry a series for at least a couple of seasons. Note that I distinguish crime-fighting from detective work here and throughout, as the latter is about solving the crime using intellect—something women detectives in books and later on-screen have been doing since the 1800s—whereas the former is about actually apprehending the bad guys and requires physical involvement. By the 1980s, the big screen had also introduced audiences to the baddest badass woman yet, the Blaxploitation fighting female, whom Sims rightly argues "changed American popular culture" with her action-oriented persona, fabulous beauty, and righteous spirit. Essentially, the violent woman began to inch toward the mainstream, no longer portrayed as just a deviant female or relegated to the role of the villain, like the *femmes fatale* of film noir (though examples of both remained on film and television). Consequently, the violent woman character became the kind of heroine who could fulfill the escalating interest in strong, independent female roles.

So, we have the initial popular embrace of the independent woman occurring in mass media that, increasing over the decades, has become what Jowett refers to as proof "that feminism or some feminist ideas have been incorporated into hegemony" (5).[6] This allows for willingness in some arenas of the popular imagination to comprehend an empowered female identity where some versions of femininity could absorb characteristics of strength and female desirability rather than be lessened by aggressive or violent abilities. Additionally, the 1980s were also a time in which massive changes in the workforce had impacted American society. By 1982—the year that the first full love-buddy program *Remington Steele* premiered—51.5 percent of women had entered the American workforce,[7] indicating what economist Claudia Goldin calls "a quiet revolution" that affected both the economy and heterosexual relationships. More women, including married women, were working than ever before, but more notably, more women were working in "careers" rather than "jobs." This meant that the female workforce expanded from being populated primarily by women who "work because they and their families 'need the money' to those who are employed, at least in part, because occupation and employment define one's fundamental identity and societal worth" (Goldin 1).

More women also owned their own businesses or worked as management than ever before. In 1972, women only owned 4 percent of American businesses (Linard). By 1980, the number had risen dramatically to 26.1 percent ("Facts on Working Women"). Between 1960 and 1970, the number of women in management positions rose a modest 3 percent, from 15 to 18, but between 1970 and 1980, that number shot up 12 percent to a total of 30 ("Percentage of Women"). The numbers would continue to increase, year after year, through the decade. Even so, there remained plenty of concerns about the repercussions of career-bound women, and while these numbers represent a big change, they still show that women were well below the level of parity with men. As Professor Alice Kessler-Harris wrote in a 1982 article for the *New York Times*, working women had to shoulder the burden of being marginalized as "peripheral workers" or as an "inconvenient aberration" (A21). They also had to take the blame for the increase in men's unemployment and the economic fears attending the loss of male breadwinners. As we can see, by the 1982 love-buddy debut, some people struggled not only with lingering concerns about whether women should be in the workforce but also with concerns about how to deal with it now that there seemed to be no signs of their leaving.

The 1980s Love-Buddy Fighting Female: Where There's a "Will they?" There's a "Won't they?"

The conflicts raised by women's increased entry into the workforce and their greater participation in management positions shaped the two 1980s love-buddy narratives that bookended the decade: *Remington Steele* and *Moonlighting*. In *Remington Steele*, private investigator Laura Holt (Stephanie Zimbalist) opens her own detective firm. She invents a male boss, Remington Steele, and names the firm after him because she can't get clients as a female P.I. During a case, she meets a charming interloper and thief (Pierce Brosnan) who discovers her secret and takes Remington's name and position. (We never do learn his real name.) Laura and "Remington" become business partners and a detective team. In *Moonlighting*, ex-model Maddie Hayes (Cybill Shepherd) loses all of her money to a thieving accountant. She has to close each of the failing tax-write-off businesses she owns that have become financial burdens. She intends to close her detective agency, but she meets the boss, David Addison (Bruce Willis), has an exciting adventure on a case, and ends up becoming his boss and taking over the business—renaming it the Blue Moon Detective Agency (to cash in on her celebrity as the once famed "Blue Moon shampoo girl").

On the one hand, both narratives promote acceptance and even celebration of the burgeoning vision of the strong, independent woman, symbolized by the professional successes of its fighting females. These narratives are the beginning of the contemporary feminist-friendly love fantasy, in which the successful woman partners with a dashing, enlightened male in a symbolic nod to equality: equal representation (female and male co-stars), equal opportunity workplace (male and female co-workers), and companionate intimacy freed from the monetary, legal, and gender restrictions of the traditional heterosexual contract. On the other hand, the fantasy is portrayed as extremely tenuous, where failure constantly threatens the successes of both the workplace and the intimacy. This tenuousness can be seen as representing some people's lingering fears that the strong, independent career woman will undermine social traditions as much as it can be seen to represent other people's experiences with the realities of the strong, independent career woman who tries to negotiate those traditions.

Testing Female Authority

In a sense, the fighting female was on trial in the popular media of the time because she didn't fit into an easily classified gender role. Her presence on screen ebbed and flowed throughout the 1970s and 1980s—a media experiment, a blip in a popular culture almost entirely inhabited by fighting males and victim females. This tentative quality made her the perfect character to showcase the career woman whose social presence was also considered by some to be an experiment doomed to fail. *Remington Steele* provides a good example of this. Not only is Laura one of only a few examples of working women to own her own business on primetime at this time, but her business is in a predominantly male field, meaning her character treads on unsettled cultural ground. The show depends on her ambiguous position and actually emphasizes it in the opening monologue:

> I always loved excitement, so I studied, and apprenticed, and put my name on an office. But absolutely nobody knocked down my door. A female private investigator seemed so ... feminine. So I invented a superior. A decidedly MASCULINE superior. Suddenly there were cases around the block. It was working like a charm until the day he walked in with his blue eyes and mysterious past, and before I knew it he assumed Remington Steele's identity. Now I do the work, and he takes the bows. It's a dangerous way to live, but as long as people buy it, I can get the job done. We never mix business with pleasure; well, almost never. I don't even know his real name!

The beginning of her monologue reminded viewers, week after week, of both her failure and her success. She was not able to get a company running under her name based on her own merit because of her sex, but thanks to her ingenuity and her implied abilities as a detective—doing the work, getting the job done—she found a way to make the success happen. She also has earned the right to success, thanks to her apprenticeship. Her position is, therefore, defined by the tensions between traditional sexist assumptions about women in the workforce and newly enlightened realizations that women might be capable contributors.

These tensions remain a theme throughout the series, ranging from Laura's concern about losing clients and cases in the early seasons to Steele's spending habits or criminal past bankrupting or otherwise threatening her business. In "Tempered Steele" (01.02), Laura has to dress Remington down for spending lavish amounts of agency money on a woman (one he was tasked to distract while Laura investigates a case). Because he gets mad at her attempts to restrict him, he ruins the case Laura is about to complete. In "Thou Shalt Not Steele" (01.05), Laura worries about money and fights with Remington for saying no to a client's case without asking her, when she would have taken it for the much-needed income. At the beginning of season two, we learn about another threat to the agency because Remington is being audited, and Laura must come up with a way to prevent his identity and their fraud from being discovered.

Moonlighting also portrays the failure/success tandem, as Maddie Hayes goes from a successful professional model and savvy investor to being the struggling owner of an insolvent detective agency. Failure defines the very basis of the series, from her entrée into the detecting profession through her tenure as an investigator. Bankruptcy hovers over every case and new client she dredges up, every success she and David Addison have, and every executive decision she makes. In "Brother Can You Spare a Blonde?" (02.01), Maddie almost loses her house. In "Atlas Belched" (02.09), competitor Lou LaSalle wants to buy the agency, and Maddie almost capitulates because it's so close to bankruptcy. To pay the bills, Maddie often has to take cases that she or David finds distasteful, as she does in "The Bride of Tupperman" (02.11). In that case, a man wants the agency to find him a perfect wife—and Maddie scoffs at being a professional pimp. Every episode raises the question of whether the agency will close; remaining open hinges solely on the outcome of the current case.

There are two overall implications to the will-she-won't-she-be-a-success theme enacted by Maddie's and Laura's struggles as business owners. First, and important to note, is that to a certain extent, the struggles are results of circumstances beyond the fighting female's control. Laura's failure to dredge up clients for an agency under her name isn't actually her failure. It's society's failure. By noting the oversight of clientele who automatically think a woman can't be a good detective, the monologue highlights the wrong-headed sexism behind that assumption. Remington himself refers to the ill treatment Laura received trying to open a business under her name, saying, "Tawdry thing this male chauvinism" (01.01). Their first client together is a chauvinist who insists Remington lead the investigation, even though Remington says, "I never involve myself directly in a case. I function best in an advisory capacity." Even so, the client likens Laura as the second string to Steele's quarterback (01.02). Her struggles here are specifically gender-related and evidence of the obstacles women face in the workplace.

Maddie's situation is the result of a corrupt accountant who runs off with all of her money, so her circumstances don't implicate gender inequities. She does not have clients who question her abilities as a woman detective, as Laura does. Yet, the tenuousness of her business does not have to be directly tied to her position as a woman in the narrative to still implicate her position as a woman in the media represented as a business owner. Laura's unfair circumstances more explicitly point the finger at prejudice, but the key issue at hand in the struggles facing both businesses is the way they highlight the competitive and difficult nature of a capitalist business force (a common concern in 1980s mass media) in which women have to be able to stand up to challenges that aren't always fair—it's just business. Maddie actually makes this very claim in episodes one and nine of the first season, noting that the events occurring around the agency—the possibilities of liquidating the agency or selling it, respectively—are "just business." But it's not just business—it's a new popular representation of a female-run business that must navigate conflicting audience views of women as capable *and* as a threat. As female business owners, both characters held a conspicuous place in the television schedule in a decade when only a few other female characters ever had their own businesses.[8] Their positions then as owners/bosses only highlighted their token—and thereby tentative—stance.[9]

The second implication of the will-she-won't-she-be-a-success theme in these two 1980s love-buddy programs emphasizes the uncertain basis of female authority being explored for the first time in the workplace during this period, both on-screen and off. The question not only of whether women possessed the business acumen or assertive nature to be leaders but also of whether they could apply leadership skills cropped up in the popular media, contributing to the sense of experimentation circumscribing representations of working women on-screen. The media paid a lot of attention to women in positions of authority, like British Prime Minister Margaret Thatcher and the first female Supreme Court Justice, Sandra Day O'Connor, appointed in 1981. In 1984, the first major-party female vice-presidential candidate, Geraldine Ferraro, ran with Walter Mondale and instigated a very public debate about (and an unprecedented amount of focus on) whether women could be successful in authoritative positions. During a debate with then-Vice President George H. W. Bush, the moderator inquired if Ferraro thought "the Soviets might be tempted to try to take advantage of you simply because you're a woman"—and in one interview on *Meet the Press,* correspondent Marvin Kalb asked Ferraro if she was "strong enough to push the button" (Braden 109–10). In 1985, the crime-fighting profession even saw its first female police chief, Penny Harrington, in Portland, Oregon. The appointment made national news, as did the federal sex-discrimination suit she brought against the department (shortly thereafter) for the poor treatment she experienced—perpetrated by the vice squad under her command—and for being forced to resign.

In a decade in which only one woman held a CEO position in a Fortune 500 company, it was not unusual in the '80s to wonder if women had what it took to get the job done. Businesswomen had to face and overcome long-held stereotypes about females. They were thought by many to be "too soft to be hard on crime, too emotional to be trusted with the nation's checkbook or defense, too disorganized to be effective because of their family responsibilities or mysterious biology, and too idealistic to play the hardball insider game" (Witt et al. 211). The mass media highlighted every blunder as a reflection of women's abilities in general. As Ferraro lamented, "[T]he defeat of one woman is often read as a judgment on all women" (qtd. in Faludi 269). Since women, in general, had very little representation in public business and political office, they received extra scrutiny from those who saw them as role models *and* from those who questioned their right to authority and ability to lead in their positions.

The 1980s love-buddy narratives mirror both of these tendencies: the willingness to represent a woman with authority as a business owner but the lack of conviction about that authority. Returning to Laura's monologue, we can see that even as she informs the audience about how she made her business work, she betrays her lack of autonomy over that business because a complete stranger could so easily usurp her control. Her claim that "before I knew it he assumed Remington Steele's identity" highlights her powerlessness in the situation, as does the phrase "as long as people buy it." Laura is at once Remington's boss and subordinate—both in the role she plays as his employee and in her forced capitulation to his scheme. She creates his role but then has to rely on him to perform it properly and not endanger *her* business. Remington's rogue power is particularly a problem in the first two seasons, when he constantly keeps her leadership abilities in check. When the sexist client in "Tempered Steele" insists that Remington lead the case, Laura is forced to guide him on the side and hope that Steele can complete the con. In "Steele Waters Run Deep" (01.03), Laura has to scramble to cover a boring security job that Remington doesn't feel like doing, even though it will fill the office coffer for two years. Laura regularly can't get Mildred Krebs (Doris Roberts), the office assistant starting in season two, to give Laura things she needs (like a photo of a suspect, as in "Red Holt Steele" 02.03) or tell her important details—sometimes because Krebs' first loyalty is to Remington, whom she calls "the boss," much to Laura's dismay. (Krebs isn't in on the ruse until later in the series; then her attitude toward Laura changes accordingly.)

Laura is also the effective crime-fighter and detective who has to give Remington all the credit—in spite of his bumbling, which continues until he decides to become her apprentice and learn the detective trade from her. In "Tempered Steele," Remington's name is the one in the papers being credited for foiling the murder, though he wasn't the one to figure out the correct culprit. In "In the Steele of the Night" (01.09), Steele must uncover a murderer at a reunion of detectives, but he relies on Laura to guide him through the whole process and also to make him appear legitimate amongst other professional investigators. Remington merely performs the role of the knowing detective, or he just plays around while she actually solves the crime, as in "Heart of Steele" (01.14); often when he does help, it's accidental, as when he takes down a bad guy Laura was chasing after accidentally dropping a pencil for which he was looking. Because Remington is a male and Laura is a female, it's impossible to ignore the implications of sex conflict as the basis of this authority/dependence struggle, a point to which I shall return.

Maddie Hayes takes on the role of an amateur detective, but she owns the Blue Moon Detective Agency. She is the one who decides to keep it running as a legitimate business. However, various elements throughout the series clearly put her ability to manage an office and maintain authority in doubt. Her employees consistently mock her or resent her leadership. In the episode "My Fair David" (02.05), Maddie catches David in a limbo party with the other employees. She's angry because he needs to act more like a "boss, not a buddy," and she bets him that he can't be serious. If she wins, he has to fire the unnecessary employees he has insisted they keep on. The employees, dissatisfied with the new somber David, badmouth her for "de-Daving" him. Another instance of the employees' disrespecting her authority is when Maddie fires the troublesome MacGillicuddy (Jack Blessing) in "It's a Wonderful Job" (03.08). The entire office revolts.

David, the insubordination ringleader, disrespects her from their very first meeting, at which she informs him of her plan to dissolve the company. He calls her a "cold bitch" for her business decision (01.01). David also encourages unruly behaviors from other employees by treating the business, and her authority, as a game (as the aforementioned limbo incident indicates). In the majority of episodes, he lounges around the office playing with his toys, nursing hangovers, and singing ballads. The more she yells at him and at the employees—and the more the unprofessional dynamic stays the same—the more ineffective her authority seems. For all her professionalism and knowhow, and for all the respect she earns from clients, she still can't control the business. For all of David's goofiness and lack of business acumen, the employees respect him more. The "It's a Wonderful Job" episode makes David's underlying authority explicit when Maddie imagines never having started Blue Moon (in an homage to *It's a Wonderful Life*). David ends up being the successful business owner, and she's the sad, lonely drunk. The episode portrays her business choices as interfering not only with her success but also his. In the end, this storyline has her respecting his choices more than hers, thereby degrading her authority, as happens in "My Fair David," when Maddie herself apologizes for wrongly trying to make him more serious and businesslike because she misses the "old David." She is often wrong in her interactions with him, even though her expectations for a responsible, respectful, and reliable business partner are more than logical and reflect the reality of any professional workplace.

Taken from only these perspectives, these two love-buddy programs might seem more aligned with backlash oppositions to the burgeoning strong, independent woman ideal rather than representations of the feminist-friendly love fantasy. Critics were quick to point out problems with Maddie's authority that stemmed from David's chauvinism. As Susan Faludi characterizes the show, backlash exists throughout the ways David "ultimately tames his 'queen bee' boss" as part of the show's "long-running campaign to cow this independent female figure" (*Backlash* 157). Elaine Warren, writing for the *Los Angeles Herald Examiner* in 1986, saw a softening of Laura's authority and, as others have since pointed out, believed Holt's "overall strength of character has been noticeably diluted" from her portrayal in seasons one and two, specifically because Laura "has come to depend on Steele" more, as exhibited in her "cuddling up to him at trying moments" (qtd. D'Acci 144).

However, there's more to consider that complicates these critiques. Where each of these females does earn respect is in her fighting abilities and/or in the work she does to catch the bad guy, in successfully closed cases at the end of each episode. Of the two, Laura is definitely the better crime-fighter. She almost single-handedly closes each of the cases that come to her agency. She saves Remington regularly, and while there is relatively little violence enacted in the narrative by any character in the show compared to other crime shows of the period, Laura is comfortable handling a gun and wielding punches, kicks, and weapons, including a purse (01.05), a hypodermic needle (01.13), and a knife (01.18) to take down criminals. Maddie also fights in a variety of ways, though *Moonlighting* includes even less explicit physical violence than *Remington Steele*. Maddie will do anything from bite a killer she's fighting (01.04) to wrestle guns from bad guys (01.01 and 01.06), and she actually throws as many punches as David does—though both tend more toward slapstick than serious fighting skills. They are just as likely to take down a culprit together by slip-sliding through a mess of bubbles on a tile floor and falling into a pile (02.02) as by having a long fight scene. The key here is that she's just as *in*capable as he is. For example, in the pilot, David punches and wrestles with one villain, knocking him out, while Maddie wrestles with another and takes away his gun. But David's nemesis gets the better of David, and Maddie shoots wildly and gets taken down by the one she fought. They both prove incompetent. Nevertheless, Maddie is definitely more aggressive than David is and has a penchant for yelling, growling, snarling, slapping, and doggedly chasing the culprits. She's a woman with determination and physical assertiveness that leaves little uncertainty about her strength. Thus, no matter what hesitations arise about Laura's or Maddie's business success or authority as a boss in each episode, there is no question as to whether these two fighting females will succeed for the client, find and often fight the culprit, and close the case.

As mentioned previously, the strong and independent characteristics that made these successes possible are integral to the allure of both of these love-buddy fighting females, and that is what works in service of the burgeoning feminist-friendly love fantasy. These women flouted the popular status quo of the period but were not subject to typical narrative punishments. They were aggressive, driven, and capable without being exaggerated as monsters (which happened with certain other 1980s narratives, including transgressive women, like those showcased in *Dynasty* and *Falcon Crest*). Even Maddie's "cold bitch" persona was just one facet of her personality and didn't preclude audience sympathy for her.

Additionally, Maddie and Laura enacted feminist values by calling out chauvinism and making feminist choices—though the word feminist was never actually used in either program.[10] Maddie constantly calls David out on sexist behaviors. As Laura's *Remington Steele* opening credits monologue repeated weekly, she is forced to build a grand deception because clients are too sexist to work with women dicks. Both characters also exhibit sexual desire and have sex out of marriage without being portrayed as deviant. They are attractive, and there are instances of sexual objectification—more so for Maddie, whose beauty and modeling background are referenced regularly. However, they are objectified considerably less than their 1970s fighting sisters, and they often criticize such objectification—again, more so for Maddie, who regularly calls David out for his sexist ogling. Finally, both women crave emotional connection and the vulnerability involved with intimacy, but they do so without making themselves appear fragile and in need of protection that they can't otherwise provide for themselves. They are emotionally mature, expressive, logical, professional, romantic: in other words, they are complex beings expressing agency in their personal lives (even when they continue to struggle with it professionally).

If there remains any uncertainty about how both of these women presented new and inspiring fighting females for an audience starved for intelligent, strong, and independent women, then just look to the many websites, social media outlets, and fan fiction dedicated to these shows decades after they hit primetime. Stephanie Zimbalist still gets fanposts (today's version of fan mail) thanking her for what she represented. Brenda Holmes writes a Facebook post stating:

> Your character in Remington Steele, I thought of as a partial role model back in the day. (That character, along with my own mom.) That's because she could be her own person (strong and independent), while also having an incredibly handsome guy in her life. From what I've seen since those ep[isode]s years ago, few women are that strong. I've tried to be one of them, but have struggled with it for years. I've come quite a ways, but still have some road ahead of me. But I just wanted to thank you for setting one more example for me at the time.

In her comment, Ms. Holmes echoes what many women might have found so fascinating about *Remington Steele* and its 1980s companion—the presence of a "strong and independent" woman who also has romance in her life. There's also an entire page dedicated to Maddie on the very thorough and well-researched website *DavidandMaddie.com,* celebrating all things *Moonlighting,* where fans share their fascination with her complex character and the way romance contributes not to her story but to her personality. One describes Maddie by saying, on the one hand, "She has extraordinary strength—an iron will—and an outlook that is occasionally inflexible," while on the other hand, "When the ice begins to thaw, we get a look at the Maddie who often seems afraid to come out and play [...] the woman who is soft-hearted and vulnerable" (Klauss and Hopkins).

These are very different responses than what some feminist critics have said about the show, then and now. Warren addresses the "traditionally feminine, vulnerable ways" (qtd. in D'Acci 143) romance defines Laura. Faludi and more recent fan critics like KC Lynch focus on the backlash machismo of the male characters by providing behind-the-scenes production stories that highlight producer Glenn Gordon Caron's desire to bring a real man back to television (Faludi 144) or conspiracies to "curb the single Shepherd's 'aggressive' personality" by rejecting her attempts to define Maddie's character (Faludi 157) or by blaming Shepherd's pregnancy for ruining the show (Lynch). Such criticisms reflect the difficulty of pinning down any one reading of these programs. Still, they neglect the insights that the pleasures viewers experience bring to readings of the program—viewers who recognize that there's more going on behind the hetero-relations for the fighting female than simply the production company's attempts to moderate the threat she poses (to allow for a broader audience appeal that includes those who may not have been ready to celebrate a woman in charge).

The combination of independence and intimacy in these stories makes for a powerful appeal to women who, in the wake of feminism, claim a right to their own lives and to building their own identities outside of romance, but who still desire intimacy, hetero or otherwise. Amidst a popular media culture filled with stories about newly liberated women having trouble with romance—as single or married women seeking higher education or new levels of previously unattainable career goals—a heroine who beats the odds does seem inspirational. And there were plenty of articles printed during this period that "reported" on the relationship between women's increased independence and their dwindling romantic prospects. What woman of the eighties doesn't remember the extremely misguided 1986 *Newsweek* cover story on the "Marriage Crunch" that famously and mistakenly warned women that they were more likely to get killed by a terrorist than to get married after 40?[11] Another article, "The Changing Women's Marriage Market: Later May Mean Never, Study Says" from *The New York Times* February 22, 1986, notes how women who get college degrees and start careers have only a 50 percent chance of getting married once they hit 25 (W. Greer). That same year, the *Times* also published "More Women Postponing Marriage," which includes data about women *and* men getting married later in life, but it ends by referring to the diminishing ratio of single women to single men after the age of 35 (Associated Press). The *Times* trend continues into April 28, 1987, with an article that describes "Single Women: Coping with a Void" and ends on a section called "Independence or Intimacy" that characterizes women's growing lack of desire for sex or love the longer they are out of a relationship, of women gratefully going into the office on Sunday to avoid the cute brunching couples and families, of women praising the pleasures of living how they want but secretly yearning for someone to share their lives with (Gross). As still tends to be the case, there is an assumption that independence and intimacy are mutually exclusive terms, particularly for women.[12] These references provide just a small sampling of the obsessive reports being published all over the country and throughout the decade.

When taken in relation to this negative cultural context, it makes sense that women then and now might seek narratives where the fighting female nabs the bad guy *and* gets the good guy without having to use typical feminine wiles, sacrifice her principles, or hide her ambition; without suddenly having to become incapable, afraid, or fragile; all while remaining the hero of her own story and even saving the good guy from time to time. These are all crucial characteristics that set the love-buddy fighting female apart from the few other strong, independent female characters of the time, like Claire Huxtable (Phylicia Rashad) of *The Cosby Show* (1984–92), Ann Kelsey

(Jill Eikenberry) of *LA Law* (1986–94), and Alexis Carrington Colby (Joan Collins) of *Dynasty*. While not all women focus on cultivating romantic relationships, the search for and enjoyment of intimacy is part of the majority of women's lives. Many women do struggle to find a balance between the desire for romantic relationships and their professional ambitions. Because of this, it also makes sense that the media-cultivated tension in the independence/intimacy opposition would be reflected in those fighting female romance narratives, where the question of the crime-fighting woman's career success nestled comfortably among the will-they-won't-they question of relationship success made popular by the love-buddy storyline.

Thus, the love-buddy fighting female fantasy can be seen both to reflect and to cultivate a perception of heightened intimacy conflicts that were—and continue to be—stressed by portions of the mass media in a turbulent postfeminist period. People could be enthralled as much by the examinations of the fighting female's desirability in the intimate sphere and her ability to fulfill the role of a lover as by interrogations of her authority in the business world and her ability to fulfill the role of a partner. That's why the ups and downs in intimacy mirrored the ups and downs of the businesses in both shows: added to bankruptcy threats, lost clients, and amateur mistakes was the threat of the relationship breakdown in which each moment of intimate progress (a lingering look, a spontaneous hug, maybe even the first mistaken kiss) might be stalled by the fighting female's doubts and fears about losing control and power.

Flirting with Power

In these narratives, the female protagonist's fears are quite well-founded, what with the struggles to maintain authority that define her tenuous position in the work partnership with a man. Thus, a return to a previous point about *Remington Steele* (that also applies to *Moonlighting*): power struggles over authority in the workplace occur within a sex hierarchy that still privileges the male partner. This privilege is true even for male characters, like Remington and David, who are decidedly more enlightened than the "traditional" male and who arguably combine sensitive qualities with their rakish and even chauvinistic behaviors (respectively).

Both men profess to support their "partners" wholeheartedly. For example, when clients overlook Laura's authority and demand he work on the case, Remington is just as frustrated and tells them she's in charge. Of course, he also wants to avoid responsibility and simply enjoy the spoils of his arrangement. Also, as much as some critics want to paint a picture of David as "hardboiled," he constantly undermines his own chauvinism with moments of sincere and supportive behaviors toward Maddie, as when he tells her, in the pilot episode, that he'll respect her wishes and wait for her to decide about staying in business. Of course, this is undercut by his having to shoo away reporters because he called them assuming he could get Maddie to make an announcement to keep the agency open.

This contradictory interplay in the male personalities not only develops their dynamic qualities as co-leads but also reflects the way that, as men, they are automatically afforded the privilege in the authority hierarchy because of the traditional heterosexual contract, even when that privilege is unearned. As I pointed out previously, for a good part of the series, Remington does little but spend the company money, and Mildred automatically accepts him as "the boss." David comes to work unkempt and hungover and exhibits no kind of management ability, and the employees afford him much more respect than they afford Maddie.

The narratives make it difficult to forget that even though these men aren't the bosses, the success of the business resides entirely on them—keeping up a stolen role (Remington) or controlling the employees and the tenor of the office (David). The workplace dominance/submission relation then gets intermingled with the issue of heterosexual intimacy, bringing power struggles into romance (or bringing attention to the way power already defines romance relations). Thus, the authority, independence, and control the fighting female struggles to maintain on the job and in her work partnership becomes part of her struggles in her romantic partnerships because they are with the same man. This dynamic plays on the fears within certain arenas of American culture that were undecided about what women's increased public presence would do—not just to the economy or the structure of the domestic sphere, in general, but also to the intimate relationships between men and women. Would the threat and uproar the working woman caused in the public economy happen in her private relationships? How would men and women relate to each other if they both possessed the traits required to be self-reliant and successful career people? What would romance look like? Moreover, what would be the benefits of such a change *for men*?

As men faced greater competition from women in jobs, competition became part of the romantic fantasy, where the professional woman and man as business adversaries translated into intimate adversaries. Films like *Woman of the Year* (1942) and *Adam's Rib* (1949) explored a related strong, independent woman fantasy decades earlier, during a similarly tense economic period when women had entered the workforce not only in higher numbers but also in more technological and dangerous jobs—as opposed to the domestic and other low-paying jobs poor women had always had to do—in response to World War II.[13] Such an archetype flourishes particularly in periods like the Great Depression and World War II, when "tougher" women, as Gates puts it, were "not only admirable [...] but necessary" (110) to step up to new demands in the workforce. Heterosexual competition as an intimacy standard, thus, emerges during periods when gender roles become destabilized. Consequently, one common love-buddy fighting female trope has been the obsessive inquiries about the problem of what Laura Holt repeatedly referred to as "mixing business with pleasure." Business and pleasure are competing notions that don't mesh intuitively with traditional romance because the tradition began long before the personal and private spheres overlapped for the majority of women. Blurring the lines of emotional and professional experiences—where it would lead, what it would threaten, how it could happen—defines the basis of the romantic clash for the 1980s love-buddy fighting female. After all, her position symbolizes the way the professional woman's personal feelings are at stake but also her career, where a failed relationship could lead to a failed partnership and a failed business endeavor.

In the pilot episode, the first time that Laura sees the stranger who will become Remington Steele, she finds him attractive and alluring in his role pretending to be a South African government agent. When he takes over the imaginary role of Remington Steele that she created, she is frustrated and angry with him, until the end of the episode when he is about to leave both her and the role behind, when she is free to flirt with him and even seem sad at his departure. But in the second episode, he returns to her and the role and immediately begins causing problems. He spends money wildly, forcing her to close his accounts. In his anger, he then ruins a lead in the case she was working, making her look bad to an already sexist client. Steele then ingratiates himself with the client by offering his own plan without Holt's approval. The two have a heated argument back at the office, an exchange that starts with a frustrated Laura chastising him for his inappropriate behaviors and ends with the two discussing the possibility of going to bed together. Laura very openly declares that she would like to sleep with him but that she won't let pleasure get in the way of business, ending the discussion. Her secretary Bernice (Janet DeMay) encourages Laura to go for it and enjoy herself, but Laura demurs, in part because she's unsure of what she wants and what indulging her desires would mean for the business, and in part because she thinks that not sleeping with him will keep him interested.

These two episodes set the tone for the remainder of the series, as Laura moves seamlessly between competing emotions: resentment and appreciation, frustrated anger and attraction, and worrying about the state of the agency and her own personal needs. Remington does help the business, if only because of sexist clients who refuse to work with a woman unless she's working for a man. The only way she imagines herself able to exercise "control" over Remington—to both keep him helping the business and sticking around for a possible relationship—reveals how the fantasy of competitive romance is just another power play that requires manipulation and calculated denial. This sounds very much like tactics from the old heterosexual contract: a woman denying sex until the security of a commitment can be obtained. Only this time, her feminine wiles exist side-by-side with her determination to follow her dreams and be a success. Moreover, it's understood that Laura denies herself pleasure as well. Make no mistake: this play is not about making Laura seem prim. Other episodes show us that Laura was once something of a wild thing, a partier; she has had past lovers, and she will have other potential lovers during the series.[14]

What's particularly interesting about the will-they-won't-they aspect of their relationship isn't so much about either sex or commitment, even though it professes to be, but rather is about trust and sharing, the real basis of the power problems between them in the realm of intimacy. Laura insists on knowing who Remington really is before she can consider maintaining a relationship of any kind with him, outside of the workplace. He refuses to give her this knowledge for most of the series. They continually contest each other's reasoning and positions on this: he says that she's being too rational, and she says he needs to commit, at the very least, to sharing his story with her. The narrative continually positions them on opposite sides of each other, even at times when they share the same desires—though, of course, at different times. This keeps the competitive edge to their interactions. For example, in "Signed, Steeled, and Delivered" (01.04), Laura is excited when Remington asks her out on a date until she learns it's only because his previous date canceled at the last minute. Here, she seems the most interested in moving things forward with them romantically. Then, in the very next episode, Remington is the one who wants to make a date of their evening work as they steal a painting to foil an art thief—he shares cognac with her from a thermos, toasts to their "first time" (committing a crime). Laura, however, says very clearly, "This isn't a date, you know" to cut off the romance, this time to his disappointment.

These power plays certainly can be seen to reinforce the notion of traditional gender roles in hetero-romance as a salve to the destabilized gender roles portrayed in the hetero-partnering in *Remington Steele*, just as the critics mentioned earlier note. Hence, the show traverses the murky line dividing the burgeoning ideal of feminist-friendly love just finding a toehold in arenas of 1980s popular media and the rigid standards of intimacy based on gender opposition and unequal sex relations favoring male privilege and control. The same dynamic occurs in *Moonlighting*, but the competitive, power-play romance takes a hostile turn. Maddie actually despises David from the beginning—with good reason—unmoved by his immediate attraction for her. David constantly goads Maddie with his oafish passes and chauvinistic objectification of her. The perfect symbol of their hostile romance occurs with the first big love scene between them in season three's episode, "I Am Curious …

Maddie" (03.14). They argue—David thinks she should choose him since she dumped Sam Crawford (Mark Harmon), but she wants to choose based on what she needs rather than what she feels.

David goes on about how shallow she is, how she looks for men who look good on paper, and how she's all business, no "pleasure"; Maddie complains that he lacks culture, doesn't take work seriously enough, isn't driven. He calls her a "bitch," and she calls him a "bastard" and tells him to leave her house. She slaps him, repeating her demand, twice. The third time she begins to slap him, he catches her hand. They stare at each other, and in a moment that viewers like myself had waited for—a moment that 60 million viewers tuned in to see, one that a 1996 issue of *TV Guide* ranked as number 77 of the top "100 Most Memorable Moments in TV History"—they finally kiss—passionately, tenderly—and end up in bed together. The next episode begins where this night leaves off, the morning after, and it starts with another argument. Maddie wants to pretend nothing happened, David doesn't want to pretend, and the two fall into bed together again. And so it goes. Moments of passion and attraction, peppered with door slamming, slaps, punches, objects thrown, and lots of yelling.

The extremity calls to mind the traditional love-hate romance plot where a slap, a shouting-match, or another hostile gesture often functions as a prelude to the kiss and true love. It's a trope that has existed since Shakespeare, one that *TVTropes.org* refers to as the "slap-slap-kiss."[15] This narrative convention has been described as symbolically enacting the similarity between love and hate, which is certainly a worthy point. Yet, there was so much more going on behind Maddie's two very powerful slaps, so much so that it garnered a good deal of media attention and caused quite a stir amongst viewers. Many found the violence off-putting and thought it didn't reflect the kind of true affection the characters felt (or should have felt if they were going to fall into bed together). I think what is so troubling behind what the website calls the "slap-slap-kiss" is how it bares the power dynamics behind the romance, particularly in *Moonlighting*. It enacts violence very much in keeping with the hostile back and forth between Maddie and David and reflects their relationship/work struggles. The slaps are also a gender-bending act. When the slap comes from a woman trying to maintain control instead of from a woman who has been offended, it symbolically depicts social confusion about the empowered woman who at once presents an alluring ideal but also poses a threat to traditional heterosexual romance. The slap is, of course, another power play, one that attempts to assert her frustration at the threat David poses to her independence because, as she mentions during the fight, she feels like he keeps choosing for her by asserting his attraction against her will. Her slaps result from his once again not respecting what she says because he won't leave. His emotional power over her is furthermore tied to the overall power he exerts in the business as well, which I addressed earlier, and the "slap-slap-kiss" ultimately reminds viewers of the uneasy competitive basis of post-women's liberation hetero-intimacy. It can be solved in the moment, but the relationship, like the future of the Blue Moon Detective Agency, remains unstable in the long run.

Yet, the extremity also emerges from the show's satirical basis, which includes a progressive mocking and unraveling of romance conventions as much as detective show traditions that we don't see in *Remington Steele*. Thus, Maddie and David are more like caricatures than characters at times, but caricatures that eventually develop into more complex characters and thus break down the stereotypes informing perceptions of their behavior. I would say that their emerging intimacy shows its greatest potential for feminist love through this breakdown, as they learn to relate to each other as two subjects rather than defaulting to the typical subject/object dynamic characteristic of male/female relations traditionally represented in mass media.

In the moments when they aren't fighting over work, values, or romance by taking stereotypical male-versus-female positions, they become sensitive, supportive, communicative, even tender human beings. These moments encourage the audience to look beyond their exteriors: the cold, driven professional Maddie (functioning emblematically as the feminist career woman who threatens heterosexual traditions) and the goofy, irresponsible, and sexist David (functioning emblematically as the entitled, traditional career man who threatens career women's success). They reflect at once the worst and best of the roles they embody. These moments also encourage seeing that the sex-based power competition only exists when they perform these stereotypical roles. Eventually, we see a man and a woman who accept each other for who they really are and can forgive each other for the mishaps caused when they are in caricature, so to speak. Their most intimate moments aren't when they are in bed together but in other situations of difficulty and joy when they can mourn, weep, or celebrate together. Their real potential for intimacy is not in the partners they are initially or the lovers they are periodically: it is in the friends they end up becoming, in the camaraderie that outweighs the competition and gives them common ground but doesn't necessarily erase their individual differences.

The same breakdown of the subject/object divide and the non-sexual intimate dynamic that contradicts the elements of competition are also very much a part of the *Remington Steele* narrative, though both are less drastically enacted. Laura plays the business-minded woman focused on her career. Remington plays the charismatic troublemaker who focuses more on being entertained than on being responsible, at least early on before he becomes a true detective. They may lack caricaturistic excess, but Remington and Laura make up for it in their flipped work positions. After all, in spite of

Remington's challenges to her authority and her need of him to role-play, she is actually the professional detective, and he the amateur. He may make her position difficult, but he ultimately does have to follow her lead. In fact, she is the one who provides him the opportunity to become a crime-fighter and inspires him to be her apprentice. That's one of the reasons why I don't put as much stock in oft-stated criticisms lobbed at the way the series changed from the original premise (pitched in 1969 by Robert Butler, the eventual creator of *Remington Steele*, along with Michael Gleason) of a series featuring only the female investigator. That they eventually added a male "boss" to the show to get a green light on production is a capitulation, but having Laura be the one with the skills and the successful business acumen still flips the gender roles and asserts her subject position in a way that had not been done before on primetime. Considering the period, having a woman be a man's professional better was a bold sex-role statement.

Their intimacy is established as a process of getting to know each other, solving crimes together, and sharing moments of triumph—experiences that go a long way toward undermining the competition that incites power struggles and, thus, is reminiscent of traditional sex-role divides (even if the roles are reversed). In the scene in "Thou Shalt Not Steele" in which Remington treats their stealing a painting together as a date, it's not a kiss or any other kind of sexual expression that he finds enticing in the moment. It's that she's sharing for the "first time" what is implied to be his professional talent (stealing). His reply to her statement that they won't be making a habit of such capers is "Pity, really. There are so few forms of true intimacy left." This statement is both playful, in keeping with his troublemaker character, and sensitive because it is sincere; he wants to share this with her. He enjoys working with her and comfortably expresses that—the job offers moments when he can let his guard down, just like it does for her, and they can stop competing and playing at whose gender wins.

Examples like these problematize the readings that the shows only favor the male characters and do whatever they can to lessen the feminist impact of the female characters. The interplay of these intimate roles, with their fluctuations and contradictions, shows how unstable gender roles are and undermines the traditional notions of male/female romance. Both results are essential to the fantasy of feminist-friendly love, which occurs through alternative forms of feminist-friendly intimacies that had yet to take hold in other arenas of the popular imagination before the love-buddy narrative.

The first version of feminist-friendly intimacy occurs in *Remington Steele*, where the strong, independent Laura does find romance and ends up with a well-matched partner, whom she actually helps cultivate through the series, both professionally and relationship-wise. The show ends on an assertion of couplehood that essentially offers a straightforward and typical view of hetero-romance, only with new co-protector male/female identities that assert compatibility. From the start, the attraction was mutual, and over a shared dinner during the pilot, Laura and Remington flirted openly with each other. The series encouraged focus on their being well matched romantically by maintaining the focus on this attraction as a pleasant experience for both parties (as opposed to the reluctant attraction Maddie felt toward David). Even more so, as the series continued, they became more well matched through shared principles—Remington giving up crime to become a crime-fighter, and Laura learning to embrace the criminal within to improve her crime-fighting—and, eventually, through shared abilities, as both were closing cases in the final seasons, rather than Laura's being the one to piece everything together. Though the plot finalizes with Holt and Steele finally going to bed together—having resolved Remington's unwillingness to open up emotionally by reuniting him with the father he never knew—the ending remains ambiguous about the fate of their working relationship. Will they return to the States and continue to work as partners? It seems likely, but who knows? Suddenly, this information is no longer as important as Laura getting her man and the series getting a storybook happy ending, castle and all.

Moonlighting ends with a very different, but still important, assertion of feminist-friendly intimacy, one that offers a critique of the classic storybook ending. In a self-referential move typical of the series, during the finale's last scenes, the "producer" Cy tells them that the show died because the romance was over. Maddie responds, "But it's not over. David and I are still friends." Cy sarcastically responds, "Oh goodie, that's exactly what America wants to see. David and Maddie, friends." In reality, a number of issues contributed to the show's cancellation, issues ranging from long-term writing and production problems and delays of the desires of Bruce Willis and Cybill Shepherd to move on to other endeavors. Still, the narrative choices made in this final episode to explain the ending emphasize the problem with society's ideas of love as traditional romance, showing how it is based on unrealistic expectations that a fulfilling intimacy between men and women can only be sexual and romantic. The finale does so by turning the other characters into the voice of society—Cy saying that Maddie and David needed to stay in love to stay on-screen and Agnes tearfully criticizing them for ruining everything because they ruined their romance. In other words, with its final breaths, the show critiques the same kind of heteronormative assumptions that some feminists note are a problem in representations of women in the media in general in the male and female protagonist being destined, basically through their sex roles, to end up together in a romantic relationship. The show critiques this in favor of another kind of hetero-intimacy: platonic partnership. Very few television programs involving fighting females have explored this possibility, and most of those began after the turn of the new century.

The final scene has Maddie and David sitting at the front of a church, holding hands, looking at each other tenderly, before a montage of happy, sad, romantic, angry, and intimate moments throughout the series. By not bringing these two together at the end of the series, in spite of the characters' best final efforts,[16] *Moonlighting* ultimately cannot imagine a feminist romance, but it does give us a glimpse at a feminist-friendly love as hetero-intimacy. As for the issue of whether or not the Blue Moon Detective Agency would prove solvent, that became about as moot as the will-they-won't-they trope (because they did get together for a time, and it still didn't matter). Like with *Remington Steele*, the final emphasis is the state of the union, so to speak. What ended the agency wasn't Maddie's poor business skills or lack of authority but rather the show's cancellation, for the reasons listed above. The network closed the agency as part of the finale, freeing the show's narrative arc from the will-she-won't-she-be-a-success trope as well. Does that change the fact that there were consistent male challenges to her authority throughout? No. That remains problematic as far as the professional woman she represented. Still, *Moonlighting* offered audiences a kind of partnership between men and women that explored multiple elements of female identity that would make possible a stronger, more complex female character.

Overall, the potential that these fighting females' personal relations and business interests may be undermined or may unravel at any time shapes these 1980s love-buddy narratives. From this perspective, these early love-buddy programs are really about the fighting females, even though they include male co-stars, and the shows reflect contemporary questions about female identity in an age struggling with working women. More than anything, this social and economic disruption—encouraged by feminist movements and also by a changing financial system—weakened gender roles and put into play conflicting expectations. Firmly entrenched beliefs established through the heterosexual contract—beliefs about a woman's place being in the home, being protected and supported by a man, or about a woman's not being able to do what a man can do—were being undermined with every statistic: even those news reports that promoted panic about women's marital status included proof of their rising educational and career successes.

One effect of orienting these love-buddy narratives around the fighting female is that she often comes off as being emotionally reluctant at best or cold at worst. Hence, Laura's repeated refrain about not mixing "business with pleasure" turns out to be a defense mechanism to ensure that she remains in charge of the business. Maddie's "cold bitch" persona in the first episode, when she dispassionately informs David that she is closing the agency, turns out to have been another defense mechanism, a result both of her being swindled out of everything and of her being put in charge of firing a bunch of strangers. These women don't always have the luxury of seeking fun or catering to their emotional whims. This reality indicates that the struggle to maintain authority and to balance the intimate desires with the business work is the woman's alone. As Mizejewski points out in her discussion about Maddie's unwillingness to give in to her desires for David (a point that also applies to Laura's resistance to Remington), "her resistance symbolized not virtue but hard-earned lessons from 1970s feminism: independence, self-protection, and integrity" (*Hardboiled* 79).

Remington Steele and *Moonlighting* also reveal a new expression of privilege for the male characters who function in these love-buddy fantasies not only as semi-enlightened men—because they are sensitive, more emotional, and find the empowered woman desirable—but also as men who are more enlightened than the women. Both Laura and Maddie are uptight about and determined to control the terms of their relationships with men. This determination is indicated in their romances with other men during the show, men who tend to be drudges and dullards. Laura is linked to her ex, the dull banker Wilson Jeffries (David Huffman) and has a flirtatious relationship with a season-one employee, the by-the-book investigator Murphy Michaels (James Read). Maddie marries, briefly, Walter Bishop (Dennis Dugan), during a period of emotional confusion because he seems stable and, compared to David, dispassionate. Remington and David, on the other hand, tend to be more easy-going and cavalier because they can be. It's simpler for them to incorporate non-stereotypical gender traits because they already occupy the superior position in the sex hierarchy. Both Remington and David are portrayed as playboys, linked to beautiful and exciting women either in their pasts or in the present. The men's free-wheeling emotional lives, whether in their determination to seek pleasure at work or off the clock, tends to highlight the excessive self-control practiced by their partners who work long hours with little social life and who temporarily end up with the dull men. And the women's temporary choice of dull men highlights the way the non-traditional female seeks emotional protection against intimacy or in practical intimacy the way the traditional female sought economic and social protection in intimacy.

David and Remington don't need to resist because the stakes aren't as high for them. This differential becomes a key problem in the love-buddy narratives to come. Whereas once the ideal traditional heterosexual relationship was presumed to ensure a woman's social and economic protection and security as well as the fulfillment of her feminine role (whether or not this was the case), in the world of the strong, independent woman, the heterosexual relationship presents a threat: to her career, her autonomy, and her self-respect. In *Autonomy, Gender, Politics*, Marilyn Friedman situates this fear as being related to one of the many possible ways people "merge" through romantic love. Here, she distinguishes the results of a healthy merger from an unhealthy one, stating, "Romantic mergers that nurture and affirm us can promote our autonomy as individuals by promoting our self-understanding, self-esteem, and capacities to act effectively in concert with others. Romantic mergers that drain or erase us can reduce our autonomy as individuals by diminishing those same attributes" (123–4). Nevertheless, the potential romantic merger "can threaten the personal autonomy of either partner in a heterosexual romance." Further, as "[t]raditions of love and gender still hold women more responsible than men for sacrificing their independent selves to sustain" the relationships, there *is* an element of personal peril, one that both *Remington Steele* and *Moonlighting* clearly remind us poses a bigger threat to women's autonomy at the office or in the home (132). This is why Laura and Maddie are so serious about the business of love and worry about getting involved on a whim or purely for pleasure.

The 21st-Century Love-Buddy Fighting Female: "You just can't stay out of my personal life, can you?"[17]

Both of these 1980s love-buddy narratives reoriented the popular boundaries of femininity for white, professional women in order to make room for strength and independence in their female protagonists' identities. They contributed more proof that such a woman's drive, assertiveness, and intelligence were not entirely threatening, did not deserve punishment, and could, in fact, be very desirable traits that fit snugly within her femininity, rather than automatically being opposed to it. As crime-fighting characters, Maddie and Laura provided an excellent counterpoint to the less nuanced macho crime-fighters popular at the time, including those in *Magnum P.I.* (1980–88), *Columbo* (1968–2003), *The A-Team* (1983–87), and *ChiPs* (1977–83). They were different from many other female characters whose hetero-romances were emphasized in the narratives—like thinly-veiled damsels-in-distress Jennifer Hart and Amanda King and eye-candy playthings proliferating on the big screen in films like the *Police Academy* franchise. Maddie and Laura also provided a contrast to the negative portrayals of the violent or aggressive woman as a driven, manipulative bitch character found in just about any soap opera (in primetime or daytime) and in more extreme forms in films like *Fatal Attraction* (1987). But the unique character of the love-buddy fighting female took a nearly sixteen-year hiatus after *Moonlighting* ended in 1989.

One could argue that the break ended with the 1993 premiere of *The X-Files*, which provided a varied take on the love-buddy, with the will-they-won't-they tension between the dual protagonists Dana Scully (Gillian Anderson) and Fox Mulder (David Duchovny). However, there is little interrogation into their relationship, no agonizing about whether they want to or should become a couple, even if there are enticing moments. When they come together near the end of the series, it happens obliquely, behind the scenes, sometimes to confusing effect (for example, it's unclear whether Mulder fathers Scully's baby). The same case goes for *Fringe* and the partnership between Agent Olivia Dunham (Anna Torv) and Peter Bishop (Joshua Jackson). Both shows include elements of science fiction that impact the basis of the hetero-relations in ways beyond the scope of this study. As far as Scully's and Olivia's positions as fighting females, both fit more within the fraught narratives that began to preoccupy the cultural imagination of the 1990s, which Chapter Four addresses. Thus, it wasn't until 2005, with the premiere of the long-running series *Bones*, that another love-buddy narrative hit the small screen. The series *Chuck,* which premiered in 2007, and the also popular *Castle,* which premiered in 2009, brought audiences other new primetime love buddies.

Bones features forensic anthropologist Dr. Temperance "Bones" Brennan (Emily Deschanel), who works for the Jeffersonian (a fictionalized version of the Smithsonian). Along with a crew of "squints" (Jeffersonian scientists), she also assists FBI Agent Seeley Booth (David Boreanaz) in solving murders. Amidst their crime-solving and fighting, Booth and Brennan eventually marry and have two children. *Castle* is named for the male protagonist, Richard "Rick" Castle (Nathan Fillion), a best-selling crime novelist. The series begins with his using his connections with the New York City mayor to be assigned to the NYPD as a consultant so he can research a novel. He is assigned to Detective Kate Beckett (Stana Katic), who becomes the muse for his latest detective hero, Nikki Heat. Castle and Beckett solve crimes together first as partners, then as lovers, and then as husband and wife. *Chuck* is also named for the male protagonist, Charles "Chuck" Bartowski (Zachary Levi), though, as with each love-buddy narrative, there would be no story without his fighting female partner, CIA agent Sarah Walker (Yvonne Strahovski). In the pilot, Chuck accidentally downloads into his brain the Intersect, a top-secret security technology that encodes vast amounts of data; thus, he becomes an unwilling asset of U.S. intelligence. Walker and NSA Agent John Casey (Adam Baldwin) are assigned to protect Chuck and also to use the knowledge he's downloaded to complete missions. Chuck and Walker also end up married by the season finale.

In spite of the years that passed between them, the new love-buddy narratives aren't necessarily more progressive than the previous ones. They play on many of the same issues regarding the threat love poses for the empowered woman and the male/female negotiations on-screen that emerged from the 1980s narratives and vacillate between progressive and regressive. However, it is the representation of these issues that changed. The questions of female success have been downplayed. Also, these newer stories reflect an increase in television violence and different hetero-intimacy standards that have implications for today's feminist-friendly ideal.

As contemporary love-buddy narratives, *Bones*, *Castle*, and *Chuck* include fighting female protagonists who are far more violent than their 1980s counterparts. From the very first episode of *Bones*, Brennan shows she can take care of herself and fight criminals. In the pilot, she wields a bat against an assumed intruder. Another time, she shoots a criminal in the leg to keep him from destroying evidence, proving her comfort wielding firepower (01.02). In the season nine finale, Brennan saves her partner and husband, Booth— who's pinned down in a gunfight in their shared home—by "toting a shotgun *like a boss*," as one excited fan reports (Mitovich, emphasis in the original). She also knows three kinds of martial arts (01.19). Brennan is actually less combat-oriented than the other two love-buddy fighting females, and she's the only one who has not specifically trained as an agent or cop. As a police officer, Beckett shoots to kill in the line of duty, throws punches, and chases down and tackles perps (wearing stilettos no less) so many times that a list would be impractical. As a trained CIA agent, Walker regularly kicks some serious criminal ass, punching, kicking, and shooting people in almost every episode (also often in stilettos). As the most violent of the three, Walker even kills an unarmed villain at one point (02.11).

Moreover, these three fighting females can take a beating in ways that their 1980s counterparts didn't, which indicates an increase in primetime audience tolerance for female violence, not only in what women perpetrate but also in what they can handle as part of their strength and independence. In addition to the normal scrapes and bruises that come from physical battles, all three of the women are either shot (Beckett and Brennan) or otherwise hospitalized from injuries at some point during the series (Walker), and they make full recoveries. Hence, they continue to reflect the gender-bending qualities of the fighting female and also reinforce the compatibility between strength and femininity that has become more and more apparent in on-screen female characters.

Variations on a Theme

As with the early narratives, these three love-buddy series also focus on the fighting female's negotiating the threat of heterosexual intimacy for the successful, driven professional woman. Still, some important modifications indicate a shift in fantasies about empowered women, in general, that relate to the feminist-friendly love potential in these more recent series. First, these new characters represent the strong, independent woman as highly successful as well as authoritative in her career, unlike her predecessors, whose empowerment was still under explicit interrogation and thus represented more ambiguously. The shows characterize the female protagonists as brilliant women in fields that are male-dominated. Brennan is one of the foremost forensic anthropologists in the country, holds three doctorates, and speaks six languages. She is also a novelist, and her own character is based on an actual anthropologist and writer, Kathy Reichs. Beckett has the honor of being the youngest person to make detective in the NYPD (04.01). She's college-educated, highly intelligent, and she speaks Russian from a semester between her junior and senior year spent abroad (02.01). She's eventually promoted to work for the Attorney General in Washington, D.C (06.01), and by season eight, Beckett is the captain of the precinct. Walker is experienced, talented, fluent in several languages, and regularly praised as an excellent spy by her colleagues and her superior throughout the series. The hard-to-impress Casey even calls Walker the "best damn partner" he's ever had (02.18). Her potential and talent were noted early on by the CIA, who recruited her when she was still in high school (02.04).

As the women in these three shows are part of a larger group of accomplished female characters being broadcast on television and in film,[18] they also no longer occupy only token—and therefore more tentative—power positions the way Maddie and Laura do. Brennan regularly works with two other talented female "squints": Angela Montenegro (Michaela Conlin), an artist who renders forensic reconstructions and knows all things cyber-tech, and Dr. Camille Saroyan (Tamara Taylor), the head of the Forensic Division. Beckett works with medical examiner Dr. Lanie Parrish (Tamala Jones) and Captain Victoria Gates (Penny Johnson Jerald), who joins the precinct in season four after the death of the previous captain until Beckett becomes captain. Castle's daughter and mother are both portrayed as driven and successful women, particularly as the show progresses when his daughter Alexis (Molly Quinn) becomes Castle's PI protégé. The series includes a bevy of other successful crime-fighting women with whom Beckett and Castle join forces, including female FBI and CIA agents. Walker becomes friends with Chuck's sister, the accomplished doctor and occasional CIA asset Ellie Woodcomb (Sarah Lancaster), and Walker was once a member of an elite squad that included three other kick-ass women. Chuck's mother, Mary Bartowski (Linda Hamilton), turns out to be a deep-cover CIA agent who features in several episodes later in the series.

The second important change that's occurred in the love-buddy narrative is the focus on the marriage and family aspects in the partners' lives, as opposed to just the wooing phase or romance and sex that occupied the earlier two series. After Brennan and Booth fall in love, they end up having a baby together and get married. Rather than signaling the end of the series, they continue their crime-fighting partnership even as they work on the complications of parenthood. We get to see them negotiate parenting styles, as they do when their daughter, Christine (Sunnie Pelant), begins cursing (10.07), and they disagree about whether that is a problem. After a few seasons of wedded bliss, they have to face Booth's gambling addiction. Brennan kicks him out when his debts endanger the family (10.19), though they are able to work it out by the end of the season. They also have to decide about changing their careers—together—an issue I examine in more detail later.

Castle, Beckett's partner in crime-fighting and love, comes with his own ready-made family—a teenage daughter and a mother who lives with him during the early seasons of the show. Even before Beckett and Castle become an item, Beckett gives Castle parenting advice, and his daughter Alexis readily accepts Beckett into her life when Beckett and Castle affirm their love. The problems they face in their romance, just as Brennan and Booth do, are very much reflective of "real" relationship problems involving two independent people making their lives work. For example, Beckett is offered a job working for the Attorney General in Washington, D.C. (05.23), and Castle proposes (05.24)—not, as he makes clear, to keep her with him but to ensure that they can stay together after she takes the job, which he encourages her to do. Thus, the two have to decide how to work out the long distance. In a testament to how well the love-buddy narrative has absorbed the career woman ideal into the fantasy, there is never a question that Beckett must choose one or the other. Instead, the partners make it work.

Family plays an important part in Walker's story, too, as we get to know more about her background. Raised primarily by her paternal grandmother when her grifter father is in jail or away on a scheme, she and her father become estranged when a young Walker rebels and joins the CIA (and is able to use the grifting skills she learned growing up in her work as a spy). Walker reunites with her father during the series—and also with her mother, from whom Walker also became estranged—but only to protect a refugee whom she adopted a sister and left in her mother's care. As the series progresses, Walker's real family expands to include: her partner and eventual husband Chuck; his family, including his sister and his sister's fiancé (and later husband), with whom Chuck lives for a few seasons; and Chuck's best friend, Morgan Grimes (Joshua Gomez). Eventually, Walker and her other partner, Casey, become like family, too, in spite of Casey's professed distaste for all things personal and emotional (which begins to change later in the series when he discovers he has a grown daughter and when he becomes Morgan's handler, taking a comparatively nurturing role to help Morgan ease into his agent responsibilities and to protect him). Walker and Chuck also marry in the season four finale, while continuing their work/love partnership for the final fifth season. Their relationship trials are less "realistic" in the sense that Walker ends up being brainwashed and turned against Chuck (though some of us have probably had experiences with exes that could only be explained by a brainwashing theory). However, they do remain together and still are married in the end, in spite of the difficulties.

The will-they-won't-they allure of the love-buddy narrative remains an important part of each series as a whole. In this way, little has changed from the time of *Moonlighting* and *Remington Steele*, whose producers reportedly agreed that "keep[ing] relationships interesting and honest is the trickiest element of producing a continuing series in which romantic tension is a critical element" (Holston). Walker's relationship with Chuck is very much up in the air for the first three seasons as she considers a romance with another spy, and Chuck meets other love interests. Brennan and Booth each have romances with other people, ignoring the sparks between them and their growing intimacy. Beckett and Castle play an infuriating amount of back and forth: Castle proves ready and interested in a relationship, but Beckett gets a new boyfriend; then she's ready, just after Castle reconciles with an ex-wife; Castle tells Beckett he loves her (but doesn't know if she is aware because she is shot and bleeding out at the time); and by the time she's ready to acknowledge that she did hear and says it back, he's moved on again.

The wedding part is also drawn out in all three series, as a number of professional issues interfere. Villains always pop up at some inopportune time to prevent smooth nuptials. Beckett learns she didn't properly annul a previous marriage. Castle is kidnapped on their first planned wedding day. A serial killer blackmails Booth to postpone the wedding (without an explanation to Brennan or anyone) to prevent the death of five innocent people. Walker is poisoned right before the wedding. Thus, the narrative relationship tensions remain intact, only expanded to allow for what these shows assume is the natural progression after wooing and consummating—the wedding.

In 1986, writing about the way "Sexual Tension Teases Stars and Viewers," Noel Holston voices a common question about the will-they-won't-they plot and whether showing "commitment would fundamentally alter the relationship, perhaps destroying what made them popular." Critics would often cite the lackluster relationship between Sam and Diane on *Cheers* as an example of how commitment ruins the storyline. By the new century, as we see in the contemporary narratives, the answer to this question seems to be a resounding "no." That's because tensions remain an integral part of the storyline and still invoke the tentative nature of the empowered woman's romantic future, as with the early love-buddy series. They're just varied tensions that reflect more contemporary popular culture.

Having It All-or-Nothing

One such variance indicated by the love-buddy narrative development of family and marriage symbolizes the influence that the have-it-all ideal has had on the concept of feminist-friendly love, itself an ideal based on popular media interpretations of feminist agendas. The concept had only just emerged in the 1980s. One of the first uses was of it in the title of Helen Gurley Brown's book *Having It All: Love, Success, Sex, Money ... Even If You're Starting with Nothing*. There was also a film in 1982 titled *Having It All*, starring Dyan Cannon as a successful businesswoman juggling two husbands (one on each coast, no less!). While there had been women juggling family and work in lower-income households literally for centuries, this was not considered a noteworthy feat until women had the option to choose their careers and work as professionals, either in addition to or instead of having a marriage and a family. Movies like *Baby Boom* and successful career moms in television shows like *Family Ties* (1982–89), *Who's the Boss?*, and *The Cosby Show* brought images of the mother-nurturer/careerwoman-achiever into many families' homes.

However, these women, while certainly not stereotypical, were not fighting females and thus didn't reflect the same challenge to gender norms as Maddie and Laura from the same period. Those two characters existed in a time when, in order for women to be able to have it all, audiences had first to imagine them having a successful romance and a successful career, both of which had not been combined in crime-fighting, action-based narratives. As shown, neither early narrative was able to represent that combination completely. Laura and Remington did end up in bed together, and Maddie almost had a child (as well as a brief, ill-considered marriage), but they never went beyond the most uncertain early stages. The relatively swift cultural reorientation of a woman's success in love and life toward having it all, a reorientation that followed the 1980s, both reflects and reinforces the ideal of the empowered woman in that only a strong, independent woman has the necessary resources to juggle both the career and family that are supposed to define having it all. By achieving this, the love-buddy fighting female of today reassures audiences it *is* possible, which thus paints a picture that the mass media fantasy banks on and constructs the allure of this possibility.

At the same time, however, the lingering attributes of intimacy-based tensions in today's storylines—not just in the question of their getting together but their staying together and having a family, the themes of interference keeping them apart, making them even question each other's loyalty—reflect the more recent realization in certain arenas of the popular imagination that the "have it all" dream is just that, a dream. The 21st-century love-buddy narratives emerged after this dream had not only been inflated as the goal of the contemporary empowered woman but also deflated by a good deal of media scrutiny involving the unrealistic fantasy it offers.[19] For some, the idea of women having it all became less a goal and more an obstacle.

Probably the most important critiques of the having-it-all fantasy have come from black and other women and feminists of color who recognize that, as a priority, it centers more around white, leisure-class, college-educated (potentially aspiring professional) women. This fantasy has little to do with the experiences and immediate needs of the women bell hooks describes as those "who are most victimized by sexist oppression," the women who make up the "silent majority" left behind in what is not only a sexist but also a classist, racist, ethnocentric, ableist American society (2). Hooks is neither the first nor the last to identify this problem, which is generally a problem with white and/or leisure-class feminism, where the "plight" of some women who exercise the most privilege becomes "synonymous with a condition affecting all American women," even though those women are not in the majority and often don't have much in common with other women (2). This restricted/ing focus on what must change in the workforce to make it more "equal"—namely, access to opportunity, equal pay, and an end to the glass ceiling—does not reflect "the pressing political concerns of masses of women" (2).

Patricia Hill Collins identifies a similar problem with too much emphasis on gender, at least when it's extracted from the matrix of domination responsible for other inequities women and men experience that demand change, including "[p]overty, unemployment, rape, HIV/AIDS, incarceration, substance abuse, adolescent pregnancy, high rates of Black children in foster care, intraracial violence, and similar issues" that make up only a small portion of experiences for historical marginalized classes and groups (8–9). These problems within America's social infrastructure and cultural climate do take a "gender-specific form" (9), as gender shapes all encounters, but such problems are often rendered invisible when compared to the concerns about the professional workplace, where the option to *have* it all to determine success seems to take precedence over *having to do* it all to determine survival.

So, this love-buddy fantasy effectively rests on a bourgeois notion of white womanhood (the cis-gender aspect of which I'll address more in the final chapter). That doesn't mean it necessarily holds less power for those who are woman-identified and heterosexual, no matter their backgrounds or other identities, as they are the ones who are exposed to the brunt of much of the romance and love narratives. Even if those women don't necessarily believe it will happen for them, they still tend to expect if not idealize it. Hill Collins shares a story from the first day of her first "Introduction to Black Gender Studies class," as her students discussed their general expectations for marriage. She notes that "African American women in particular did not hold out much hope that they would find suitable partners" (247), but that "[t]heir responses suggested that they had considered these questions more thoroughly than either African American men or White students" (247). This additional consideration likely occurred because of the excessive number of obstacles those Black women knew they faced in finding not only a suitable partner but also in avoiding the extra risks racism poses to the relationship once it develops. Certainly, I have had white female-bodied students lament what feels like the impossibility of finding a man who can handle their autonomy, but nowhere near to the extent of my Latina and Chicana students who voice similar concerns (always in their journals, which only I read), concerns about how they will find a man who doesn't expect them to play a traditional domestic role, to give up their own dreams. Why wouldn't these students feel this way considering that women of color have even fewer blockbuster or mainstream examples of successful romantic relationships (much less one where the female protagonist isn't expected to subordinate her strength and independence) because of the white-centric mass media of the 1980s–2010s.[20]

We can see how the have-it-all dream can apply to women in a class- and-race-divided culture when we consider some other criticisms that have arisen regarding this fantasy. Probably one of the first critics of the have-it-all concept to gain popular attention was Arlie Hochschild, the author of *The Second Shift*, who pointed out that as women attained more responsibility in and access to the public sphere and became part of a dual-earner partnership, their home life responsibilities didn't budge. In essence, women doubled their work time and responsibilities by balancing career and family (an issue that will crop up in the romaction fighting female narratives discussed in Chapter Three). This problem was one that already existed for women of working-class and other households where there was no question that both parents had to work, assuming there were two parents available in the home. Yet, the second shift didn't lay claim to the American cultural imagination in the same way until the extra responsibilities began to weigh on the new working women. And the solution to this problem—outsourcing home and/ or family care—was usually a woman of more vulnerable class and race category, which basically guaranteed a second and sometimes third shift for that woman.

More recently, Debora L. Spar argues that the dream of having it all made possible by feminism has become a nightmare of perfectionism. Young women set unrealistic goals for themselves and take the responsibility for success wholly on themselves without being aware of the social, cultural, political, and biological limitations that make those goals incredibly difficult to achieve even for the smartest and most capable women. Thirty years ago, the Superwoman identity was invented. She could raise her children, take over the corporate world, and even find a nice, sensitive man who would stand by and watch her succeed (but contribute startlingly little to either endeavor). Even if this perfectionism extends to her role as a wife and/or mother, making her more likely to feel responsible for the domestic sphere herself—and even if this perfectionism masks the classism apparent in a Superwoman ideal that still applies to middle-class women who have to juggle child or family care with their jobs because of rising childcare costs—the specter of perfectionism hangs primarily over the heads of women who have access to the kind of education and support that would allow them to rise into the super ranks. Today, more critics recognize the mystique behind the have-it-all concept (Martin). Yet, it remains an alluring fantasy, one still associated with an idealized goal for women's liberation that is limited/ing.

The contemporary love-buddy narratives navigate both sides of the dream and walk a very fine line by giving these fighting females everything their hearts might desire—the fantasy—but also by reflecting the complications of this fantasy. Ultimately, as tentative as the notion of "having it all" remains for a plethora of reasons—as problematic as this ideal might prove to be—and as fraught as putting the woman back into the family narrative to which she has long been linked might also be[21]—the very presence of popular female characters who are accepted to possess a range of roles represents a change in certain areas of the mass media that is in keeping with many feminist interests related to undermining the gender divide. Now, with regards to women's options in relationships, we can rightfully argue for both the importance of the career woman and for the woman as a stay-at-home parent while recognizing women's abilities to be both at once or at different times in their lives. We can also tout the advantages of remaining single or ending up coupled, going back and forth between the two, or even extending the romance to polyamory. At the very least, this change authorizes the presence of new mass media identities for women who have the privilege to choose; thus, the change can be seen to reflect an increased acceptance in certain arenas of popular culture of women as capable contributors in the workplace but also an acceptance that a woman who is strong and independent on the job can still be a wife and/or mother if she desires—even if this acceptance exists in conjunction with media examples to the contrary in other arenas of popular culture, and even if this acceptance oversimplifies or ignores economic realities and other forms of oppression that women experience.

The latest love-buddy narratives resolve the tensions associated with the strong, independent identities they produce in ways that are unique in recent programming: by creating narrative worlds where the fighting females can have it all by turning the workspace into a home and creating one big happy career-oriented family revolving around the partner-couple. Also, there is a third distinction between early and contemporary love-buddy narratives—following the assumption of the successful career woman who's no longer a token and following the narrative beyond the marriage—in that today, the lines that once divided the crime-fighting, action-based excitement from the family drama blur. Both David R. Coon and Ien Ang address the budding trend, which Ang notes began in the 1980s, of personal struggles becoming part of workplace dramas like *L.A. Law* or *Cagney & Lacey* (more recent examples include shows like *NYPD Blue* or *Grey's Anatomy*). However, as Coon observes, while "these series move easily between the domestic and professional spheres, they generally maintain a distinction between them" because doctors and lawyers don't deal with patients or clients in the home. Police units and detective agencies tend to remain only in the public sphere (241). In these love-buddy narratives, there is no retreat for the fighting female from work or home, from public or private.

For the fighting female, the public and private spheres collide. First, work becomes a home away from home, and colleagues become family either in addition to or in place of actual relatives. Beckett and Castle's colleagues at the precinct—her best friend Lanie, and their other partners, Detectives Javier "Espo" Esposito (Jon Huertas), and Kevin Ryan (Seamus Deever)—support each other through good and bad. They stand by each other, fiercely loyal. When Beckett suffers from PTSD after being shot by a sniper, and she freezes when faced with taking down a sniper during a later episode, Espo talks her through it and helps her face her fears (04.09). When Beckett takes a dark turn while investigating her mother's murder and goes rogue, all of her partners support her, even after she alienates them. Espo, Ryan, and Castle don't tell on her to Captain Gates. The one time that Ryan does inform Gates, after Beckett's gone off alone to face the sniper who shot her, it becomes a source of contention between Ryan and Espo, who thinks Ryan betrayed Beckett. But Ryan's betrayal was in service of their friendship and actually allowed him to save Beckett from falling off a building. The situation ends up giving them all a chance to talk it out as friends later (04.23). Beckett also spends her free time with her colleagues outside of the workplace as they regularly end cases with plans to meet at the bar, and none of them are presented as having any friends outside of each other. Ryan even proposes to his girlfriend Jenny in the middle of the precinct and, of course, everyone is part of the wedding party later on that season (03.11).

The same goes for Brennan's and Booth's colleagues at the Jeffersonian and for Chuck's and Walker's team. Their colleagues are also their main source of social and emotional life. Many of Chuck and Walker's dates and social events occur in the apartment Chuck shares with Ellie and Devon (Ryan McPartlin), and each season, there's a Thanksgiving episode revolving around completing the mission in time to attend the family dinner. Before Ellie marries Devon in season two, Chuck makes it his mission—literally, as he ends up using CIA resources—to find their long-lost father to walk Ellie down the aisle. In these shows, characters all attend each other's weddings, celebrate births, and mourn losses together, as when the character Lance Sweets (John Francis Daley) on *Bones* is murdered by the serial killer Christopher Pelant (Andrew Leeds). Everyone rallies together not only to take Pelant down but also to help Daisy Wick (Carla Gallo), Sweet's girlfriend and the mother of their unborn child. At one point, when Brennan asks Daisy if she has any family who can help out, Daisy replies, "It's here [the lab]" and that they are all her "family" (10.02). In fact, the characters in each of these series refer to each other as family, as when Beckett tells Espo, Ryan, and Castle that "no one outside of this immediate family" could know of Captain Montgomery's betrayal (03.24). In other words, there are multiple forms of intimacy being explored in these shows, in conjunction with the love-buddy relationship, though the couple relationship remains central.

Because of this family dynamic, the second collision of the public and private spheres occurs: personal problems enter the workspace, and professional problems enter the home space. A good example of this is when colleagues discuss relationships as they work, as when Beckett talks to Lanie about the men they date in between discussing clues revealed by a body Lanie autopsies while they chat. Castle also talks with his friends Espo and Ryan about relationship issues. Castle often seeks the advice of Beckett, Espo, and Ryan when faced with parenting conflicts. And everyone comes together to help Beckett find the killer of her mother—a woman who was murdered while investigating political corruption—which indicates how the professional and the personal have been a mix for her from the beginning of her career. This mix, however, is not unusual in the way that many series bring personal relationships into the workspace.

It's when the work space becomes part of the domestic sphere that a difference in the love-buddy narrative emerges. There are times during the series when Castle's family is threatened, as when Alexis inadvertently is taken when her friend is kidnapped for ransom, and Beckett and the team work to save her (05.16). Then Beckett's apartment blows up during a failed attempt to assassinate her (02.18). Both Castle and Beckett set up their own separate workstations in their separate homes to continue investigating the murder of Beckett's mother. Alexis even works an internship for Dr. Parish while she tries to decide what she wants to study in college, bringing the family directly into the precinct and placing them at crime scenes. Job and home spheres overlap in these instances, and even more so when Alexis starts to help solve crimes as a budding PI.

Similar meldings occur in *Bones*. Bones' and Booth's wedding is postponed when a psychopath threatens to kill people if they marry (08.24). Additionally, their home becomes the setting of a nasty gunfight after Booth is mistaken for an assassin and set up for murder (09.24). Chuck's apartment is invaded throughout the series—the first time by Sarah before they began working with each other when she was tasked with stealing his computer. Walker's father helps out on missions, using his con-man skills. By the end of the series, not only Chuck but also Casey, Morgan, Ellie, and Devon all live in the same apartment complex at some point. Civilians Ellie, Devon, and

Morgan are regularly—often unwittingly—ensnared within missions. Morgan becomes a pseudo-agent on Team Bartowski with some training from Casey. Ellie becomes an asset, briefly, for a group she thinks is the CIA. Devon is mistaken as a spy and has to help on a mission. Chuck and Ellie's parents even turn out to be spies. By the end of the series, not only has home been occupied by work, but work has been occupied by home, as the whole family regularly spends time in "The Castle," the spy team's secret base located under a Buy More store, where Chuck works his cover job.

Role Play and the Changing Workplace

These collisions of public/private interests and experiences have two effects that reinforce the way the love-buddy partnership attempts to conceive of and capitalize on a fantasy of feminist-friendly love by undermining the traditional heterosexual contract. In this public/private mingling, the lines dividing the sex roles through the separate spheres blur. Coon notes this kind of blurring in *Alias* (a narrative to be examined in Chapter Four), but his conclusion relates to the gender work occurring in the love-buddy narratives as well.

> By using the home as a setting for professional concerns and the workplace as a location for familial battles and negotiations, *Alias* challenges the binaristic view that imagines separation between the domestic and professional spheres. In doing this, the series also breaks down the gender division that parallels the split between spheres. Both men and women are free to move through domestic and professional spaces ["Putting Women in Their Place" 242].

Because of this freer access, both sexes navigate domestic and professional roles interchangeably. Nurturing emotional labor focused on relationships and connection (presumed to be the central work of the domestic, private sphere) coincides with intellectual and service labor focused on developing society (presumed to be the central work of the public sphere). The work is also shared by both sexes in tandem instead of separately. This indicates the ways that gender roles are not static and that the gender divide itself is specious. Consequently, we can see that the impetus to protect (considered a primary masculine trait) is actually an impetus to nurture (considered a primary feminine trait) and that the presumed strength of the former is compatible with the latter. So, there are times when Beckett saves Castle, Castle helps save Beckett, Ryan and Espo save Beckett and Castle, and vice versa. One episode, after Beckett saves Castle, he jokes that this is her eighth time saving him, but he's saved her nine (04.07).[22] All of these characters are impelled not just by their professional duty (as detectives) or their creative passions (for Castle as a writer) but also by their love and caring for each other.

The protection dynamic with Brennan and Booth is a little different in that they are not always out in the field together when it comes time to bring down the villain. They both perform generally equal protective roles in their work as crime-fighters, and they both save each other from the Gravedigger serial killer (Booth saves Brennan—02.09—and Brennan saves Booth—04.14). As the series progresses and they become the parents of two small children, both of them also work in the field less and don't really participate in combat to bring down the bad guys anymore—Booth takes a desk job, and Brennan works almost entirely in the lab. Booth's protective skills are his instincts and emotional intelligence, his ability to rely on his gut. Thus, he functions as the predominant nurturer and often saves Brennan not physically but emotionally. When she's upset over the loss of the dog Ripley (04.04) or when one of her most favored interns, Zack Addy (Eric Millegan), is found guilty of aiding a murderer (03.15), Booth supports her. His protection tends to focus on nurturing Brennan's emotional growth, as the show regularly establishes that much of her cold, logical demeanor reflects an attempt to cope with difficulty. But even though Brennan may lack obvious markers of nurturing, her dedication to Booth and her friends and her tireless energy for solving crime and identifying bodies—indicated more than once by her remaining at the lab alone at the end of an episode to identify unclaimed remains and give families closure—reflect the blurred lines between protection and nurturing.

In *Chuck*, Walker and Casey literally are assigned to protect Chuck, and Chuck is the primary nurturer. He has talks both with Walker and Casey about the importance of sharing their feelings, while early in the series, both tend to see "feelings as liabilities," as Walker says (02.09). This dynamic also changes throughout the series, as their protection and nurturing blend. Even Casey, the hard-nosed NSA agent with a soft spot for Ronald Reagan and the good-old Cold War days, exhibits the protector/nurturer combo when he recognizes Chuck's feelings of inadequacy as an asset (from witnessing Walker and Casey in full action all the time doing things Chuck can't do for himself). Casey lets Chuck appear more competent in front of people Chuck wants to impress by giving Chuck spy-cred (02.04 and 02.06). Even when Walker can't express her own feelings for Chuck, she still makes an effort to protect Chuck's ego and to help smooth family squabbles (which often arise when his sister or Morgan gets upset when Chuck misses an important event because he was on a mission he couldn't tell them about). Chuck's nurturing tendencies eventually extend beyond emotional care into physical protection work when he gets an Intersect upgrade to learn combat skills, so he relies less on being saved. Blurring public and private in this way at once privileges collective action between men and women as it highlights the interdependence between the personal and the social, rejecting the notion that the public sphere is the primary site of social development. Both of these notions coincide with key feminist beliefs about social justice and equality.

Additionally, blurring spheres justifies the assumption that dedication to work means long hours. Once upon a time, this assumption justified the sex sphere/role divide. There could be only one career in a traditional household because the dedication required for success required personal sacrifice—something that men were assumed better-suited to do because women, as nurturers, were the champions of hearth and home. However, now, introducing private, personal issues into the workday turns this rationalization for living to work into a rationalization for women's success in the workspace because it seems to eradicate the need for personal sacrifice. Women can have it all because the workspace can be an appropriate place for intimacy and because both kinship and coupling can fit in with a career, providing multiple sites for identity. These elements have implications for both male and female roles, which brings us back to the tie-in between the early and the contemporary love-buddy representations. Both are dependent upon a combination of a new type of strong, independent female identity and a new type of supportive male in order to produce an idealized co-protector identity for both.

Thus, on the one hand, the love-buddy narrative conjures aspects of the fighting female identity at least enough to give it some basis outside of her intimate relations; her strength and independence indicate that she has no need for a man to support her or to protect her. Brennan, Beckett, and Walker all have lives and careers of their own—and are even more set than Maddie and Laura—because their jobs would continue if the men were not involved. Each of the three is also a dedicated crime-fighter who won't sacrifice her career for her relationship, indicating that justice is as much—or more—a passion for her as the love that the narratives also emphasize. Relationships for each of them, then, are not about dependence but about desire and choice and thus function as a symbolic representation of one kind of women's liberation. The only difference we see over time is that today's love-buddy narratives assure audiences that a woman can achieve success on her own in her chosen field, offering a feminist-friendly ideal that the early love-buddy series couldn't quite obtain. The authority of Brennan, Beckett, and Walker as professionals isn't as subject to doubt in today's narratives.

On the other hand, the love-buddy narrative offers the ideal mate for the empowered woman. David and Remington were sensitive, more emotionally open, and attracted to (rather than put off by) strong women, which was no small thing in the 1980s. Neither of them portrayed entirely traditional male roles (even if the roles they played still emphasized that they had conceivably more agency and/or influence on the business side). Booth, Castle, and Chuck share these qualities. Still, these men offer more respect for the fighting female's authority, even count on it, making them symbolize stronger versions of the co-protector partner and equal, making the sex-power divide less stark than it was in the 1980s narratives. These more recent fighting-female mates also have more drive and personal success. Booth already has a thriving career in the FBI when he starts working with Brennan. He is not reluctant to work, inept, or comical, and he is eager to work with Brennan because of her expertise, which leads him to pursue her as a partner. She helps him catch criminals, making her an asset in his goals to fight crime. Castle also has an established and prosperous occupation as a popular crime writer. He seeks out Beckett because of her own successes as a detective. Because Castle is not a cop and has no professional detecting skills (until season seven), he relies on her expertise as well as her professional standing—not only so that he can earn the satisfaction of fighting crime but also so that he can continue his writing. After all, Beckett is the inspiration for his most successful character, Nikki Heat.

Throughout the series, Castle and Booth stand on their own in their careers. Booth receives commendations and promotions that still never interfere with his ability to support Brennan as a partner. Even when the opportunity to become the head of a new German field office presents itself to Booth, he is reluctant because he doesn't want to break up the team and have his career interfere with Brennan's ability to work for the Jeffersonian. Brennan is the one who has to convince him to take the position, which she does by reminding him that, because her talents are in demand, she can have just about any job, anywhere she wants. After Castle and Beckett marry (07.06), Castle is forced out of consulting for the NYPD because of a scandal, and he becomes a real private investigator, keeping both his equal status as a crime-fighter and independent character (07.11). In comparison, David and Remington are far less driven. Remington wants to enjoy the fruits of Laura's labor to live well. David just wants to have a place to party—he had never had a client before Maddie showed up. Both are less capable as business people and rely on Maddie and Laura to keep the books and run the companies; their careers before the women enter their lives are dubious at best, or in the case of David, were entirely based on Maddie's patronage. The power divide was much more explicit.

The one exception in these relationships is Chuck. When the series begins, Chuck works as a nerd herd computer technician for Buy More. He had to drop out of Stanford because of a cheating scandal (that later turns out to have been a setup). He has a brilliant mind for computers but is decidedly not accomplished at anything except being a good brother and best friend. However, thanks to a classified computer system, he accidentally uploaded into his brain (which also turned out to be a setup)—an accident responsible for bringing Sarah into his life—he becomes an asset. Sarah, as a CIA operative, is sent to protect the asset, and Chuck readily accepts the protection. Much of the series shows him developing his skills to become a spy. Consequently, he becomes successful by learning from his agent partners Walker and Casey. He

Two. Mixing Business with Pleasure　　73

becomes a trustworthy partner in crime-fighting and, eventually, the perfect romance partner for Walker, who, because of the secretive nature of her job, could never have an effective relationship with a civilian. In fact, a significant portion of season three hinges on whether Chuck will pass his spy exam as he thinks his becoming a spy will allow Walker finally to acknowledge and consummate their mutual attraction.

What Chuck does share with Booth and Castle, and to a lesser extent with David and Remington, is emotional intelligence or openness, another key to their being ideal mates for the fighting female. David and Remington do get to express more of their personalities more freely, as mentioned previously, because they have the luxury of male privilege. Still, they don't present the most reliable choices for romance because they aren't stable. Fun and charming? Yes. Ready for commitment and a relationship beyond sex? We're not really sure. They do grow to some extent by the end of the series, as Remington finally shares his story with Laura, and David, thanks to becoming an accidental Lamaze partner to a stranger, wants to step up to help Maddie with the baby. The more recent shows, however, emphasize the way these men not only accept and appreciate their partners' strength and independence but also emphasize the men's roles as emotionally stable people who are skilled in intimacy, even when they lack other skills, as Chuck does. All three men either seek out or gladly accept the work partnership before their female partner does. They recognize their feelings for their partners first. They pursue and are rejected by the fighting females—in the cases of Castle and Chuck, several times.

The emotional intelligence of these men is the biggest contribution they make in their partnerships with the fighting females; it is an intelligence that reflects the overlap of nurturing and protection elements upon which I remarked previously. The starkest example of a differential in emotional intelligence in these couples is between Brennan and Booth. Brennan is an analytical thinker of the highest order. She is extremely literal, practical, and logical. Her blunt and often careless comments, particularly at the beginning of the series, indicate a clear lack of social intelligence. She doesn't understand people very well. For example, she struggles when talking to the families of victims because she tends to tell too many gory details. At some point in the series, she belittles each of her very intelligent and capable colleagues—unintentionally—because she believes her own intelligence to be superior. Sometimes she belittles things that are deeply important to them, as when she regularly mocks Booth's faith in God—he's Catholic, and she's an atheist—and when she disparages psychology as a "soft science," as she frequently does when she talks to Sweets, a psychologist and an agent for the FBI. She doesn't apologize easily—again, because she believes she is always in the right.

Booth is almost her polar opposite in that he is much more sensitive and attuned to people. In the pilot episode, Brennan herself characterizes their difference when she identifies him as a "heart person" and herself as a "brain person" (which she very clearly means as an insult to him). Booth relies on gut feelings for his investigations and comes up with theories about motives that constantly irritate Brennan because they lack any evidence. He puts a lot of faith in faith—whether religious or personal. Also, in the pilot episode, Booth offers Brennan her first lesson on emotional intelligence by encouraging her to lie to spare the feelings of the parents of a murder victim. She displays her ability to learn from him in episode three when she makes an effort to say something nice to a victim's mother, for which Booth later congratulates her. At the end of the pilot, he schools her in social interaction by saying that if she's going to ask someone a personal question, she needs to "offer something" of herself first. She then obliges, and he responds in kind. In episode two, Booth teaches Brennan that "partners share things" in order to get her to be more of a team player. His role as an emotional support coach continues like this throughout the series.

Neither Beckett nor Walker is insensitive to the same degree, even if they are often equally as serious and direct. However, both exhibit a reluctance to be emotionally open, much like Maddie and Laura. They worry about getting involved with their partners because they fear vulnerability. At the end of the season three finale, Castle tells Beckett he loves her as she lies on the ground critically wounded from a gunshot. Throughout season four, she pretends that she can't remember anything. During sessions with her therapist, required by the department after she's shot, she frankly explains that she can't indulge her emotional attachments while she's still consumed with finding her mother's killer. Beckett also tends to be a very serious professional, a trait of which we are reminded when Captain Montgomery tells her that the reason he assigned Castle to consult with her in the first place was because as good a cop as she is, she wasn't having any "fun" with her job until Castle came along (03.24).

Walker's fears stem as much from her belief that emotional attachments are a problem for spies as from the belief that she can't be involved with Chuck because he's basically a civilian, and she would never be able to be her real self with him. During "Chuck Versus the Sizzling Shrimp," Chuck is desperate to learn something about her that's real because, after all, her cover role is as his girlfriend, and they have to work together (01.05). She balks, saying it's for security reasons, but really, it's a personal struggle. Walker can't even tell him her real middle name—she can only whisper it, looking forlorn, after he is out of earshot. She has dark secrets from her past that she can't willingly share, not without his coaxing or being forced to by circumstances beyond her control, as when Chuck meets her father because he shows up out of the blue. Walker is also vulnerable and afraid to open up because her last partner, who was also her boyfriend, was killed in action.

Both Castle and Chuck, like Booth, are responsible for helping the women embrace their emotional vulnerability, indulge their fun sides, and learn the value not just of trust but of intimacy as an element of their partnership. These men are the "heart" of the team (a term used in episodes to describe both Booth and Chuck). Of course, it's both progressive and problematic that in these narratives, the male partner mentors the female partner in emotional growth. After all, attributing emotional intelligence to men who value attachment and commitment certainly breaks down the binaries apparent in more traditional thinking about male/female relationship roles. Showing that a heterosexual relationship isn't the primary motivator for the female character, that she won't go to any lengths to "get her man," does the same thing. Finding a male *partner* in love is now being touted as one of the primary ways women achieve having it all— career success, intimacy, and a family life. It is a claim that successful corporate entrepreneurs Sheryl Sandberg and Ursula Burns both have made, and it has more recently become a bigger part of discussions about women's success in the working world. Both Burns and Sandberg highlight the important role their "partners" played in their success: Sandberg writes of it in her book, *Lean In*, and Burns, the first black woman CEO of a Fortune 500 company, has spoken of it in interviews in which she discusses her appointment as CEO of the Xerox Holdings Corporation (Berman).

In each of these shows, the male partner does not dominate the female through his knowledge, at least in terms of crime-fighting. Also, other characters in the shows act as emotional counsel for the fighting females, like Brennan's best friend Angela and Beckett's friends and partners. Chuck's best friend and his family help out Walker. There are also examples of emotionally stunted men— like Casey in *Chuck* or Zack in *Bones*—who have the same problem as the fighting females.

Still, in general, the male love-buddy partners come off as the more open-minded and well-rounded people in comparison to the women and contain the smidge of a suggestion that Susan Douglas sees in the enlightened male trope: "that it is smart, modern men who will set women free" (*Where the Girls Are* 214)—though these men are a far cry from the distant, paternal Charlie, of *Charlie's Angels*, whom Douglas uses to make this assertion. Nevertheless, the fact that these love-buddy male partners are comfortable with accepting their feelings and make attempts not only toward intimacy but also toward commitment—while nevertheless being a productive, skilled, and capable figures—implies that "having it all" comes more easily to the men. The fact that the men entered their partnerships with their emotional skills already developed, rather than having to learn them through their relationships as the women do, indicates that their identities were somehow whole from the beginning.

Now, instead of questioning the woman's position as an authoritative, successful career figure, it's her ability to open up and to be whole that is at issue. There is still a sense of lack in the narratives about these otherwise amazing fighting females, who do not "need" a man, that then makes it seem as if they do "need" one, at least to fill in their gaps. In the end, the fantasy tells us that yes, she can overcome her limitations, but it assumes those limitations from the get-go. Still, the love-buddy fighting female is portrayed as an engaging character before she develops these traits. As this development will occur over the long course of the different series, they must bank on the fact that she has enough appeal to keep audience interest. Additionally, as mentioned in the discussion of the way nurturing and protection skills blur, her emotional intelligence isn't always as weak as it seems.

Finally, the fighting female is always desirable to the leading male, even before she can open up (even in her most callous, driven, and serious state, as with Maddie, Brennan, and Beckett). This attractiveness further reinforces the idea that there is more to her than just her ability to feel; immediate accessibility and approachability (personality traits long required for a woman to be appreciated) are not requisites for her to have value. In fact, access to her has to be earned by the male partner, as he proves himself worthy of her trust. The fantasy seems to work because it allows us to believe that women have changed to correlate with our desire for empowered female models but also that men have changed to make room for that empowerment and meet women's desires for partnership, as intimates *and* colleagues. The love-buddy narratives cater to and reinforce these beliefs.

Still, more than thirty years after the first love-buddy narrative premiered, it all comes down to two sides of the same concerns about women in the workplace in relation to the heterosexual contract. After all, the fantasy developed amidst many other media attempts to interrogate both the efficacy and the desirability of female breadwinners. This interrogation has not ceased; it has just taken on new forms. The idea of women "opting out" of their career goals to become mothers and homemakers is one of the more recent popular interrogations of women's place in the workforce—and yet another one that is only an option for women of the leisure-class. Opting out has been presumed to result from the impossibility of a woman's achieving "work/life balance" (even though in cases of middle- and working-class women, it is sometimes because child care expenses would drain more than a job would add to the family's finances). Rather than directly questioning women's aptitude (because that would be offensive as we all supposedly know now that women can achieve whatever they want), the assertion is that they might prefer to be with their families or prefer not to sacrifice their personal lives.

So, there is the problematic part of the fantasy of the strong, independent heterosexual woman who gets her career and her man (and today, a family to boot). Getting it all happens only thanks to the presence of enlightened colleagues, a husband who's in the business, and a 24-hour workday. It is not thanks to changing workforce policies that would make parenting on the job easier or that would pay individuals a high enough wage to support themselves and others without resorting to the discrimination tactics that maintained the heterosexual contract and previously divided work and home by gender. So, the empowered woman's success relies on an apparently gender-liberated space that looks nothing like a real job. Getting it all also happens for her only after she learns to trust her partner in work, only after she works through the threats that intimacy presents to her work partnership, and only after she learns how to be vulnerable and intimate. However much her power and abilities can be more readily assumed, there remains ambiguity about whether she can deal with her empowerment, whether the strength and independence of the modern woman's identity, the authority she's achieved, and her accomplishments require too much sacrifice or struggle.

Likewise, there is the problem of the implied questioning as to whether women in the workplace are stunted emotionally and whether their identities are fractured without male guidance. This is a tricky issue because the narratives don't question that women are in the workplace—these contemporary love-buddy fighting females are presented unequivocally as effective partners. Rather, they subtly privilege the male as complete, more integrated, by making the female constantly a work in progress. This preserves a mysterious sense of male experience and knowledge, upholding some sense of male authority, even as his authority in other areas, such as being the sole protector and provider, becomes less assured.

We Can't Forget the Fans: Feminist-Friendly Intimacy and Viewing Pleasure

In *Enlightened Sexism*, Douglas rightly explains that popular culture is full of embedded feminism, much more so than it was even thirty years ago, a fact that requires us to interrogate, ever more deeply, any seemingly feminist-oriented fantasies we see. Douglas writes, "[W]hat the media giveth with one hand (which is why we love them), they taketh away with the other hand (which is why they endlessly piss us off)" (9). The mass media creates images of rebellion and enlightenment right along with images of conformity and tradition, endlessly crafting contradictory messages about who women are (or who women should be or want to be). One implication of these messages is that because there are representations of professional, liberated women on-screen, the culture at large readily embraces women's rights; another is that equality has been achieved because we see it being enacted on-screen. Thus, the message is that nothing needs to be done to change reality because it's expressed in the fantasy.[23] This caution readily applies to images of fighting females and their hetero-romances.

Still, even with the ambiguous representations of female empowerment as the ideal and the questionable assertions of hetero-intimacy as the source of female transformation or male emotional authority, key elements of the love-buddy fighting female's relationships do support what I have termed feminist-friendly love and indicate a growing presence of seeing some feminist-supported identities being desirable rather than punishable. A female protagonist who is assured in her identity as a smart, accomplished, strong, capable, physical, sexual person doesn't rely on a relationship to orient her sense of self or give her life purpose or direction. Additionally, positioning hetero-intimacy within a sphere of multiple intimacies undermines the limitation of the isolated couple. The couple may remain primary but does not have to be the only source of affection, closeness, or even emotional security. Also, as the love-buddy moved into the 21st century, the fighting female's intimacies began to include not only supportive male characters but also female characters (a trend we'll see again in Chapter Four). These women were no longer tokens, and many of these supportive females are strong and independent themselves. All of these narratives pass the Bechdel Test, and the elements respond to vital concerns of feminists who question traditional notions that romance is assumed to be the primary source of women's identity or experience, as addressed in the introduction.

Also, encouraging women and men to relate as partners, to develop trust and intimacy, to protect each other, to come together from shared values that include equality and justice, is essential to the ideal of egalitarian intimacy that would reduce reliance upon traditional sex roles that are inherently hierarchical—another concern feminists have had about how romance and heterosexuality subjugate women. This partnership orientation goes a long way toward undermining the heterosexual contract and the characteristics that have long been tied to definitions of female identity because the partnership orientation relies on definitions of femininity that connote strength and independence. Watching the love-buddy fighting female, in narrative after narrative, negotiate the fine line between independence and intimacy, engaging in the pleasant titillations of will-they-won't-they narratives, gives us a more rounded version of female identity; these narratives also help us imagine the possibility of feminist-friendly love even as they remind us that such a love is at best hard-won (more likely for only a small population of women) and that we still have work to do.

The love-buddy fighting female character reveals both cultural fantasies and anxieties about the empowered woman that coordinate with the growing number of fans, like Brenda Holmes (the Laura Holt fan) and I, who seek strong female roles on-screen and who do find real partners, male or female. The interplay between the fantasy and the fears can make for cautious viewing but doesn't erase the power of the fighting female. Problems aside, the contemporary love-buddy fighting female does get to have it all, falling more on the side of fantasy-fulfilling than fear-mongering. Having it all in a culture that makes work/life balance either difficult or unimaginable is the ultimate fantasy erasure of the reality that many people experience in balancing their home and work lives or in breaking relationship traditions.

For many women, such an idealized hetero-partnership is just a fantasy. Few women are anywhere near to being as attractive as these five leading ladies—one was a model (Cybill Shepherd), and one plays a character who was a model before she was a cop (Stana Katic). Also, all women are not forgiven for their gender transgressions so readily as these women are, and many women don't have partners who are as enlightened, available, or desiring of a strong, independent woman as their leading men are. The fantasy makes egalitarian intimacy seem like the way to be, like it's already the new status quo, so if it's not a woman's reality, then it can be easy to assume the problem is unique to her (or her responsibility alone).

The love-buddy fighting female character inclines more toward the "superwoman" cited earlier, whom Douglas describes—"the size-six CEO with a Ph.D., two perfect children, a doting husband, not a line on her face, and the ability to rebuild the car's engine on the weekends"—than the "bionic bimbo" pop version of the liberated female—a "superhuman woman with lots of power, maybe even a gun, flouncy hair, a mellifluous voice, and erect nipples" (*Where the Girls Are* 211). Yet, not everything comes easily to her—her triumphs are always hard-won—and nothing in her life is actually perfect (except, of course, for her looks). Presenting such an ideal does more than create a feel-good smokescreen because it nonetheless asserts an ideal that's alternative to lingering traditional representations of hetero-relationships and gender roles. Sometimes, we need to see a fantasy working before we can embrace it as a reality. All in all, the love-buddy fighting female remains a unique character. She constructs an empowered female identity as a co-protector and as a successful working woman that defies the longtime stereotypes of heterosexual women on-screen and has immense appeal for both female and male viewers.

The popularity of the love-buddy helped usher in a variety of different television programs featuring men and women in partnerships. In addition to the contemporary love-buddy narratives I've mentioned, there have been at least twenty-two different series since 2000 that have relied on male and female partners, many of whom are platonic but still intimate, a rare pairing before now. There are shows with dual leads, like *Elementary* (2012–19),

Sleepy Hollow (2013–17), *Warehouse 13* (2009–14), *Blindspot* (2015–20), and the unfortunately short-lived *Whiskey Cavalier* (2019). There are also shows with a primary female character and a male partner, like *Veronica Mars* (2004–07, 2019, and a 2014 film), *In Plain Sight* (2008–12), or *Covert Affairs* (2010–14)—and ones with a primary male character with a female partner like *Burn Notice* (2007–13) or *24* (2001–10).

Not all of these series promote the same fantasies of feminist-friendly love or are equally progressive, which isn't to say they aren't compelling in different ways. Yet these types of narratives are absolutely important for showing men and women as being able to work and to succeed together, for they are showing strong women not as strident man-haters or villains or sidekicks but as equal partners who can be independent and still enjoy hetero-intimacy. Conceiving such an interdependent relationship belies the inaccessible, separatist, man-hating feminist stereotype that still maintains an unfortunate hold on the cultural imagination, for as addressed in Chapter One, these fighting females often function as the media archetype of a feminist; even if they never apply the term to themselves, they perform as a liberated and liberating character. Considering the female partner as a hero, then, proves to be as essential as discussing narratives focusing on just women as the hero. Interrogating on-screen hetero-romances as an element of that partnership might reveal representations of female empowerment as a double-edged sword, but it's at least a sword that she gets to wield while wearing her heart on her sleeve.

Three

The Struggling Romaction Genre
Love-Warrior Fighting Females and the Politics of Romance on the Homefront

This chapter addresses fighting females in romaction, a hybrid film genre that combines the plots of both the romantic comedy and action narrative forms. While the genre has antecedents in the 1980s and 1990s, it first emerged in 2005 with the blockbuster *Mr. and Mrs. Smith*. In 2010, three additional romactions hit the screen: *Date Night*, *Killers*, and *Knight and Day*. The romaction fighting female shares the lead with a male co-star as a partner in action and love. The romaction is symbolically similar to the love-buddy narratives addressed in Chapter Two because the romaction also attempts to establish a liberated quality to the male/female pairing. For love buddies, the effect comes from storylines that revolve around the public sphere and foster a fantasy of an egalitarian workplace that maintains feminist-friendly hetero-intimacy for the strong, independent woman. In romactions, the storylines commonly revolve around the couple's domestic life, often taking place directly within their home, and construct a fantasy of an egalitarian domestic partnership ideal wherein an empowered woman can thrive. In other words, the hybrid genre attempts to envision a successful heterosexual relationship that stresses what sociologist Kathleen Gerson refers to as a "flexible, egalitarian partnership with considerable room for personal autonomy," which her research leads her to claim both men and women seek and which has become essential to feminist-friendly media iterations of women's empowerment (11).

Like most of the other fighting female types, the romaction fighting females are all white career women, and they are portrayed at some point as natural aggressors who step up to the challenge of the action plot and can at least throw a good punch, even though romaction heroines exhibit very wide-ranging levels of violence, from professional assassin to amateur civilian. They are at least somewhat ready to fight when the fight comes their way. Unlike the other fighting females in this study, the romaction fighting females are also in some way associated with the most traditional feminine role: that of homemaker and/or caretaker. The unusual combination of combatant and nurturer is probably the clearest indicator that certain arenas of American popular culture over the last few decades have begun to incorporate the strong, independent woman ideal into female identity, blurring lines between the traditional masculine/feminine divide. The result, however, is not without problems: the more the narrative highlights the female character's nurturing qualities and emotional work, the more likely she is to reinforce her male co-star's authority and to take a back seat in the action—though this is not true for all romaction fighting females.

The increased attention to the romaction fighting female's role in the home is key to any potential feminist-friendly love fantasies that might emerge through romaction narratives. These fantasies expose and endeavor to resolve male/female antagonisms prompted by a changing domestic sphere, the flip side of women's greater participation in the workforce and the corresponding love-buddy fantasies. The romaction achieves this resolution in three feminist-friendly-informed ways:

First, the romaction appears to indict traditional forms of hetero-romance for defying egalitarian partnerships that would serve both women and men. Throughout the different romactions, certain themes can be interpreted as attempts to present more progressive and liberated co-leads who do not easily fit into a gender hierarchy that privileges male authority—characters who reject stereotypical domestic roles—and whose antagonists often espouse old-fashioned notions about hetero-relations.

Second, the romaction resolution asserts an empowered hetero female identity, the love-warrior whose strength and independence work in conjunction with her role as lover/wife (and sometimes mother). This identity authorizes her to take down threats not only against herself but also against her partner. In other words, she's a woman who can fight for love as her primary goal. Being able to function as a fighting female co-lead is integral to this identity and reflects her character's position of parity with male action heroes who have characteristically been in charge of fighting for love, in one way or another.

Third, romaction resolutions seem to emphasize gender flexibility for men and women and similarities between men and women as the basis of their hetero-compatibility. In the ideal romaction fantasy, both the female and male characters must embody aggressive and nurturing abilities, and both must pursue and protect the relationship through emotional work and physical combat.

Before examining these themes, it's necessary to explain, briefly, how combining plotlines from two genres, action and romantic comedy, relates to the egalitarian hetero-intimacy fantasy. The hybridization increases the narrative tension regarding the romaction couple's domestic life to reflect a sense of crisis in hetero-intimacy that the story can then remedy. The next section outlines the progression of the action film toward the romaction in relation to the fighting female's evolution as a romantic interest and capable combatant through the 1980s and 1990s. The analysis follows this outline, focusing on the way romaction, at its best, constructs hetero-intimacy as a level playing field upon which the women are empowered, the men are enlightened, and both are equally capable of love and heroism.

However, as pointed out in the final two sections, the romaction genre tends to remain problematic in terms of a full-fledged, feminist-friendly romance. First, the majority of the romaction narratives cannot portray a truly egalitarian ideal. Second, even the most egalitarian romaction featuring the most accomplished female love-warrior identity renders a somewhat paradoxical version of liberating love because of the way non-traditional, egalitarian intimacies intersect with implications of hetero-romance as a war of the sexes. As I will argue, this problem contributes to the struggles romaction has faced in developing as a genre.

Hybridity: Where Oppositions Meet

In June of 2010, *Washington Post* staff writer Ann Hornaday explored the budding romaction trend in Hollywood films noting, "Action and romance are tying the knot, brought together by a movie industry desperate for product that will appeal not just to one demographic group (say, teenage boys) but two (teenage boys and their girlfriends, sisters or even moms)." For Hornaday and the Hollywood studio execs she later quotes, the hybrid genre merely represents another blockbuster gambit that says more about production companies' desires to fill the seats than their desires for unique plot lines.

However, the romaction does more than direct women's increased box-office spending toward the action blockbuster. Rather, the hybrid both responds to and constructs expectations that have arisen in certain areas of American culture for representations of liberating love, which *can* be achieved in narratives that include more equally matched couples and that assert shared authority, or dependent autonomy, as central to hetero-intimacy. By including fighting females in the romance narrative and by relying on tropes of romance as partnership, the romaction continues and contributes to the still-burgeoning postfeminist discourse that suggests the desirability and achievability of feminist-friendly intimacy for women and men. In the article "Action-Adventure as Ideology," Gina Marchetti offers some insight into the way genres function—insights that may relate to understanding the romaction as hybrid and the importance of the development of romaction—when she explains how

> [p]articular genres tend to be popular at certain points in time because they somehow embody and work through those social contradictions the culture needs to come to grips with and may not be able to deal with except in the realm of fantasy. As such, popular genres often function in a way similar to the way myth functions—to work through social contradictions in the form of a narrative so that very real problems can be transposed to the realm of fantasy and apparently solved there [187].

What particular contradictions do romactions work through? Today, many men and women don't want their roles or behaviors to be dictated by their gender, yet they still want to be free to choose conventional roles if it suits them. Some women want to take care of themselves but also want to be able to depend on men when necessary. Some women want to be seen as nurturing wives and capable mothers but do not want to be defined purely by their domestic roles. Some men want to be more nurturing and sensitive, yet they want to identify themselves as masculine and tough. Also, like many women, some men want to take on more responsibilities in the domestic sphere, but they also do not want to be defined purely by the role. It was only a few decades ago that reconciling these perspectives was not possible, and it often remains a problem because traditional ideas about separate spheres and gender roles in heterosexual relationships are still prevalent. Even feminists and feminist allies who believe wholeheartedly in complete male and female equality struggle to reconcile their personal and professional lives, their independent and interdependent selves, and the ideals of equality they seek with the experiences of inequality they often experience or witness. Essentially, there remains a sense of conflict for anyone who desires to benefit from new identities that are more gender-flexible and from different possibilities for hetero-relational behavior that don't rely on gender-divisive roles.

An illustration of the entrenched conflicts between liberation and tradition can be noted in the way the mass media addressed the recent economic downturn. The recession in 2007–08, dubbed a "mancession" by Catherine Rampell writing for the *New York Times* in 2009, rearranged male/female divisions of labor and intimate relations in the home and recharged many people's uncertainties about gender roles. For a time, the job sectors in which women have a larger presence, sectors like health care and education, fared better than sectors like construction and manufacturing in which more men work. Men were characterized as at-risk by much of the media. Then, in 2011, as the economy showed signs of improvement, it turned out that men fared better overall than women. Rampell then coined the term "hecovery" to reflect this phenomenon because men gained jobs not only faster than women did, but also women ended up with fewer jobs than before the recession. The disparity retrained the focus on women's still-precarious position in the workplace in general. Rather than simply asserting a sense of competition between the sexes, the reports of how "men's jobs" and "women's jobs" fared differently provided constant reminders of men and women's divided roles in the workforce and left an impression that hetero-relations had degraded as a result. In effect, the media response to the economic downturn was filled with a sense of impending doom for men and women on a personal level.

One of the most common concerns addressed by commentators and journalists was the family burden—caused as much by the challenge to both sexes in their roles at work and at home as by the loss of financial security. In particular, the media fixated on the ways men's mental health suffered from a loss of the breadwinner identity or from the humiliation of becoming dependent on their wives. Even stories that reported men's increasing appreciation for their role as a father or full-time parent still addressed their emotional struggles and the toll that takes on the family.[1] Conversely, those reporting on women's small gains in economic influence generally qualified the reports with reminders that women still don't share an equal place in the workforce, at least in terms of management and high-ranking careers.[2] All in all, the mass media's treatment of the recession and its effects addressed both men and women but did so by treating it as a gender-divisive issue. In so doing, the coverage added another facet to the general sense of crisis in heterosexual relations that has been a regular theme of postfeminist culture.

These private and social conflicts are examples of the "very real problems" Marchetti mentions that the romaction fantasy attempts to work through and resolve. The romaction addresses individual conflicts in intimacy brought about by two equal, independent, desiring people trying to negotiate interdependence without losing any of their personal autonomy or agency.[3] It also addresses public conflicts regarding intimacy caused by the traditional ideas, values, and expectations about gender and sexuality that many still hold and that can interfere with a couple's efforts to achieve a more egalitarian relationship. In other words, the contemporary romaction hybrid offers a different ideological space in which to imagine the fighting female and also to work through what Gerson identifies as "tensions between changing lives and resistant institutions [that] have created dilemmas for everyone," including in particular the ways "entrenched conflicts between work and family life place mounting strains on adult partnerships" that are necessary for a family's success (6).

The romaction's dual plot structure and combination of two typically gender-divided genres allow for the possibility of a unique resolution, which is the key aspect of the cultural work occurring in the romaction film-as-myth and is central to any potential feminist-friendly fantasy it may portray. By combining comic circumstances and romantic action with more equally-matched female and male protagonists than the average action film and by portraying more explosive, fast-paced action than the average romance, the romaction hybrid enacts the way today's bigger intimacy conflicts need bigger bangs to resolve them. Additionally, by offering two equally developed plot lines, the romaction doubles the impact of the resolution: that of the threat to the couple's lives through the action and the threat to their intimacy through the romance. Kiss, Kiss! Bang, Bang!

Romaction Emerges: The Rise of Female Love-Warriors

The ideological work accomplished by romaction hybrids would not be possible without the inclusion of a fighting female in the narrative. The empowered female identity she represents as the love-warrior is, conversely, enabled by the hybrid, which requires her to face two crises (one internal to the couple and one external) and to fight for life and love, equally. Until the relatively recent emergence of gay and lesbian rom-coms that have emerged in streaming networks, romantic comedies have required hetero co-leads, but the action genre has always been more male-centric. In both genres, the male tends to be more responsible for ensuring the future of the romance, either fighting to get the girl back or to save the girl, respectively. Also, the action genre has often marginalized the woman's position in the narrative and has tended to rely upon traditional stereotypes in women's roles, ones in which the female character inclines toward passivity and victimization. In order for the romaction hybrid to work and a woman's empowered identity to be enacted, a co-lead fighting female needs to be introduced into, and remain throughout, the narrative—at the very least so that she could be there throughout the action to participate in the relationship drama (instead of being hidden off-screen until the hero's triumphant finale when he saves her).

Romancing the Stone and *Jewel of the Nile* probably come to mind for many as 1980s romaction films, as they did for Hornaday. Both films do provide a fighting female, and Joan Wilder (Kathleen Turner) is most certainly a co-lead as opposed to a sidekick or supporting role, which was extremely rare—if not brand new—in an action film when the movies were released. Plus, a romance novelist who refuses to give up her search for the right man seems a good candidate for a love-warrior. However, neither film quite fits the romaction category. Both fit better into the more typical action-adventure or fantasy/sci-fi genre in which the story's motivating influence is some quest or mission and in which the romance occurs as a consequence of rather than an equal or even primary motivator for the events. Joan doesn't fight for romance. In *Romancing the Stone*, she fights to save her sister, who has been kidnapped by a Columbian drug cartel. Additionally, Michael Douglas' character tends to be responsible for most of the fighting and saving until the film's end. In *Jewel of the Nile*, Joan fights to get an imprisoned dissident, the "jewel" of his people, to his rightful place in power. She is duped by the dictator currently in power and is herself imprisoned. Jack comes in to save her, though she is already in the process of saving herself and the jewel. Consider these two films in relation to the *Indiana Jones* franchise, the Allan Quatermain movies, *Cherry 2000* (1987), and the like. The women in these are feisty and definitely ready for adventure. Yet, they contribute little to the action and even less to the heroic resolution of the plot; they must regularly be saved, as much from their misguided assumptions of invulnerability as from harm; and love is often a convenient subplot.

Kathleen Turner's character grows from a mousy, housebound novelist into a gutsy heroine, and she does shoot the bad guy at the end of *Romancing*, so she certainly fits the fighting female bill. Still, she's a far cry from the passionate, calculating, and substantially more violent character she plays in the critically acclaimed 1985 film *Prizzi's Honor*, which offers a closer prototype for the romaction, though it doesn't quite get there. With its more supposedly masculine-characterized ties to the mafia/gangster/crime film being combined with a central story of romance, *Prizzi's Honor* was really the only 1980s film that included the kind of male/female couple dynamic that would become integral to romactions—and that is central to the feminist-friendly fantasy of hetero-intimacy that romactions attempt to enact. Turner's character Irene Walker is a freelance mafia assassin, and her paramour, Charley Partana (Jack Nicholson), is an enforcer for the mob. They are essentially equals as professionals and in their capacities for violence, qualities that reflect the romaction theme of gender-flexibility and non-stereotypical gender roles as a basis for hetero-attraction. However, Walker pays dearly for her abilities and gets killed by her husband Charley, who has been ordered by the Don to take her out (for the good of the family). Interestingly, Inness reads Irene's performance of "the perfect wife and sexual partner" as detracting from the character's "tough self-presentation" because it enacts "stereotypically feminine roles" (70). However, before her death, her relationship with Charley is transgressive because those roles are expanded by the strength and independence implied by her job as an assassin. Her fate can thus be read to imply that the cultural imagination of America in the 1980s was not yet able to envision a fighting female fantasy in which the exuberantly violent independent woman is not deviant and does not pay for her transgressions. In the end, Irene's fate parallels that other notorious 1980s twisted femme fatale, Alex Forrest from *Fatal Attraction* (1987).[4]

In general, the 1980s were a decade when the mass media struggled to find a place for the fighting female in love, even if the character had achieved a modicum of popularity in *Moonlighting* and *Remington Steele* and in narratives that didn't involve romance. For the most part, the most violent fighting female action protagonists in the 1980s were single females like Sigourney

Weaver's Lt. Ripley—though she didn't kill people, only aliens—and Brigitte Nielsen in *Red Sonja* (1985). The 1990s were really when the first versions of violent fighting females in love emerged in a few proto-romaction movies, but almost none of the women held co-star status.

The third film of the *Lethal Weapon* franchise, released in 1992, was the first mass-media movie to introduce a fighting female action character who was a successful love interest: Rene Russo's tough, high-kicking Lorna Cole. The plot is basically that police officers Roger Murtaugh (Danny Glover) and Martin Riggs (Mel Gibson) team up with internal affairs officer Lorna Cole to uncover corruption in the department relating to an illegal arms dealing scheme. Cole, however, is far from a leading protagonist in the film—her name didn't make it onto the poster head, and her romance with Riggs stays firmly in subplot territory, on the margins with Riggs' previous supporting ladies (keeping good company with his partner Murtaugh's family and with Holly Gennero from the *Die Hard* films).

The *Lethal Weapon* franchise did, however, introduce one element that created an inroad into the romaction narrative by bringing the domestic sphere into the action—rather than merely putting the ladies in danger, which had been done in the first and second films with Murtaugh's daughter and Riggs' paramours. The franchise also literally brought the family abode into the picture: Murtaugh's house is blown up in the movies, and the family station wagon is totaled. Situating the action in the private sphere, instead of in some random public or foreign place, reflects what Elizabeth Abele describes as "a reclamation of home, creating a place for the hero at the hearth, in a more intimate community, with less restrictive gender and racial boundaries," which is an important advent in action and the development of both the romaction fantasy and its love-warrior woman (9).

Additionally, like *Prizzi's Honor*, *Lethal Weapon 3* emphasizes the similarities between romance partners as a positive basis for their relationship, rather than as a source for conflict or dislike. Riggs and Cole are equally stubborn, gruff, and non-nurturing; both tend to be loners; and both are capable fighters who use a lot of martial arts moves. They aren't particularly well-liked by their colleagues. They'll both do whatever it takes to get the bad guy. They have similar battle scars, which they compare during a moment of intimacy (a move that would reappear in the first full romaction, *Mr. and Mrs. Smith*). The film also emphasizes that Riggs is attracted to Cole's fighting ability and trusts her to take care of herself. When some thugs they are questioning accost Riggs, Murtaugh, and Cole, Murtaugh wants to help Cole, but Riggs stops him, saying, "No, I want you to see something. She has a gift. Watch this." Lorna then proceeds to take down five guys, breaking bones and destroying property, in true Riggs style. Ultimately, the movie depicts the first version of a truly violent fighting female in a hetero-romance who gets to have the happy romantic ending (and by *Lethal Weapon 4,* who gets to "have it all" when she and Riggs have a baby). Still, Cole's character remains firmly on the sidelines of both films featuring her.

The same sidelining occurs for Jaime Lee Curtis' character, Helen Tasker, in *True Lies* (1994). Yet, the movie is important in the romaction development timeline again for integrating the hero's home life into the action narrative. Harry Tasker (played by classic action hero Arnold Schwarzenegger) is a run-of-the-mill CIA agent who must save the world by preventing Islamic jihadists from obtaining nuclear weapons—only Harry also has to deal with an unruly daughter, a bored housewife, and typical family routines. These establish Harry not just as a super-spy but also as an average Joe. Furthermore, the home life enters Harry's workplace when he uses his CIA resources to help with his marital issues and when his wife Helen becomes a spy and his partner for the same government agency where Harry works at the end of the film.

True Lies also establishes some important tropes that are replayed in romaction themes and that set the movie apart from other action or romantic-comedy genres. First, and most importantly, there is a double-threat: their marital relationship is rocky, *and* terrorists endanger the family's lives. The action resolves both. Specifically, the marriage has become dull and routine. Because of this, Helen lets herself be enticed into a (fake) spy scheme by Simon (Bill Paxton), a car salesman who pretends to be an agent to pick up women. When Harry learns of her boredom, he decides to set up his own scheme to rekindle the romance. In a sense, their relationship puts Helen, and later, their daughter, in mortal danger because Harry accidentally puts her on the enemy's radar with his plan to seduce Helen using the agency's safe house. He must act to save both the romance and the world with the action by fighting the terrorists who have his family. Thus, the internal relationship work and the external problems entwine in a dual narrative.

The movie furthermore projects an assumption that even the most unassuming, domestic women prove to be natural, enthusiastic fighters, tying two opposing roles together. Helen seems more than prepared for a more exciting life outside of domesticity and the humdrum of her clerical job. That's why she agrees first to Simon's ridiculous scheme and then later to the mission she thinks she's being given by the government (even though it's actually her husband creating a ruse to romance her with excitement). As soon as the going gets tough, Helen has no problem kicking balls, punching her husband (for lying to her), smashing chairs against mirrors (or a phone against a face, again, her husband's), slapping a villain, or handling a gun (even if she handles it poorly). When Harry sees a room full of dead men, thinking that Helen was responsible for killing them all (even though it was a random act committed by an Uzi tumbling down the stairs), he is visibly impressed. Helen is violent mainly by accident, but by the end of the film, she has become a full-fledged agent and partner to her husband, gaining an important egalitarian position from which the romaction fighting female would later climb. This resolution establishes another important romaction theme, one in which violence acts as the precursor to rekindled passion. The fighting female must prove herself capable of action violence before she can be a match for the action hero so the romance can gain narrative prominence.

However, *True Lies* remains firmly in proto-romaction territory because it lacks the full egalitarian basis of co-leads who work together throughout the narrative—a lack also made apparent by the movie's production details. After all, as great as Curtis is in her supporting role, *True Lies* is undeniably a Schwarzenegger film (only his face and name grace the cover of the movie poster and VHS/DVD cover). Additionally, the film focuses more on masculine crisis than on the couple's shared struggle toward egalitarian intimacy. The overarching theme is that Harry is not man enough to have a full work and home life, that he is to blame for his wife's boredom and his daughter's disrespect, and that he must fulfill his masculine role as protector to make things better. Schwarzenegger's position as the primary hero is highlighted by the fact that near the final climax, he leaves his wife to save their daughter, without even informing Helen that their daughter has been kidnapped. As he flies away, Helen has a bewildered look on her face. So, aside from the machine-gun misfire incident, she never has a chance to save him, she has no input in the fight, and we don't see her again until after Harry has saved the world. In other words, she contributes almost nothing during almost all of the action and never quite enacts the love-warrior identity. One might say this is because she's an amateur, but that doesn't stop some of the later romaction heroines from at least being given the chance.

The box-office successes of *Lethal Weapon 3* and *4* and *True Lies* certainly contributed to their influence as test cases for the love-warrior woman—after all, as Hornaday mentions, Hollywood likes to pursue the tried and true. Still, the imbalances in these proto-romactions qualify the egalitarian potential of the intimate relationships and the requisite basis of gender-flexibility for a successful hetero-romance the later romaction films attempt to present. Thus, they undermine the fantasy the fighting female portrays, overcoming obstacles to feminist success in order to imagine the strong, independent woman in love.

The only killer woman character who gets to have it all as a co-star came out a year after *Lethal Weapon 3* in the box-office disaster, *Undercover Blues* (1993). The movie is about two married spies who are happily retired after the birth of their daughter; they must come out of their retirement to take down an old arms dealer who has returned to the game. The fighting female, played by Kathleen Turner as Jane Blue, is capable of as much violence as her husband, Jeff Blue (Dennis Quaid). The film paints an idyllic picture of their marriage as true equals, emphasizing the similarity in both characters' gender-flexibility as they take turns caring for the baby and shooting bad guys. Yet, the film has no romance drama: it has no inflections of the crisis in hetero-relations that are integral to interrogations of hetero-intimacy in the romaction. They are happily married at the start, and they don't have a single fight with each other. It's really more of an action film that just happens to have a married couple as protagonists. Unfortunately, not very many people enjoyed it as much as I did. The film didn't make much of an impact on general audiences and received lackluster reviews as "a perfectly enjoyable, completely forgettable hour and a half" (Horwitz). Its poor box office returns ensured that studio executives would not see it as a template for success on which to base future action movies. Still, the fact that it included a co-lead violent fighting female in a happy relationship was notable and in keeping with the other experiments with fighting females in love during the decade.

What we see happening in the early 1990s is evidence of the difficulty action had being extracted from the traditions of its genre, at least in terms of female representation. None of these women are love-warriors: all tend more toward the sidekick position, usually as a token character. Still, the narratives attempt to navigate the fighting female character who gained more status during the latter part of the decade. However, until the 2005 release of *Mr. and Mrs. Smith*, the majority of the fighting females in the period tended toward the lone-wolf hero. Hilary Neroni overviews a few exceptions to the single fighting female during this period, including characters played by Juliette Lewis in *Natural Born Killers*, Angela Bassett in *Strange Days* (1995), Frances McDormand in *Fargo* (1996), and Geena Davis in *The Long Kiss Goodnight* (1997). All of these women play fighting females who have successful romances (and three of them are extremely violent). However, as Neroni points out in her admirable analysis, the narratives go to great lengths to erase the "trauma" of their violence and make them suitable partners, measures that include disjointed narratives, separating their violence from their femininity, or flipping gender roles with their paramours rather than blending with them (113).

Also, only two of the narratives had the fighting female sharing the lead with her love interest. In *Fargo* and *The Long Kiss Goodnight*, the romance was all on the margins. It wasn't until *Mr. and Mrs. Smith* that a fighting female shared a co-lead position in which both characters shared gender-flexibility, finally breaking down the action genre's gender hierarchy and tendency to rely on traditional depictions of hetero-intimacy. In 2010, three additional romactions hit theaters: *Killers*, *Date Night*, and *Knight and Day*, each presenting a variation on the *Mr. and Mrs. Smith* theme. Before turning to these most recent romactions, this discussion will first focus in detail on *Mr. and*

Mrs. Smith to establish its position as the romaction standard that presents a feminist-friendly love fantasy based on an egalitarian couple and the new conflicts they face together.

The Egalitarian Couple: Hot and Deadly

Mr. and Mrs. Smith differs from most of the preceding proto-narratives first in that the stars are on equal footing as co-leads in the film. Brad Pitt and Angeline Jolie received equal salaries of $20 million each for their roles. They are both on the movie posters and VHS/DVD cases, posed as mirror reflections, aside from the wardrobe. From a professional standpoint, they thus have equal status in the film's production. They are pictured together at the film's beginning and ending, the majority of the scenes feature both characters at the same time, and all of the plot advancement relies on both characters. Additionally, the film is a true hybrid, seamlessly intertwining the rom-com and action narratives by affording as much screen time to violence and action as to the romance and reconciliation—even better, the latter occurs *at the same time* as the former. As characters, *Mr. and Mrs. Smith* are equal in skill, equally responsible for the misunderstandings that lead to their intimacy problems, and equal in efforts to repair the relationship. They are both empowered individuals who empower each other as partners throughout the film. By the end, they come together to represent an enlightened couple because they are liberated by egalitarian intimacy that matches their strong, independent qualities. All of these aspects establish *Mr. and Mrs. Smith* as the über-romaction.

Here is a quick précis of the film: The story begins "five or six years" into the marriage of John (Brad Pitt) and Jane (Angelina Jolie) Smith, as they sit in a counselor's office to discuss the proverbial lost spark. Flashbacks show us that they met in a city under siege (Bogotá, Colombia) and fell in love while a revolution raged in the background. Back in the States, they had a short courtship and married after only a few weeks. Returning to the present, the narrative reveals that they both work as assassins for different firms and that neither knows about the other's real job. Unfortunately, their companies are competing firms (like "Macy's and Gimball's," as one character later describes it) that put bounties on the couple's heads to end the unsanctioned union. John and Jane, upon learning they are both assassins, first have to learn to trust each other again before they can fight to save their lives and their marriage, which they do, producing a fantastic amount of carnage.

As this is a study on fighting females, it makes sense to begin with the character Jane Smith. She is depicted as one of the most violent fighting females ever to find and keep true love on the big screen and to be alive by the

Three. The Struggling Romaction Genre   93

end—at least at the time of the film's release.[5] While her violence is justified by her work as an assassin, she has no conflicts about her work—she enjoys it, she's good at it, and she has no regrets (and no trouble sleeping). The full expression of the romaction hybrid as feminist-friendly love fantasy would not be possible without just such a violently empowered woman as Jane represents. Her violence aside, she also emblematizes the modern woman who has achieved full equality in life and has a strong, independent identity.

Consequently, Jane suffers none of the crippling practical circumstances that disempower modern women—for example, physical or intellectual constraints and economic dependencies. Additionally, Jane offers a blend of typically masculine and feminine traits, combining violent actions with allure, strength with beauty. Jane's physical prowess, emotional fortitude, and gender flexibility are confirmed in scenes in which she breaks a target's neck with a swift but somehow delicate twist; in which she calmly smashes a stalling informant's face with a telephone; in which she refuses to fall apart after she thinks her husband, John, has tried to kill her; and in which she tells John that she doesn't have trouble sleeping after a kill. She never once screams in fear, though she grunts and growls with rage. The film casually celebrates and naturalizes her violence. Far from making her seem threatening or transgressive for her easy killing ways, her violence defines part of her personality as no-nonsense and powerful—and this is part of what makes her so compelling as a character and so alluring to John. The audience also sees that Jane is equally versed in complex technology through her use of myriad computers, gadgets, and guns; in strategic planning based on her ability to organize intricate assassinations with clockwork precision; and in current events that keep her up late reading the newspaper and able to coolly answer a Jeopardy question as she's heading to complete an assassination. Jane has not just risen beyond the glass ceiling; she has blasted through it with a tactical shotgun.

As if her capabilities needed any additional emphasis, the financial independence and success in Jane's work life as a professional killer—with a swank downtown New York office and what seem to be several other brilliant and attractive female employees or associates ready to follow her every command—appears to balance perfectly with her idyllic suburban personal life. She has the white clapboard house, the lovely décor (including new curtains that she wrangles from a "tea sandwich of a man" who also wanted them), a big kitchen, and the requisite hubby. At every turn, she projects a version of the superwoman mentioned in Chapter Two who has and can do everything, including achieving the mythically desirable balance of personal and professional success. And her capacity for ruthless violence balances with her romantic capacities, without her being punished for a killer status that rejects conventional expectations of women as nurturing. She may have people to kill and danger to face, but she will always have dinner on the table by seven or be home in time for the Colemans' party.

Further evidence of the empowered woman ideal informing Jane's character is that she proves to be non-maternal—as shown by her clear discomfort with and lack of interest in children when she is forced to hold a neighbor's baby. She is also non-domestic: we find out later in the film that all of the dinners she "made" were actually made by one of her employees because she "has never cooked a day in [her] life." She also does not have to suffer for her gender transgressions "the trauma of being alone" fate that Neroni notes often occurs for the truly transgressive violent woman (150). When the façade of domestic bliss crumbles, Jane's personal life actually improves, fitting better than ever with her professional life. These traits don't mean a woman can't be maternal and domestic and still be empowered. Rather, they reflect an acceptance of her non-conformity, freeing her from traditional conceptions of what an appropriate female candidate for romance should resemble.

Lest I forget to mention an important part of the fighting female, feminist-friendly love fantasy, I must note how Jane manages to have and do it all while remaining impeccably, effortlessly gorgeous and with a comfortable sense of her own sexuality—no frumpy or frigid off-putting feminist stereotype here. While detailing Jolie's own attractiveness seems unnecessary, Jane's appearance deserves notice, as her costumes connote an intriguing mix of gender-blending influence. In one of the film's early scenes, we see her in a sheer white cotton tank and skirt—certainly appropriate for the assassination work she apparently just completed, as inferred from the sleek knife she slips into a thigh holster resembling a white garter. Then, following another kill scene in which she dresses as a dominatrix in a black patent-leather merry-widow, the accompanying thigh-high boots and fishnet hose become part of the pink and frilly outfit she wears to the Colemans' suburban mixer. For work, she wears visibly high-end, designer power outfits—sleek, in monochrome beiges and blacks—with impossibly high heels; in the field, she wears sweat-stained camo with military-issue boots. Then there is the classic man's suit that both John and Jane don for the climactic fight scene (though hers covers a midriff-baring Kevlar)—chic, no-nonsense, and semi-androgynous.

The juxtaposition of her wardrobe styles, in which masculine blends fashionably with feminine and conservative mixes with sexy, emphasizes the posturing quality of contemporary women's clothes and aligns with feminist readings of gender as a masquerade, a construction people slip into and out of with ease. The way Jane wears each outfit, exuding confidence, unself-consciously captivating, asserts her sexuality as power, not something to be ashamed of or to hide, in a way that would make Germaine Greer or Madonna proud. From the outside in, Jane seems in complete control and fully emancipated/empowered. She is the product of the feminist dream or at least some versions of it. All in all, Jane is a model example of Susan Hopkins' girl hero, who "has entered virtually every sphere of male power" and become "a heroic over-achiever—active, ambitious, sexy and strong. She emerges as an unstoppable superhero, a savvy super-model, a combative action chick" (1). What's more, there is no question that her sex or gender in any way holds her back, making her further proof of feminist success.

After all that, what better to top Jane's tasty feminist sundae of a life than the proverbial cherry of a hot, progressive hubby? Enter male protagonist John Smith, the man with everything to complement the woman who has it all, and the other integral number to the egalitarian romaction equation. The narrative portrays John as independent and accomplished like Jane. He is a partner in another successful assassination firm, he is equally skilled in guns and combat, and we know he contributes a fair share of financial security to the home, as one might assume upon seeing the large stash of cash he keeps literally "buried under the tool shed." It might be fair to say that the movie more explicitly emphasizes Jane's success by showing all that she can do well, but one could argue that what John *does* is not as important as *who* John is. Certainly, John proves himself talented in many of the same ways as Jane: there's no question of his own success, strength, intelligence, or sex appeal. Instead, the narrative focuses more on establishing his position as the new male, the complement to Jane's empowered fighting female, a character of distinctly gender-blended nuance who functions to empower his heroine partner further.

With the metrosexual's flair for nice clothes and good cigars and the action hero's total cool, he can kill four men without mussing his dapper business casual attire (no bloody white tanks and bare feet for *this* John). Refreshingly sentimental, he can then forgo piles of cash flying around in the violent aftermath for the engraved flask given to him by Jane, "an anniversary present." With the stud's sexual appeal and the romantic hero's chivalry, he not only woos the independent and exciting Jane with his playful and passionate sexuality but also sticks around to make her breakfast the next morning—after the rest of the hotel staff have fled because of the revolution. (He jokes about having to milk a goat to make her coffee). Jumping right into a marriage proposal after six weeks of courtship, we see this new man isn't afraid of commitment: nary a stereotypical scene of pre-wedding jitters or post-wedding regret spoils his enthusiasm. Even the dissatisfaction or frustration he feels about married life, which Jane also feels, isn't something he experiences with cynicism about how awful marriage is supposed to be (a stereotypical male refrain in much of popular culture). He is sad and ready to work to improve things.

The narrative regularly emphasizes John's own liberated masculinity (and thus liberat*ing*, for her) by contrasting him with Eddie (Vince Vaughan),

John's friend, who is a typical male chauvinist type: bitterly divorced and living with his mother "because that's the only woman [he's] ever trusted." Eddie, as a sexist foil, continually discourages John's impulses toward commitment and intimacy with his wife. When John says he'll "talk to the missus" about attending a barbeque at Eddie's house that is for "dudes only," Eddie stereotypically denigrates Jane's position as the old ball and chain by asking John if he needs to "give her a call in case you decide to scratch your ass ... make sure she thinks it's okay." Eddie also eagerly calls for John to kill Jane, in return for her confused attempt to kill John because wives "all try to kill you—slowly, painfully, cripplingly." Eddie's exaggerated misogyny further highlights John's position as a female-empowering male. As John never once dignifies Eddie's digs about John's masculinity with any kind of response, the audience can infer that the old relationship models and their related conflict rules—which echo much of Eddie's amusing, stereotypical rhetoric—don't have anything to do with John.

Another important aspect of who John is in this new female-empowering male persona involves his comfort with his wife's many successes and abilities. Describing Jane to Eddie, to justify his whirlwind proposal, John says, "I'm in love. She's smart, sexy." Such a response seems fairly generic—who wouldn't say as much about her or his betrothed? But when he continues his explanation, he shows appreciation for her passion: "She's uninhibited, spontaneous, complicated." Finally, when he describes her professional expertise—based on what he thinks her real job is when they start dating—by saying, "She's like Batman for computers," his appreciation takes on more weight. After all, he has just situated his respect for her by likening her abilities to those of a superhero—a male one at that—with nary a concern about "masculinizing" her or, rather, emasculating himself by association. Later in the film, after he has become acquainted with her violent profession as an assassin for a rival company, his appreciation for her skills becomes the most apparent. At different moments, he looks at her with a variety of pride, amusement, appreciation, lust, and yes, some fear, as she exhibits her violent talents. None of this changes his feelings for her or makes him feel she is unfit as a partner. He easily negotiates her multi-faceted identities and accepts her as a lover and a threat, as a wife and a fighter, as flawed and capable, and as desirable and desiring. Such traits in a woman partner need not be mutually exclusive for the liberating man.

In addition to what I see as representations of gender flexibility that are important to the feminist-friendly love fantasy, the narrative continually emphasizes similarities, how Jane and John are alike, without apparent regard to their sex, specifically in terms of their action-embedded intimate relations. This crucial element in the romaction works toward establishing their equality and contributes to readings of the liberated and empowering nature of their union. They both take pleasure in what they do, as indicated by shared moments of whimsy as they fight against their enemies together in the warehouse store; by their shared look of amusement when John breaches Jane's workspace and she cleverly escapes; by their mutual flirtatious taunting, calling each other's bluffs, when John falls into Jane's elevator trap. They also both take equal responsibility for the relationship work. For instance, there are several decisive moments in their relationship trajectory, points in the plot at which the action and intimacy most thoroughly coincide, where it would be very easy to have one or the other protagonist take the lead (which was the typical tack in the proto-romactions and could signify a power imbalance that would contradict the level partnership fantasy the narrative promotes).

When John and Jane meet for the first time in Bogotá, and even though they are strangers, they simultaneously approach each other in an unspoken, shared "cover" as a couple to avoid police who are searching for "tourists traveling alone." Quick close-ups for the audience's eyes only flash from Jane's thigh, where she slides a knife into a hidden holster, to John's back, where he covers a gun sticking out of his belt. The association of shared violent purposes and initial coupling stresses their similarities as does the fact that they are both turned on by combat, either against others (as in Bogotá) or against each other (in a later—dare I say epic—foreplay fight scene in their own home). Then, there's the moment near the film's end when the couple faces a final attack from the mass of assassins their companies hired to kill them. John and Jane storm out of their makeshift shelter together, having agreed to fight their way out as a team, defeating the enemy as total partners—emphasized by the way their movements are initially synchronized, then coordinated, like a violent dance.

Returning to the epic combat scene in their home as one of the decisive moments for their fate as a couple, John does, in fact, initiate the ceasefire. The scene follows Jane and John's house-wrecking, fight-to-the-death cum foreplay-to-reconciliation. When face to face and gun to gun, John lowers his weapon first, while Jane angrily yells, "don't ... come on," unwilling until the very last moment to concede to romance and the powerful "key kiss," defined by Mark Rubinfeld as "signifying an end to resistance, a recognition of romantic love, a declaration of commitment, a portent of permanent union, and a pleasurable closure to the narrative" (6). Admittedly, John's refusal to "take the shot" could be seen as a typical enactment of male privilege and control, in which he feels an innate "masculine" responsibility to protect her or in which he steadfastly refuses to listen to what she says she wants and denies her autonomy, respectively. Referring to just this kind of typical masculine posturing in romantic comedies, Rubinfeld sees that such an "insistence on male persistence, of course, reinforces male dominance, just as the heroine's 'giving in' reinforces female deference" (10).

However, by the time this scene plays, the narrative and characterization have established that Jane does not need to be protected. She can more than fend for herself and can even be a serious threat. She also very clearly loves John and has no intention of actually killing him. (Otherwise, why would she have been upset when, at one point in the film, she thought he was actually dead?) Also, after she has suggested they take their individually planned escapes, she doesn't really want him to leave when things get really dangerous for them. (Otherwise, why would she have stuck with him so long in the conflict before suggesting the out?)

While these characters are problematic, in and of themselves, they fall on the constructive side of fantasies about feminist intimacy that leans toward modern romance as a place in which couples meet and work together as equals, not as traditional patriarch/wife or as two halves of a companionate whole. They do not complete each other, and no one has to change or teach the other person to become more than what they are. Each is whole and capable, and they choose each other for their personal qualities, not for the gender-prescriptive role each wants the other person to play. The hybrid nature of the romaction makes such an emphasis on egalitarian compatibility more feasible than it would be in the regular romantic comedy or action narrative structure. Love occurring between equally talented men and women working together happens in both, but the gender flexibility and balance of power tend not to have nearly the emphasis that becomes possible in Romaction specifically because the partnership can be more explicitly enacted through shared action prowess as much as actual characterization.

Liberating Conflict: New Relationship Rules

> "Are you getting enough action at home?"[6]

Mr. and Mrs. Smith's romaction protagonists affirm the modern egalitarian couple who are equally empowered and who are freed, eventually, from the constraints of unenlightened gender politics. At the same time, the film satirizes conventional domesticity and traditional intimacy roles, thus underscoring restrictive cultural norms that, from the perspective of the narrative, encourage intimacy conflicts. Through this, the romaction demonstrates how feminist-friendly intimacy must authenticate itself against a backdrop of restrictive cultural norms.

Even though the Smiths seem to have it all, something is missing: the perfect balance all turns out to be a charade—literally, in the way John and Jane perform their married roles. Early in the film, the narrative relates evidence of John and Jane's dissatisfaction about and dissembling within their marriage to scenes of traditional or "normal" relationship encounters like couples therapy. The more within the ranges of the norm they seem to be, the more out of sync and unhappy they are. At the same time, those social norms are shown in direct contrast to their private longings and interests as individuals and, thus, as part of a liberated couple. Following a short opening scene where John and Jane have an initial meeting with a couples therapist, the narrative flashes back to the couple meeting in Bogotá amidst the dangerous chaos of revolution, the romaction's version of the "meet cute." They dance in the rain, finish a bottle of hard liquor together, and greet the morning together drinking coffee while the walls of their hotel shake around them from bombs going off nearby. They are happy being themselves, connecting through their shared fearlessness and playfulness, and their interaction follows no traditional script for either the romantic comedy or the action film. Surrounded by danger, they seem comfortable, companionable and passionate, as though their individual danger-seeking natures fit well together. I don't know about other viewers, but I can say I generally don't associate the kind of people who would find this kind of risk exciting with the kind of people who would attend couples therapy.

What happens between Bogotá and their first therapy session? John and Jane get married. Only after marriage enters the relationship does the couple start to perform the traditional gender roles that eventually translate into the conventional—and restrictive—domesticity that dismantles the egalitarian basis of their intimacy. The first indicator of trouble ahead is when John and Jane are on a date at the carnival, presumably shortly after they met. They play a shooting game. Jane, after looking at John somewhat warily, pretends to not be able to aim well during her first attempt—she misses all the shots deliberately. When John takes a turn, he hits all but one target, claiming "beginner's luck." One could say that Jane flubs her shots not to play the typical female role but to keep her assassin skills secret and prevent John from being curious. If that were the case, then why, after John's turn, would she try again and hit every target (also citing "beginner's luck")?

My answer is that either way, she ends up deferring to John—either in shooting poorly the first time because she thought it would be expected of her or in waiting until he does well before she can. During the courtship, she has already begun performing her role as the traditional female who must nurture the male's ego and not express any kind of alpha tendencies. After the marriage, Jane takes this performance even further. Within the narrative framework, the only real skills John sees from Jane are domestic ones: cooking, decorating, and dressing. Her "real" self has been effaced, and John has felt it. He is no longer full of compliments about Jane's skills as he was during their courtship; rather, he is reduced to irregular, awkward compliments about dinner or about a dress he thinks is pretty because he has no other way to relate to or appreciate her.

The rest of the early film scenes—before John's and Jane's secrets emerge—depict their marriage as bogged down in a supposedly normal domestic routine; the scenes imply that because of this and because of the role-playing, the marriage has become oppressive. The narrative emphasizes the monotony first through a repetition that specifically implicates conventional domesticity as the source of the inertia. For example, the phrase *dinner is at seven*—"It always is," John says at one point— is repeated at least three times. Another is the phrase *perfect timing*—to which John once replies, "As always."

These moments communicate, through repetition, an effect that Virginia Wexman describes as "a quality of obsessive return that presents the characters as part of an inflexible social and psychological milieu in which they feel trapped and helpless" (174). It is as if the very fact that John and Jane replay the old marriage custom of the husband returning home from work to dinner the wife (apparently) cooked is a kind of domestic spontaneity suck. We see the same kind of repetition early in the movie when the camera focuses on the spouses touching their wedding rings, either when they are putting them on after returning from a "job" or when they are fidgeting with them while they talk to the therapist about their dissatisfaction.

Yes, for such "spontaneous" and thrill-seeking people, it seems odd that Jane and John never really smile or laugh when they are together in their home or even when they are with each other after they have married (with the exception of the large, fake smile that accompanies an equally fake sing-song greeting to their neighbors when they arrive at the Colemans' party). Not until their secrets are revealed and they begin fighting each other, that is. When the rival companies that employ John and Jane find out that the two are married, each is given 48 hours to take the other out, an outside threat that forces them to face their personal marriage problems. This rising action allows two romaction tropes to occur: first, the emotional reconciling in which they have to decide they really want to be together (strictly romantic comedy stuff), and second, the enemy face-off where John and Jane can choose to partner up (the core of action content).

Once the real action begins, the narrative combines the tension of the unspoken questions "Will they get back together?" and "Will they kill each other or be killed?" Now the audience is reintroduced to the genuine Jane and John, who return to the way they were when they met. They are playful, teasing as they egg each other on, daring each other to show what he or she's got. They are delighted competitors, all sly smiles and cheeky taunts. They have finally stopped dissembling and playing the appropriate spouse roles and have started acting like themselves. Again, while it could be seen that their secretive, dangerous jobs as hired assassins necessitated John's and Jane's secrecy about their daily life, that doesn't explain why they would need

Three. The Struggling Romaction Genre 101

to lie to each other about things as simple as where he went to college (Notre Dame for art history, rather than MIT for his engineering work cover) or that she is a Jewish orphan (who hired fake parents for the wedding) unless one takes into account their assumptions about being proper spouses. Accordingly, only from this place of liberation through authenticity can they really decide what their relationship is to be and who they want to be in it. Their decision, interestingly enough, ends up being to destroy their home and all that their domestic, married life imposed upon them: deception, consumption, and boredom.

With the house literally in ruins, the Smiths can consummate their unconventional, liberated love with that key kiss followed by passionate lovemaking. However, this is only a step toward egalitarian partnership. There are still moments when, despite the inroads they are making toward rejecting traditional romance roles, they falter and return to gender-divisive behavior that keeps them out of sync. For example, when John and Jane have to escape their house because it's under siege from the assassins their companies sent to kill them, Jane balks when John hands her a smaller "girl gun," and the delay almost gets them shot. The same thing happens when they argue over how to deal with the guy they've taken hostage (who turns out to be the bait put up by their companies), and John warns Jane not to "undermine" him. The bickering slows down the interrogation; it takes so long for them to learn that they've been set up that they almost get caught.

Not until they solidify their equal alliance by giving up the roles entirely do they work in sync. This equality is symbolized by the moment they agree, together, that they will face the enemy together—a bonding that occurs in the toolshed scene only after they face the reality of their false marriage. Now they are partners; now they can beat their enemy in a spectacular showdown at, of all places, a large warehouse store called KostMart—another consumption-and-domesticity-oriented space that ends up being demolished. All of this violent chaos satisfies an audience's craving for the exciting action of defeating an enemy, but the romance remains every bit a part of the event: even as Jane and John fight the seemingly endless stream of assassins targeting them, they still have moments of tender sharing, made all the more tender for the peril surrounding them. As mentioned earlier, the choreography of their showdown shows them fully in sync, back-to-back, and side-by-side, one ducking to reload while the other shoots, one shooting from the gun on the back of the other. It's quite elegant. And one must remember that all the action is in service of the romance because it was the very act of their being together that brought the threat into their lives.

It takes very little stretch of the imagination to see in the Smiths' intimate predicament a mockery of traditional (or in some vocabularies, conservative) gender roles that mirror the kinds of critiques feminists like Betty

Friedan and Shulamith Firestone made about divided domestic and emotional labor. Neither John nor Jane really enjoys their domestic bliss. Neither is really interested in the spoils of their suburban life: having the perfect red oak floors, re-covering the couch to match the new drapes, winning the golf trophy "again," sitting through stories of a neighbor's husband's promotion, or getting the zero-percent APR. Still, they seem compelled to continue playing along. After all, "that's marriage," as the therapist states in response to Jane's distressed description of the chasm opening between herself and her husband—a response that seems to emphasize the therapist's role in asserting a certain misery status quo, marriage as deception and separation (as if that could cheer her up).

Rather, the narrative critiques just the kind of assumption the therapist makes about what marriage is or should be, an assumption that continually re-inscribes stereotypical roles. The narrative also underlines how these assumptions are upheld by an outmoded public—society at large—that is slow to progress and that hampers private needs and desires for liberated individuals in love, like the Smiths, to structure the relationship as they see fit. The therapist represents this public voice (his presence is literally confined to his voice). Another traditional public voice comes from the Colemans, the perfect suburban couple who seem to police the Smiths' gender propriety through explicit praise (symbolized by Mr. Coleman's comments about the red oak floors that he admires) and implicit disapproval (seen in Mrs. Coleman's surprise when she sees fishnet hose peek from under Jane's pink dress). The Colemans also maintain a strictly divided gender environment in their domestic sphere, as when they organize their party: the women, wearing pretty pastels, congregate with the children and talk about their husbands' jobs, and the men adjourn to separate rooms to joke separately about golf and smoke cigars. This is the very environment that Jane and John find anathema to their more gender-flexible and egalitarian personalities.

The loudest public voices about the gender impropriety of Jane and John's union are their bosses, who assume that just because Jane and John work for rival companies, they can't be married. There was no mention of any rivalry in the companies before this, no mention of either company's attempting to kill those who worked for the rival company until John and Jane. So, it's specifically the supposed taboo nature of their relationship that makes them targets. As the agent who plays the bait (to draw Jane and John in to be killed) states, the companies can't have "two competing agents living under the same roof. It's bad for business." How's that for an indictment not just of the two-person working household (which has long been the case for all but the leisure class) but also of the modern two-person *professional* household? Such a household actually does represent an obstacle for many married couples who struggle to balance their career desires with their intimate relations even as they must continue to address lingering problems about sharing the household work and the process of making a home while holding a job. The point ends up being that none of the outsiders get it right, all of them play from an outdated set of rules, and they all try to control the relationship by defining it in ways that align with old relationship caricatures that don't fit with the fantasy of equality for the contemporary couple the Smiths represent.

Again, the romaction hybrid created by combining and reworking both action and romantic-comedy themes enables a new vantage on heterosexual egalitarian intimacy conflicts by encompassing the multiple threats unsettling the couple. So, there tends to be an element of internal, private emotional threat from within the couple caused by differing desires. This is normal for romantic comedies—in which the obstacles between men and women tend to be about opposing ideas of commitment or dependence or love that the couple overcomes by communicating or changing some aspect of themselves as individuals. For example, they clear up some misunderstanding about who wants whom, or the previously commitment-shy character decides to marry. In this case, our protagonists actually share the same misunderstanding that many viewers maintain—that a successful marriage requires a traditional gender division of labor and a stable domestic life.

The action plot, then, adds to the private conflict not only a social interference external to the couple that comes between them (not unknown to romantic comedy plots) but also a public problem in the form of a common enemy—who becomes an enemy because of the couple's nontraditional basis. The common enemy must be faced and overcome by the couple as partners, acting together against this outside force that would deny the new liberated couple's autonomy, impose restrictive social roles, and/or bring about the end of the relationship. Neroni's introduction to *The Violent Woman* provides a useful elaboration of the transgressive possibilities that action film violence presents—specifically, violence by female protagonists. Most action films portray themes in which the protagonist acts counter to socially acceptable roles and in which the plot supports the renegade or rogue approach to a problem (involving the use of violence). In romantic comedies, socially approved behaviors and resolutions tend to be reinforced by bringing the rogue character back into the fold as he or she accepts the proffered romance. At the end of the film, then, the private and public conflicts become most clearly aligned as both characters go rogue; neither conflict can be extricated from the other because the influence of the public on the private is reinforced by private reenactment within the public realm. From this perspective, the film clearly reflects a fantasy of social overhaul starting within the couple.

Throughout the film, the interactions between John and Jane, as they struggle to define their relationship for themselves, reaffirm sociologist Linda A.M. Perry's conclusion that couples need to "move beyond sex-stereotype mandates to make possible a true cultural paradigm shift into equality. This shift would free females and males from blindly adhering to the difference perspective that relies on accepting socially mandated rules and roles for each sex" (193). Audiences witness and maybe learn from the slippery slope that threatens egalitarian possibilities for liberated couples in love when they decide to "be married" if they enter marriage with expectations that they must act or appear a certain way or that they should define their relationship the way society defines it. Thus, the film critiques not marriage but rather the hypocrisy of today's culture that continually highlights the importance of individual autonomy while still clinging to restrictive and discordant expectations about being married. Such hypocrisy makes of marriage, from the film's perspective, less an egalitarian partnership and more an obstacle to authentic intimacy that occurs when we "obey social rules by adopting social roles even when the rules and roles may limit or damage our self-direction" (Perry 189)—in the very way we see those rules and roles interfere with John's and Jane's happiness.

Just as the film assures audiences that society no longer has the right to determine what interests one enjoys and what gender attributes they exhibit, it additionally leads us to believe that society no longer has the right to determine that intimacy in a heterosexual union must be enacted based on defined gender scripts, which is ultimately the basis for reading the film within a feminist-friendly ethos. In the case of *Mr. and Mrs. Smith* as romaction, the only happy ending to modern romance conflicts is one in which both partners win and outmoded society loses. As if the large body count the Smiths leave while taking out the enemy weren't enough, the film's final scene emphasizes just how little society should contribute to defining modern love by having Jane and John return to the therapist's office. This time, instead of listening to his commentary about marriage or answering his questions aimed to help them define or rate their relationship, they interrupt him to share what is important to them—they have rekindled the romance (by turning the house into kindling). Yes, the Smiths most certainly "redid the house," as Jane gleefully informs the therapist, destroying not only the hold traditional domesticity had on them but also the confining need for public validation and definition.

In the end, neither person in the couple has to conform to achieve love. Rather, both have to reject conformity in favor of their true selves before they can resolve their conflicts. This choice makes them both love-warriors, an identity they can share and use to face the challenges posed by a union that brings together an empowered woman and a female-empowering man. This choice is also what allows the Smiths literally to win back their right to stay married, to be passionate and in love, and to keep their jobs—one assumes from the fact that they return to therapy in the last scene, meaning they aren't on the run anymore. A hundred years of feminist struggle to have it all, or at least the possibility of having it all, is condensed and reenacted in two hours of romaction.

Trial and Error: The Year of the Romaction

The success of *Mr. and Mrs. Smith* paved the way for the 2010 romaction run, as producers were encouraged by the hefty returns of the 2005 film. Additionally, the film presents the most clearly imagined egalitarian space for the hybrid genre in which to represent the feminist-friendly love fantasy because Jane Smith is a very capable fighting female. In fact, she is the only professional fighting female in the four romaction films that have been released. The remaining romaction female protagonists are amateurs who range in fighting ability from basically none, for Claire Foster (Tina Fey) in *Date Night*, to a little for Jen Kornfeldt (Katherine Heigl) in *Killers*, to moderate for June Haven (Cameron Diaz) in *Knight and Day*. While *Date Night* has two protagonists who are essentially equally matched civilians, in *Killers* and *Knight and Day*, professional male action heroes lead their civilian female co-stars through the fight. Before addressing *Knight and Day*, it's necessary to address how the other two films fall short of the bar set by *Mr. and Mrs. Smith* in terms of representing the egalitarian couple and the liberating conflict.

The Man with a Plan

In *Date Night*, Claire and Phil Foster (Steve Carell) are a typical suburban couple with two careers and two children. Once a week, they have a standing date night for a movie and dinner at the local steakhouse. One night, after the shock of learning that a couple they have known for a long time is divorcing because that couple feels like they've lost the spark and become just "really excellent roommates," Claire and Phil decide to dress up and upgrade their usual date night. They head to the big city for dinner at a trendy restaurant (that requires reservations a month in advance). After stealing the reservation of another couple that doesn't show up (a couple who just happen to be in trouble for blackmailing the state's DA), Claire and Phil are mistaken for that couple by dirty cops who then threaten them. The Fosters must run for their lives. As they fight to save themselves, they come face to face with their own relationship problems and fears. By the end of the night, Claire and Phil are both rejuvenated by the action they've faced and reminded that their nice, boring suburban family life is exactly what they both want.

Mr. and Mrs. Smith created a couple of equally-skilled assassins to enact the symbolic egalitarian partnership as the basis of the modern romance fantasy; *Date Night* uses a couple of equally inept and unskilled civilians to mark the same equal standing.⁷ The level of parity between the two extends beyond their amateur status to indicate the many other ways they are alike and, therefore, equal as individuals in the couple. They are both, basically, normal individuals with very normal lives. In fact, the Fosters may be the most lackluster couple to ever star in an action-adventure. Phil's a tax lawyer who tries to get his clients excited about opening an IRA with their refunds. Claire's a real estate agent trying to deal with reluctant buyers, a busted real estate bubble, and plummeting housing prices. They both end up exhausted from work every day and struggle to muster the energy to take care of their two children and go on their routine date nights. They both show visible dissatisfaction with the lack of romance in the marriage, exemplified early on as they separately sneak a wistful look at an affectionate married couple in the steak restaurant where the Fosters usually go. Each feels overworked and under-appreciated.

Beyond the parity between them as individuals, there are moments in the action when the narrative seems to emphasize their parity as partners, albeit bumbling partners, in the battle. Phil takes the lead to get them out of the boathouse. Claire takes the lead to steal files from a real estate office, breaking the window to do so, so they can find her previous client Holbrooke Grant (Mark Wahlberg), who is a government security expert. They are both behind the wheel during the car chase (in separate cars stuck together at the bumper, so they literally share driving). They both have to "work that pole" in a strip club to gain access to the DA in order to question him. Yet, the violent action comes almost entirely from Phil. He hits the bad guys who hold them at gunpoint with an oar. He wields a (defunct) antique gun that he stole to protect them and shoots it at the corrupt cops. More importantly, Phil is the one who comes up with the final plan to foil the bad guy, while Claire remains clueless, or "lost" as she repeats in her confusion, over what happens. So, he ends up saving the day, and what was an adventure for them as partners ends up being his personal triumph.

This sense of the action empowering Phil rather than both of them, as a couple, is emphasized by the way he comes up with a plan and executes it to save them, an act that makes him the effective figure that he failed to be throughout the movie. Before Phil's success in the film, Claire had repeatedly claimed that his "plans are the worst," and he himself said, "I'm not very good with plans generally." He's mocked by a thug character for using weak "tough-guy lines" and is called Claire's "androgynous friend" in the strip club. In contrast, Claire is never expected to come up with a plan. Her ability to plan (or not) is never questioned, nor is her gender interrogated the same way. There is, in general, just no sense of her part in fixing the relationship. There is, conversely, a deep sense of his responsibility to make things right, whether it's in pepping up date night by taking his wife out to a better restaurant or in getting the bad guys arrested. This point provides an important contrast between Phil Foster and John Smith as fantasy characters. There's a level of anxiety in Phil about portraying an authority figure, particularly in comparison to the suave Holbrooke Grant (Mark Wahlberg), that John never exhibits. Phil is intimidated by his wife's obvious attraction for Grant as well as Grant's extensive knowledge and resources, which Phil and Claire rely on to get them out of trouble. In fact, the film regularly offers comparisons between Phil and Grant, ones in which Phil doesn't measure up and is concerned about it. The imbalance in character focus reduces the symbolic egalitarian basis of their relationship.

These issues undermine the portrayals of the enlightened couple's overcoming the domestic role gender divide at the base of the intimacy conflict in the movie. Traditional gender roles are a problem, but not for Phil. They are a problem for Claire, who, in turn, makes them a problem for Phil. Claire has undertaken the traditional homemaker role and has accepted that she is the one who must take care of everything in the house as well as doing her job. She's drained by a list of responsibilities, from making the children breakfast to getting them into bed at night, that she lays out during an argument with Phil in the car (while they are trying to escape the enemy). Her being drained is the reason she can't "light up" for her husband—his one desire. Her one desire? To sit alone in an air-conditioned room eating lunch without anyone touching her as she drinks a Diet Sprite. We are certainly encouraged to understand her plight, but not as much as we are encouraged to understand Phil, who does portray a version of John Smith's female-empowering man because he is willing and interested in doing the emotional work it will take to strengthen their marriage and improve their domestic life.

Phil asks Claire to put more trust in him to share the household duties, to let him do things his way, so he can do his share and also reduce some of the stress she experiences as the primary caretaker. He wants to be more of a partner in the home. We also learn that he takes part in a book night with Claire and her female friends—and reads the whole book every time—because it's important to Claire. He even uses a lesson he learns from the most recent book club reading to come up with his plan to foil the bad guys. His sensitivity increases sympathy for his character and emphasizes his role as the hero, but it does so by decreasing sympathy for her character—because she isn't letting him help. As Phil claims, and as we see evidence for throughout the movie, "You have to do it all yourself, your way. You got me screwing up before I even get a chance to come through for you." Additionally, the narrative does not emphasize any heroism on her part.

The effect of this character imbalance can be seen as an indictment of the postfeminist superwoman character Claire embodies, the woman who has it all and takes it all on because she knows she can, but who suffers for it. We see small clues that Claire creates problems for herself throughout the film: Phil says he'll make breakfast for the kids in the first scene, but Claire ends up making it. She tells him what to get for a birthday party their kids will go to, then says she'll get it, it's "easier." He claims he's ready to do more in the house and make things easier for her if she will "let" him. Her super-capability then becomes an issue of excess control—she's so empowered that it overwhelms her. Thus, the source of the conflict falls on her, for not taking advantage of his enlightenment—it's not a conflict in which they realize they are both at fault and must both make amends to correct. Their dynamic at once spreads the enlightened message that men should have more responsibility in the home and should undertake domestic responsibilities, but it also implies that women are responsible for "letting" the men. In other words, the fantasy re-writes Arlie Hochschild's "second shift" narrative, which still applies to many women who have careers outside of the home. Today, domestic life isn't a problem because men are bad partners in the home, and the world around them didn't change; it's because women are bad partners and unable to let go. This conception of the domestic divide is not feminist-friendly.

Conversely, *Mr. and Mrs. Smith* indicates that modifications had to be made by both people in the couple but, more importantly, by those around the couple—the workplace, friends and colleagues, the therapist. To further differentiate the *Date Night* portrayal of the domestic divide, consider how, despite Phil's professed willingness to do more, what we see and hear of his domestic work paints the stereotypical picture of the inept man. In his own words, he "doesn't know how to load the dishwasher," and, as Claire points out after once again bruising her shins, "You never, ever, ever close any drawer you ever open. Ever!" He says that he knows he can "surprise her" by stepping up if she'd let him, but his domestic performance makes us doubtful. Additionally, he's already exhausted from his work, indicated when he falls onto the couch twice upon returning home during the early part of the movie, so tired he has to promise his son he'll play a game after he briefly lapses into a "mini-coma." It's hard to imagine his being able to follow up on his promises. Thus, we have only a sense of him as an authority, the savior, outside of the household in the public's sphere, and her as the "total bitch," the words she uses to describe herself after she unloads her unhappiness onto her husband.

Ultimately, *Date Night* paints a realistic picture of the modern family, with two working parents struggling to navigate domestic life. That's what makes the film's inability to render a more balanced partnership for the couple in the action and intimacy work so disappointing. The film betrays lopsided anxieties about a man's ability to protect his wife and family and a lopsided fantasy where his strength as a good husband leaves more of an impression than her abilities as an empowered woman, leaving us with a weak model of egalitarian intimacy. In the end, Phil comes off as the love-warrior hero who's saving the day and the relationship, and she's the wife. A similar problem with a lack of parity in the male/female participation in the action and the emotional work—leading to another narrative that ultimately problematizes hetero-partnerships and the potential for feminist-friendly intimacy—occurs in *Killers*, by far the weakest romaction for relying on stereotypical depictions of domestic gender roles and for maintaining a divided power dynamic between the spouses.

The Overprotector

Spencer (Ashton Kutcher) and Jen of *Killers* meet and fall in love at the beginning of the movie. They are in Nice, France, where Jen is on vacation with her parents after she has had a recent breakup. Fast-forward to three years later, and Spencer and Jen are married and live in a typical suburb with friendly and prying neighbors. Jen is a successful professional who works in computer technology. Spencer, we also learn at the beginning of the movie, is a spy who's dissatisfied with his life and wants nothing more than to settle down to the very life he finds with Jen in the suburbs. However, Spencer's old handler shows up unexpectedly and tries to get him back in the business. Spencer rejects the offer. Suddenly, everyone in his nice suburban fantasy—his friends, colleagues, and neighbors—is trying to kill him. Because Jen returns home unexpectedly when she's supposed to be on a business trip, she's in danger along with him. They face numerous enemies, showcasing Spencer's fancy spy fighting skills. At the same time, Jen must face the fact that her husband lied to her and the realization that she's pregnant. Their marriage and family are in jeopardy.

In this film, there was some real potential for projecting couples rejecting standard romance tropes and outdated gender roles. For example, Spencer is another semi-enlightened man who doesn't fear settling down and taking part in family life. In fact, he seeks it, rejecting instead the macho, lone-wolf style life he had as a spy—with its glamorous travel, fast cars, beautiful women, and big explosions. He redecorates his wife's office, making it organized and attractive. He's hesitant to accept his birthday gift from Jen, a ticket to Nice, because he says, "I have everything I need right here." He even criticizes Jen's imposing father—played by Tom Selleck—for acting like Jen's a "fragile doll," saying, "I depend on her, Sir. It's not the other way around." Unfortunately, this is part of a scene in which Spencer asks the father for permission to propose (reflecting a romance throwback move that foreshadows the problems with the narrative to come).

As for Jen, she may not be a spy, but she is a very capable career woman whose boss respects her more than her slovenly male colleagues. She can also throw a punch and (poorly) shoot a gun. She doesn't freak out when the action begins. Likewise, while she's not happy about it, she deals with the violence around her surprisingly well. She even progresses by the end of the movie into a more mature and confident woman who can stand up to her solicitous, overbearing father and also make a decision about whether or not the marriage works, now that she knows her husband's secret.

That's where the progress ends. Spencer does all of the action work, and Jen does all of the emotional work. Spencer saves her. She can't properly shoot the gun she's given. Jen shoots a bad guy in the arm accidentally, just like Helen Tasker accidentally takes down a roomful of terrorists with a dropped Uzi in *True Lies*. Jen holds the gun like a rotten banana, and she carries it around in a child's stuffed animal backpack. Her one punch takes down a nosy neighbor, not an enemy. Her independence is severely limited by the fact that she maintains close ties with parents who take care of her, even financially—as we learn when Spencer cuts a tag off Jen's dress on their first date, and she freaks out saying that she can't afford the dress. She was going to take it back, but now her dad will have to pay for it.

Also, Jen only gains a backbone once she learns she's pregnant. Her goal is to protect the child, rightfully, but she then turns into a stereotypical "Mama Bear," as she calls it, suddenly snacking incessantly. That's not to say that women must be violent to be seen as strong and that motherhood automatically undermines their empowerment. However, when women enter into the action narrative, the tendency is always to play up stereotypical personalities in ways that make women appear not only dependent but also often comically incompetent. Even in *Date Night*, in which both Phil and Claire are incompetent, Phil eventually gains competence, but Claire does not. So, they fall into the category Inness refers to as "pseudo-tough," which "is one of the ways that the media perpetuate the myth that women are less capable and competent than men" or "that a woman's toughness is still not the equal of a man's" (14). The romantic comedy tendencies far overshadow the action implications in ways that reveal a heterosexual power imbalance that is the real problem at the basis of hetero-relations—and a core reason why such intimacies have been considered to undermine a fighting female's power in a narrative when it forces her back into the old romance box.

As Jen's and Spencer's story heads toward the denouement, we learn that Jen was never really in danger anyway—except for her proximity to Spencer. Her father, it turns out, is a spy who knows Spencer is a spy and has known it from the beginning. Her father—who has some serious control issues—embedded sleepers into their lives to protect his little girl should it turn out that Spencer returned to the spy life. Thus, all of the violence and attacks were the father's fault, based on his misunderstanding, and the narrative chalks up his behavior to simply being part of a "normal" dad persona. Dad is in no way held accountable for his actions. Also, the narrative emphasizes Spencer's similarities with the dad instead of rejecting the male-protector stereotype. First, Jen says she "married the one man who is exactly like my father." Then, at the movie's end, after they have the baby, Spencer sports a thin version of his father-in-law's mustache. Finally, the last shot of the film is that of the baby's crib, in the dark, surrounded by an alarm grid, indicating Spencer's father-spy protection *modus operandi* is in full swing.

All in all, this film has much in common with *Date Night* and implies that the father must protect the family at all costs. Jen and Spencer don't even share domestic work as partners. She's the one who decides to leave without him for the sake of the baby because she feels he can't keep her safe. She's the one who insists on a trust circle at the end of the movie and who requires her parents and Spencer to promise to end the fighting for the baby's sake. She changes little and realizes nothing about her role. Yet, she is in control of the home front. Spencer has to change his work, but he had decided to do that anyway. Jen chooses to leave and to come back without much discussion about it. It's a good reflection on her independence, but it's a poor reflection on her potential as a love-warrior whose independence combines with strength to change the status quo of the relationship power divide. Her character, like Claire Foster's in *Date Night*, simply reasserts the same fixed gender promoted by the action genre protector/protected dynamic that the romaction had the potential to undermine.

Missing the Mark: What Happened to the Romaction?

What contributed to romaction's unfortunate regression from showcasing the egalitarian couple to effectively replaying the typical hierarchy of male-as-action-hero/female-as-love-interest (even if now she can dabble humorously in a little of the fighting action)? It would be easy to read the change as a backlash against the gender flexibility that proves that the action genre is not conducive to progressive politics when it comes to conceiving the fighting female's place in a co-lead romance narrative. Maybe the idea of a romance on the big screen, one in which both a man and a woman get to fight for love and save each other, just proves too transgressive. This might explain the recent trend of female-led blockbuster action films like *The Hunger Games* and *Divergent* franchises and why female characters continue to gain in the action genre—and hold their reign in the romantic comedy genre[8]—as the romaction genre fizzles. These movies, like their action forbears, tend to keep the romance on the sidelines and assert that there can only be one hero fighting for love. This investigation will return to these films and this issue in Chapter Five.

Another possible reason for the change might be that as women gain more access to the action sphere and the big and small screens depict more fantasies of female empowerment, the ideological function of the romaction is no longer necessary. Perhaps audiences no longer seek fantasies to resolve the conflict provoked by the notion of strong, independent women in love because they don't see a conflict there. After all, Katniss Everdeen finds true love while leading a revolution. Yet, she faces serious hardships as she negotiates her role as a fighter with her role as a lover. Not only do the other fighting female narratives I analyze contradict any assumption that the sense of conflict surrounding the empowered woman is gone, but so do a good portion of the relationship columns out there. Take, for example, the large number of websites and blog posts dedicated either to answering the question "Can Strong Independent Women Find Love?" (Rubinstein) or to doling out advice to help men "Handle Strong Independent Women" (Sama). There definitely remains a sense of hetero-crisis to resolve; there also remains a desire for fantasies that provide the resolution in ways that assert the strong, independent woman ideal.

I would argue that the problem with the most recent romaction narratives is that they missed some mark for audience expectations, indicated by the fact that *Date Night* and *Killers*, combined, earned barely half of what *Mr. and Mrs. Smith* did. Perhaps audiences found something lacking or less appealing in the more recent films. Both 2010 films had blockbuster potential in terms of their action-packed storylines (including explosions and car chases); additionally, they fit the hybrid formula studio executives believed would draw in larger crowds. Of course, there are many reasons for the variances in film success, ranging from publicity to development to the draw of the actors involved. Critics of *Killers* almost unanimously panned it as an ill-conceived and poorly written movie. *Date Night* received more favorable reviews, however, and actually has a higher critic rating overall than *Mr. and Mrs. Smith* on Rotten Tomatoes.

The major star power of Brangelina could account, in part, for the discrepancy. True, Katherine Heigl was following up on the success of *Knocked Up* (2007). Also, both Steve Carell and Tina Fey were enjoying a good deal of media attention for their work—Carell for *The Office* and Fey for *30 Rock* and *SNL*. In fact, Fey's uncanny *SNL* impressions of Sarah Palin in 2008 further contributed to her celebrity. However, none of these actors could match the box-office allure of either Brad Pitt or Angelina Jolie, much less the two of them together.

The Freedom to Experiment

I see two other related sources that account, at least somewhat, for the discrepancy: first, *Mr. and Mrs. Smith* was essentially an experiment on the part of the writer and director. Conceived by Simon Kinberg, an energetic young scriptwriter, the film's screenplay developed out of his MFA thesis for Columbia University's film program. The story was not developed in the executive boardroom with high returns in mind. It was developed for originality and in an environment of academic inquiry. Kinberg's penchant was for action films, but his approach was shaped by what he describes as Columbia's

> attention to character, drama, dialogue, emotion. [...] Columbia forced me to go deeper with every scene, every character. I wrote *Mr. and Mrs. Smith* as my thesis project, and I know it never would have attracted world-class actors and an innovative, indie-minded director if not for my professors [...] and students pushing me to explore the characters and themes, challenging me to take the emotional drama seriously, encouraging me to start a summer action movie with a scene of marriage therapy. The questions and challenges at Columbia were never, "How do you make it bigger or louder or faster?" They were, "How do you make it deeper and truer and more original?"

The "indie-minded director" to whom Kinberg refers is the notoriously difficult Doug Liman, who tends to insist that a film fits his vision no matter the cost or the input from studio executives. This reputation earned his behavior the title "Limania," an insistence on filming or re-filming scenes on his own time and dollar to get around the producers. The only reason the studio allowed Liman to direct *Mr. and Mrs. Smith* was that Brad Pitt insisted upon it. According to the long piece on Liman in *New York Magazine,* he was basically a pariah for the trouble he caused on his previous film, *The Bourne Identity* (Fishman). Even though Liman feels he lost his "indie credibility" after *Mr. and Mrs. Smith* because it turned out to be a runaway box-office success, he didn't approach the film from the blockbuster aesthetic. He made the film according to what his interviewer calls the "Liman aesthetic," which produces "smart, stylish genre films that confound their genre." So, both the writer and director's initial impulses in conceiving the film had less to do with creating a sure hit by relying on standard tropes and proven formulas and more to do with aspirations to create something new. To be fair, neither the writer nor director make any claims as feminist allies or for feminist intentions with the film, but both are products of a postfeminist period—and Liman does note that his sensibility is informed by an identity as a "liberal New Yorker involved in politics" (Fishman). The point is that both were less beholden to the conventions to which Hollywood tends to cling, which could have translated into a willingness to envision a more egalitarian couple and unique plot.

The Romaction and Audience Expectations

The writer's and director's attention to originality may also have translated into their willingness to incorporate a more capable fighting female, which is the second important divergence that accounts for the success of *Mr. and Mrs. Smith's* romaction over its less progressive follow-ups. For people who fit into the new kind of audiences I described in the Introduction—viewers interested in blockbuster films who had been exposed to, and enjoyed, fighting female narratives and had seen what women can do in them—the damsel-in-distress-oriented female character in action movies is less appealing. So, because the more recent romactions did not exhibit the kind of fighting female many audiences have come to accept and/or expect in their action films, the movies might have had less appeal. This could be read to imply that the combination of love-warrior woman with Abele's home front hero addressed in my Introduction—who functions similarly to what I call a love-warrior—was a factor in the success of *Mr. and Mrs. Smith*, and it is this character, as Hornaday reports it, that the studio execs behind the more recent, less-successful romactions were attempting to recreate.

Angelina Jolie as Jane is not a stereotypical representation of a woman in romaction films and much more effectively demonstrates the love-warrior woman identity. Tina Fey and Katherine Heigl are far more stereotypical and don't quite capture the essence of empowerment Jolie does, at least in terms of what's required to make the mark on the action part of the romaction. Possibly this is because Jolie had already established herself as an actor who embodied the kind of blockbuster action fighting female who would work well as a partner. Possibly this is because, before *Mr. and Mrs. Smith*, Jolie had not only portrayed a fighting female as a cop and an FBI agent but also she had played Lara Croft—the infamous Tomb Raider—twice, carrying the lead in the film and earning blockbuster status around the globe for both movies. The careers of her proto-romaction predecessors Kathleen Turner and Jamie Lee Curtis also indicate the way an actor's representation of violence on-screen makes them more likely to be cast for fighting female roles. Turner's ability to portray a mildly violent Joan Wilder led to roles with more and more violence, ranging from a vengeful ex-wife to private investigator V.I. Warshawski to a serial killer in *Serial Mom* (1994). Curtis was already established as one of horror's first "final girls," beginning with *Halloween* (1978). Heigl and Fey had none of the action cred to back up their performances, not that they needed it for the roles they played.

Cameron Diaz's role in *Knight and Day* offers another example of the relationship between a romaction film's success and the fighting female's ability to exceed the traditional female role, not only in the romance but also in the action. June Havens (Diaz) collides with Roy Miller (Tom Cruise) at the airport. They are supposed to be on the same flight, but she gets bumped, and then she is put back onto the flight. There are only three to four other passengers on the plane, and June and Roy start talking, hitting it off. When she excuses herself to primp and give herself a pep talk in the plane's bathroom,

Three. The Struggling Romaction Genre

we learn that everyone else on the plane is trying to kill Roy. He's a CIA agent thought to have gone rogue, but it's a set-up by his corrupt partner. June ends up having to come along for the ride and for protection. As Roy fights to clear his name, June learns more about him, comes to trust him, and works to stimulate his affection and attention, even as they dodge bullets. In the end, she saves him from the CIA, and they drive off to see Cape Horn, a stop on her bucket list.

This film differs from the other three: the protagonists aren't married, and the narrative doesn't include a reference to or the inclusion of the domestic sphere. However, it contains equal parts of romance and action, the relationship endangers the couple as much as the external threats, and the co-leads work as partners to overcome both.

Now, there are weaknesses in *Knight and Day* that align it in some ways with the other two 2010 films. June does the brunt of the emotional work in that she initiates the relationship and pursues it throughout the film, while Roy tends only to react to her advances. June is a civilian, as Claire and Jen are, while Roy is the well-trained spy who must protect her throughout the film. He very problematically drugs her without her knowledge. However, June asks to be drugged another time to calm down, and she later drugs him to facilitate their escape from the CIA. June can also throw a punch and wrestle, she stabs a bad guy with a knife, and she has mad driving skills. She also partakes in an awesome shootout while riding with Roy on a motorcycle—he drives, she shoots—making her the most violent of the amateur romaction fighting females.

Additionally, Roy relates to her as a capable fighter. He continually praises her violent abilities and tells her she can handle things, that she's doing a great job. He treats her like she's capable by expecting her to be able to handle the gun he gives her (which she does not hold like rotten fruit) and when he needs her to shoot the cars following them on a chase. When they first run into trouble, he forces her to come with him for her protection, but then he stops forcing her and asks her to make a choice about whether she wants to stay with him. Though this makes them somewhat more egalitarian by equalizing their abilities and authority and by reducing the power hierarchy, it doesn't eradicate the divide.

The film fared better than its 2010 romaction compatriots, earning close to what the other two made combined. I would argue that this was, in part, because Cameron Diaz, despite having started as a romantic-comedy darling,[9] had some action cred, thanks to her roles in the two blockbuster *Charlie's Angels* films. Additionally, much of the publicity for *Knight and Day* references how both Diaz and Cruise did their own stunts, including the complicated motorcycle chase scene. As for Diaz's character, June represents a much more non-stereotypical, gender-flexible female more along the lines of Jane Smith.

June is good with cars, owns a car restoration shop, wears more androgynous clothing like plaid shirts and jeans (or big biker boots while trying on frilly bridesmaid dresses). However, she fusses over her looks occasionally, is prone to screaming shrilly during the early danger, and has a nurturing personality. She is gentle with her younger sister and is restoring their dad's old car to give her sister as a wedding present. Still, as a more effective fighting female, she better matches her partner (who, as with the other romaction males, was also portrayed as a more enlightened, female-empowering male).

Critics like Hornaday often lament the lack of ingenuity in Hollywood and believe the romaction trend "can be traced to the twin impulses of love and fear: the movie industry's love of a sure thing and its equally strong fear of trying something new." The return of the gender-normative, non-feminist-friendly depictions of hetero-intimacy in *Date Night* and *Killers* would seem to prove the allure of tradition in Hollywood. However, *Mr. and Mrs. Smith*, the ideal romaction fantasy, offered something very new, something that had never been seen before on the big screen: a seriously capable fighting female, violent and fierce and equal to her male co-star fighter in every way, a woman who ends up in a hetero-romance. The movie's success proves that there are enough people in the audience who are ready for more.

Missed Opportunities: The Sex Wars Aren't Sexy

"It's like girls and boys are on different sides."—(Thorne 65)

Ms. Hornaday's conviction that the romaction reflects a lack of ingenuity in Hollywood film and a reliance on stereotypical narrative conventions, ones in which the typical conventions of action simply mesh with the typical conventions of romantic comedies, makes sense for the most recent romaction experiments. Yet Hornaday's observation also shows just how unique *Mr. and Mrs. Smith* was as a film in terms of its feminist-friendly love fantasy. The level of parity between the characters—their equal participation in the action and the emotional work and their progressive insistence that gender roles are a thing of the past in the modern egalitarian romance—has not happened again in this genre.

However, for all the potential in *Mr. and Mrs. Smith*, for how differently the narrative imagines the centrality of egalitarian intimacy and the equality of the characters, it does reflect one pernicious assumption that, on some level, men and women will always be differently or oppositionally gendered, no matter how liberated and enlightened people become, and that hetero-intimacy will always be fostered by this difference—an assertion that is not feminist-friendly. At its best, the romaction hybrid as performed in *Mr. and Mrs. Smith* represents an expanded textual space in which the complications of modern heterosexual intimacy are worked through as the romaction couple negotiates love's modern minefield, scattered with threats of domesticity, power struggles, outdated social expectations, and destabilized gender roles. Thanks in part to the broader romaction narrative space, all of the romactions reflect an attempt to imagine a logical and optimistic answer to the feminist question of what heterosexual intimacy becomes when men and women achieve more egalitarian personal lives: love warriors fighting together to promote and save egalitarian hetero-intimacy. We can see this in each romaction version. All of them reflect a crisis of intimacy, played out by the private threats to the relationship—a reckoning the couple has to face about their relationship and resolve along with the external threats to their safety. All of the hybrids attempt to locate the source of the threat to the egalitarian possibilities of modern intimacy in the non-liberated public sphere with its reliance on outdated forms of intimacy and romance to control the couple. They then provide the solution to this threat in the film's particular version of the enlightened romaction couple, some more successfully than others.

Nevertheless, my overarching interest in showing how the ideal romaction conveyed transgressive potential in espousing a generally positive version of feminist-friendly love must be tempered by addressing a deeper, more destructive assumption about sex relations that is as much a part of these romactions as both the more straightforward genres of romantic comedy and action because it is an assumption held by society in general. First, the neat resolutions of all of the romactions (similar to both its romantic-comedy and action roots) tend to paint a too-rosy picture of modern heterosexual intimate relations as equal. Accordingly, audiences may be seeing the kind of equal couple they expect of modern media, but that doesn't mean those representations reflect the reality of intimate relations among men and women. In other words, seeing it on-screen makes believing it easier, even if it is not true. The construction of the egalitarian couple and the resolution affirming egalitarian intimacy may be more appealing as an ideal, but the fantasy can also offer the comfort of a progressive, liberating "reality" for love on-screen that supplants the need to change real social relations.

Melvin Donalson speaks to this reassuring aspect of film. Though his theory focuses on interracial buddy narratives, his conclusion easily applies to the egalitarian hetero-romance plot. Thus, the apparent gender flexibility and equality portrayed on-screen, like evidence of racial equality in "the interracial buddy film suggests that democracy and equal treatment have been obtained because if it exists on the big screen, it must exist in the world of those who watch. The tacit popular-culture maxim, both powerful and flawed, seems to be: *If something is expressed and/or performed in a medium, then it must be true in reality"* (11, emphasis in the original). Yet reports still reflect men's and women's struggles with the changing economy and the shifting house roles, women's continued salary disparity, the controversy of the Paycheck Awareness Act, and advice columns reflect male and female agonies over competing alpha relationship roles. There are plenty of "real" relationships that can't quite extract themselves from the binds of assumptions about appropriate gender roles, even if men's and women's daily lives no longer reflect the kinds of traditional home/work divides that contributed so much to the maintenance of those roles.

Second, despite its popular feminist savvy, the romaction fails at what some feel is one of feminism's broader aims: not only to imagine changes in the way men and women relate to each other, our *gendered* behavior, but also in the way we *think* about each other as sexes. Even in films, like *Mr. and Mrs. Smith,* that challenge our gender assumptions and promote egalitarian intimacy, audiences see that despite how equitable we imagine hetero-relations to be, we still require that this equity be established by men and women encountering an unquestioned opposition that appears inherent to male/female sex difference. Essentially, there must be a basis of conflict because men and women are and always will be on opposite sex sides, no matter how similar their genders become. This basis also applies to certain of the love-buddy narratives I discussed in Chapter Two, particularly regarding the competition that the narratives integrate into the romance storyline that regularly positions the co-leads in opposition, whether it's in being ready for the relationship to happen or determining who is saving whom the most.

Ironically enough, there have been plenty of anti-feminist critics who blame feminists for being man-haters and creating tension between the sexes, for ruining the complementary ideal of the sexes filling each other out. But the opposition between men and women has been part of the cultural imagination since at least *Lysistrata*—in which assumed differences lead to conflict (in the case of *Lysistrata*, women wanting peace and family connection and men wanting war and glory). In this sense, both man-hating and woman-hating have already been built into our notions of sex identity and hetero-intimacy, in which fighting is part of the norm.

It is actually *in spite* of feminist inroads into the cultural imagination regarding hetero-romance that the long-constituted sex divide remains intact. The assumption persists that sex difference still has to be articulated for hetero-intimacy to occur, meaning love between men and women can only be achieved by fighting it out, whether literally or figuratively. The romaction is a genre that depends on this trope, both explicitly and implicitly. What is such an exaggerated form of conflict if not war? What characterizes the exaggerations that lead to war if not consistently repeated aggravations and accumulated struggles, the kind which describe the way that hetero-relations are portrayed by the media, even if these conflicts get resolved by the end of the film (or the story or the pop song)? If we see achieving intimacy between men and women in terms of winning a conflict, then, logically, doesn't that mean there is still a sex war? And how can war lead to feminist-friendly love?

No matter the genre, romantic themes almost always arrange sex relations into an ideological mold that takes for granted not only that romantic unions between men and women cannot be understood in ways that exist outside power struggles; in turn, those power struggles somehow lead to or inform our expectations of love. Thus, when we see John and Jane Smith fighting (whether in witty repartee or well-choreographed blows), their fighting reflects their shared basis of equality, their independence, their desire to work together to resolve their intimate problems in a kind of foam "bat therapy" gone berserk.

In a chapter entitled "Games for Angry Couples," sex therapist Gerald Schoenewolf prescribes actual foam bat combat, first in his office, supervised, and then at home, in the nude, to help couples "channel aggression into sexuality" (121). This kind of therapy emerged in the 1980s, and we see Holt and Remington partake in it as an undercover couple on a group therapy retreat. They are encouraged to talk through their feelings as they hit each other, and the exercise indeed encourages them both to state their frustrations. However, the exercise quickly gets out of hand as they become increasingly aggressive toward each other and, as a result, get overly enthusiastic about the hitting in what is a perfect example of the slippery slope of any violence practiced within a relationship.

Just as Schoenewolf promises it will for his patients, in *Mr. And Mrs. Smith*, John and Jane's battles overtly seem to *inspire* their passion; because they can compete and fight, they are all the more attracted to each other. John whacks Jane's head back against a mirror as they tango and argue, and Jane's responding moan seems at once a response to the pain and possibly something more. In *Knight and Day,* Roy and June have one of their first intimate romantic moments after she has been fighting with him out of her anger that he has, once again, drugged her against her wishes. She punches him, they wrestle, and the wrestle then turns into something sexier. While this kind of violent crossover might offer a valid appeal for audiences with a taste for S&M play in the safety of a trusting relationship, it was enacted when there was *no* trust between John and Jane (each of whom suspected the other of being a spy who got into the relationship to keep tabs on the enemy) or Roy and June. Additionally, such scenes smack of domestic abuse, which could be seen as a very disconcerting result of their fighting foreplay. It doesn't matter if both people give the blows. Violence in love is not sexy; it's scary, and, again with exceptions for the S&M crowd, promoting it promotes an obviously problematic version of the heteronormative.

Our society's inability to achieve truly equitable sex relations—as indicated by this destructive sex war theme, which extends to other fighting female narrative types—shows how our enculturated ideas about passion can contradict and counteract any more positive inroads we make in audience feminist consciousness-raising. In essence, our ideas about love hold us all back. The problem with believing in the war of the sexes—a phrase that is still consistently used in any media text that speaks to male/female conflicts—is that it presumes heterosexual encounters will always face incompatible wills and desires in which men want one way and women want another, always in inverse proportion. In a postfeminist period that includes representations of more emotional and/or enlightened men and more aggressive, protector women, in which the boundaries of behaviors and capabilities have somewhat blended in certain arenas of the mass media, the opposition between the sexes in romance doesn't have to necessarily be based on stereotypical gender divides. That means that now, the specific incompatibility isn't as important as the existence of the variance between them and the presence of still sex-divided (if not gender-divided) conflict—a variance that reinforces the assumption that the driving force of heterosexual union and the foundation of any subsequent intimacy must be tension, the tension of difference to retain the thrill of romance. Yet, audiences expect that at the end of a romance story's passionate crusades, somehow, the casualties strewn about the heterosexual combat zone will provide fodder to nurture the tender garden of intimacy.

John and Jane Smith make this same kind of miraculous leap from enemy to lover, as do Roy and June, in a move perpetrated by many romance narratives, a move we'll see in certain fraught fighting female narratives to be analyzed in the next chapter. Within the transition, something important gets erased—namely, how one moves emotionally from hatred and anger to love. On a user blog posted on *Patheos,* writer Libby Anne shares a teacher's Facebook post that speaks to the problem of the violence-as-love tradition. The students tell the teacher that a four-year-old boy pulling a girl's hair means "he likes her!" and that a twelve-year-old boy wrestling a girl to the ground, even though she's not happy about it, is being "just how boys are." But the students then think that when an eighteen-year-old boy grabs a girl's arm, it is "not okay." The teacher's response is to say, "How would he know? How would she know? How would you know? You just told me that for the first seventeen years of these children's lives that you thought it was cute, sweet, and natural, for a boy to grab a girl and be rough with her." To some extent, romance portrayed in any genre often equates roughness with intimate gestures. The only difference is now that there are images of women who can be just as rough—they can be rough together, and that apparently makes everything okay.

Laurie A. Rudman and Peter Glick reveal the problem with this emotional leap when they mention how "[n]o other groups are expected to transition from indifference or even hostility (in childhood) to physical attraction (by adolescence) to sexual intimacy and love (by early adulthood) in the course of their development. Because of these dramatic changes, the transition is not always smooth, as is evident in the common expression that there is a 'war between the sexes'" (232). As children, we learn that men and women are on different sides; as adults who somehow know better, we presume that men and women are on the same side. But when we change the angle of the camera, it turns out that even when men and women appear to stand next to each other in certain representations in the mass media, there remains a very deep line separating them, and this is a line that seems still to be a norm in heterosexuality.

Considering the point Rudman and Glick make, the verbal sparring and name-calling between John and Jane, the cat-and-mouse chasing, and the destructive wrestling—all of the elements audiences read as flirtatious—sound a lot like the descriptions of primary school games. In *Gender Play: Girls and Boys in School,* Barrie Thorne describes these games as being responsible for the ways children grow up understanding that "boys and girls are defined as rival teams with a socially distant, wary, and even hostile relationship." What's more, the "heterosexual meanings add to the sense of polarization" (86), and they end up becoming both the justification for and the erasure of the transition Rudman and Glick noted. Talk about a double bind. In other words, one's presumed heterosexuality—by sheer force of attraction—is what allows one to transition from hostility to affection. But the supposed nature of differences that informs the "hetero" in some people's orientation are continually presented to people as the source of hetero-opposition, for reasons no more compelling or specific than, effectively, children's claims like "boys are yucky" or "girls have cooties."

The tendency in the certain romance fantasies that have feminist-friendly potential, including the most ideal version of romaction in *Mr. and Mrs. Smith,* is to present hetero-intimacy as having it both ways, to count on surface gender truces to cover a continued threat of sex battle underneath, thereby keeping assumptions about intimate heterosexual relations mired in traditional divides. Keeping this in mind, I cite Joan Scott's well-known suggestion to "treat the opposition between male and female as problematic rather than known, as something contextually defined, [and] repeatedly constructed" by "constantly ask[ing] not only what is at stake in proclamations or debates that invoke gender to explain or justify their positions but also how implicit understandings of gender are being invoked and reinscribed" (49).

Only then can we begin to understand what has been erased between men and women and why—and more importantly, how we can use what we find to change our expectations to promote resistance to this dangerous heteronorm and seek more feminist-friendly love and intimacy standards that will reshape future relations between the sexes.

FOUR

What Doesn't Kill Her Makes Her Stronger

The Fighting Female as a Survivor

The stories of the love-buddy and love-warrior fighting females are generally lighthearted, entertaining narratives in which a strong, independent woman saves the day and gets her man, achieving the have-it-all ideal. But popular culture has also presented us with fighting females who don't always get their man, whose hetero-relations are much more troubled, and whose stories are much more disturbing or violent. In the popular PBS series *Prime Suspect* (1991–2006), Detective Chief Inspector Jane Tennyson (Helen Mirren) deals with sexism and corruption in her department, alcoholism, and a string of broken relationships. Her American counterpart, Deputy Chief Brenda Leigh Johnson (Kyra Sedgwick) in *The Closer* (2005–12), also encounters sexism, problems balancing work with a personal life, and a serial rapist-murderer who taunts and eventually attacks her. Nikita, a character in two films and two popular television series, is a junkie who commits murder and is forced to work as an assassin for a secret agency under threat of "cancellation"; every relationship she has is controlled by the agency and beset by betrayal or duplicity.

In this chapter, I will address these and other examples of what I refer to as fraught fighting females (FFF). While FFFs have a few variations, the ones I will analyze are all crime-fighters, primarily detectives and spies,[1] who battle to save themselves and/or others, both physically—using their bodies or weapons—and intellectually, by finding clues, solving crimes, planning missions, and executing strategies that allow them to triumph over the enemy. The fraught fighting female, like the love-buddy and the love-warrior fighting female, reflects a postfeminist media landscape that naturalizes women's strength and consequently functions as a cipher that reveals conflicting expectations for and anxieties about the strong, independent woman archetype. However, the FFF is distinct both in the extremes of obstacles and limited agency she must overcome and in her status as the primary protagonist and hero. For while her relationships with other characters remain important elements of her story, it's very much her story, and the rest of the characters revolve around it.

Most significantly, unlike the characters examined in previous chapters, the FFF doesn't share the stage with a special male buddy or hetero-partner as a co-lead. Her aloneness renders her both more vulnerable and more formidable than the heroines of love-warrior and love-buddy narratives. On the one hand, FFFs are more challenged in their everyday lives and have to deal, both externally and internally, with a variety of dangers and susceptibilities. On the other hand, FFFs have exceptional fortitude, and any personal adversity or trauma they face empowers them, even if it first threatens to destroy their identities, their relationships, or their lives. Through a unique narrative interplay of breakdowns and comebacks, pains and successes, and male versus female, the FFF enacts an especially complicated version of the strong, independent woman ideal. She is a constrained hero whose strength might be assured time and again, but only at great cost, and whose independence is often limited in ways that make successful hetero-intimacies seem exceedingly difficult, if not impossible.

Positioning the fighting female as a lead creates space for more problematic and varied representations of hetero-relations within the narrative. It also signifies a representational parity in male/female characterizations in crime-fighting dramas. Only, the narratives base parity upon proof of overcoming powerlessness and limitations instead of upon representations of similar abilities in terms of crime-fighting. Yet, being fraught is a badge of difference, as the fighting female is not always fraught in the same ways as males. For every good male in her life, there is at least one (but sometimes more) bad male; for every male ally, there is a male enemy or nemesis. Even more confounding, sometimes her allies turn out to be enemies and vice versa.

These relational variations and instabilities are important with regard to the versions of feminist-friendly love fantasies the fighting female plays out. While some of the more recent love-buddy and love-warrior narratives included multiple hetero-relations, the males with whom she shared intimacies—whether romantic or platonic—were clearly the good guys. Even in the most heightened conflict between the fighting female and her leading man, as in *Mr. and Mrs. Smith* (literally, they are contracted to take each other out), there is no question from the audience's perspective that he's as much of a good guy as she is. That's the point: proving they both can be the hero, equally, together. These optimistic narratives orient around establishing assurances of an empowered woman who can be the equal of a man and still make an ideal hetero-partner. They also focus on creating narrative space within which to imagine egalitarian intimacies that further empower women. Those are the bases of the feminist-friendly love fantasies they project.

By contrast, FFF fantasies generally develop from stories of disempowerment, often implicating constrained agency as a seemingly unavoidable aspect of women's relations with men. In this way, these fantasies play on the darker existing power dynamics that regulate the sexes culturally, socially, and politically. The evidence of disempowerment the FFF faces presents male domination and authority as an obstacle to the hero's well-being or success. This connection occurs within her closest hetero-relations—whether personal, professional, or both. In these, the FFF is constrained by oppression, abuse, persecution, and/or prejudice. Her stories constantly function to remind viewers that the power she exerts is circumscribed by the power men exert over her, and this dynamic defines much of her struggle, both as a woman and as a professional. The FFF draws more attention to a darker side of the perceived crisis in hetero-relations postfeminism than we see in the previous fighting female narratives.

The FFF demonstrates the many hostilities women still face and the dilemma of representing female power. Her stories signify not only contradictory attitudes toward female power and violence but also fears of male power and violence. They also make clear the many ways in which men can still control even empowered women, ways that often play a part in the obstacles fraught fighting females face in their intimate relationships with men. This isn't to say that the possibilities of feminist-friendly love are excluded from the FFF narratives, only that they are much more, well, fraught: some render it a fiction, some reassert it in the end, but they all subject it to some serious doubts. The relatively few instances in which the FFF does end up happily coupled provide an interesting counterpoint to the majority in which she remains "consciously uncoupled," to use Gwyneth Paltrow's now-iconic phrase to describe her breakup from Chris Martin.

The doubts cultivated by the FFF once again reinforce crucial questions underpinning fighting female narratives: What compromises occur when representing women's strength and independence in relation to hetero-intimacy? What do those compromises say about the compatibility between the two? Are those compromises feminist-friendly? However, FFF relationship narratives also encourage additional inquiry: What happens when fighting female narratives consistently highlight female vulnerability and male domination? Does it diminish ideals of women's strength and independence to focus constantly upon constraints to their agency? Why are men generally shown to be culpable for those constraints? What does it say about hetero-intimacies that the FFF always gets her man, the bad guy, but she almost never gets a man—at least not in the end? What does it say about the possibilities of feminist love and our expectations of men that they can so easily occupy both the enemy and ally positions, often moving back and forth between them?

This chapter begins by exploring the cultural context from which the FFF emerged. This context is followed by an outline of the ways the character is fraught, focusing upon themes of constrained agency in detective and spy FFF narratives that invoke fears about male power. These themes draw attention to abusive dynamics that implicate male dominance in women's oppression—even as they function to assure us of the hero's strength as she overcomes that oppression—and project conflicting messages about hetero-intimacy for the empowered woman. These include sexism and objectification, sex-based violence, paternal/patriarchal authority, and male-partner betrayals. The chapter concludes by concentrating upon themes of resolution that capitalize upon or allay those fears and promote more progressive hetero-relations, emphasizing feminist-friendly intimacy as the basis for opposing male domination and for empowering women.

Female Identity and the Interplay of Strength and Vulnerability in Popular Culture

Fraught fighting females face emotional and/or physical violence that can be difficult to watch, and we cannot underestimate the impact that viewing the brutality they face can have. Of course, in today's action and thriller movies, the hero must be able to fight, but the hero must also often be beaten before the final confrontation. Further, there are still very gendered connotations that distinguish violence by men and against men from violence by and against women. However, before the 1960s, with the invention of the female super spy in *The Avengers*—and the dramatic increase of violence shown in the media—women weren't shown punching men (much less karate-chopping them). A woman being punched straight in the face by a man during a fight was still unheard of, and even the indomitable Emma Peel (Diana Rigg) or Cathy Gale (Honor Blackman) never took a hit on camera—they only doled them out. Merely seeing a woman get slapped on-screen was enough to exact an astonished gasp from audiences, and it still is, depending on the genre of the program/film. Previously, when women were hurt on-screen (or off-screen, usually), the act was always effectively abuse. Only cruel men hurt women; heroes only fought cruel men. Only women who were victims were hurt, and the heroes saved them. The lines were fairly clear.

Now it is possible to see what Sarah Hagelin refers to as images of "abused women who don't want our pity, and images of bodies in pain that don't register as powerless" (4). Even on primetime television, a woman can be tortured and still be a badass rather than automatically interpreted as an abused female. Today's torture is often also overt and goes beyond the torture women used to deal with on-screen: being tied up or verbally threatened or slapped by an evil captor who wants to prove he means business to the male hero meant to save the woman. In some of the more graphic FFF battles today, they are shot, cut up, stabbed, raped, or subjected to psychological distress, electro-shock, and waterboarding. When they fight their captors, often by themselves, their bloody, traumatized bodies exact an even bloodier payback. Still, they are women experiencing this violence, and it's still true that seeing a female get hurt can be a confounding experience for audiences.

It could be argued that the way that the FFF narratives spend so much time highlighting female victimization—either in the hero or in the victimization of other female characters—lessens the impact of female empowerment and thus promotes a kind of women-as-victim identity that is potentially regressive. In *Where the Girls Are*, Douglas pinpoints the correlation of female power and victimization that occurred in 1974 with the "debut of two new trends on television, one the mirror image of the other." The first was the development of the female cop protagonist in shows like *Police Woman* (1974–78) and *Get Christie Love* (1974–75), in which "the barrier against women having the title role in a cop show was broken." The second was the end of another "long-held TV taboo," when it became "OK to discuss and portray the crime of rape, and soon women were getting raped everywhere" on television (209). The implication here is that assertions of female strength need to be tempered by assertions of vulnerability, a reminder of where women really stand. This mirroring seems reminiscent of some FFF film and television shows being analyzed in the next section, titled "Fighting for Justice, Fighting the System." Examples are *Cagney & Lacey* (1981–88), *Prime Suspect*, *The Closer*, *The Girl with the Dragon Tattoo* films, the mini-series *Top of the Lake* (2013), and the Netflix series *Jessica Jones* (2015–19), in which rape plays a significant part in the female hero's storyline.

For the most part, the heroes in these shows rarely exhibit physical aggression or violence to counteract portrayals of male domination, even if the heroes otherwise act aggressively—the exception being the powered character Jessica Jones (Krysten Ritter). Most of the fighting for these females occurs at the level of procedure: interrogations and crime-scene investigations. These procedures could be seen as keeping the emphasis on the violence against the victim, in the same way that interactions with sexist colleagues, to whom I'll move later, keep the emphasis on the limits surrounding the hero. When the fighting female is more violent—as when Jessica Jones kills her rapist and when Lisbeth Salander (from *The Girl with the Dragon Tattoo* series) exacts revenge on her rapist-guardian—the narrative more graphically depicts the spectacle of female victimization. Thus, overall, these narratives reflect a tactic that Clover notes in "final girl" narratives in slasher films (which have their own version of an FFF): the development of the victimization occurs over an excessive amount of screen time in comparison to either "extended frenzies of sadism" that occur in fight scenes with male heroes or the actual final scenes in which the FFF triumphs over the villain (18).

Hence, female victimization is a principal impression left by the narratives, even though the impression of the hero's strength in beating the bad guy leaves the final mark. Even this strength has been seen as comparatively attenuated, particularly with regard to other male heroes because many FFFs generally rely on guns during any violent act and then only occasionally and without much spectacle. While critic Tasker in *Spectacular Bodies* has noted that the gun symbolizes phallic power that women can appropriate, in the increasingly action-oriented crime-fighting popular media, male heroes more and more face the criminals in physical fighting scenes, and hand-to-hand combat is something the majority of the detective FFFs don't do.

However, the same argument about countering progressive sexual politics by overemphasizing the spectacle of female victimization cannot be made for all FFF narratives I'll address. Movies like *La Femme Nikita* (1990), *Point of No Return* (1993), and *Salt* (2010) and television shows like *La Femme Nikita* (1997–2001), *Alias* (2001–2006), and *Nikita* (2010–13) tend to include as many scenes of her "extended frenzies of sadism" as those dramatizing the FFF's limited agency and vulnerability to male domination. These narratives give many more striking glimpses of female empowerment in the form of women who fight the enemy repeatedly, not only with guns and knives but also with their bodies as weapons, drawing blood, being bloodied, encountering explosions—all in true action-genre demonstrations of power. Yet these particular FFFs are violent fighters because they are constructed to be, by men, against their will or without their knowledge, again raising the question of appropriated power at the same time as portraying their combat abilities.

It is neither fair nor accurate to say that either one of these FFF versions is one OR the other, vulnerable or strong, victimized or empowered because they are all BOTH. Ultimately, this is what is compelling and mystifying about their demonstrations of empowerment because they embody vulnerability and strength, face limitations, and exert independence. They are certainly not helpless, but they aren't always powerful, either. They are survivors. More specifically, they are survivors of men, of male-dominated worlds. The woman-as-survivor identity constructed in the FFF narratives grows out of and reflects the contradictory experiences of womanhood and the shifting portrayals of contemporary femininity in arenas of the cultural imagination that assert the strong, independent woman archetype as an ideal.

1980s: Woman-as-Survivor Hits Primetime

Arguably the original primetime FFF narrative, *Cagney & Lacey*, was the first to showcase female heroes navigating the victim-agent divide in its interpretation of the empowered woman ideal, and it did so in service of a specifically feminist-friendly agenda on the part of the creators and writers. Barbara Avedon and Barbara Corday devised the show after they read a book that stated there had never been a female buddy film.[2] After sharing the book with producer Barney Rosenzweig, they wrote the script for what would become the TV movie that launched the series in 1981. More than once, Rosenzweig emphasized that the show was about "two women who happen to be cops, not two cops who happen to be women," which highlights the focus on the main characters' lives as women that would become central to later FFF narratives.[3]

Cagney & Lacey, traversing the new ground of the primetime female-driven detective melodrama, had the unique battle of promoting an overt feminist-friendly agenda without seeming to—meaning without being too strident, pedantic, or alienating—so it could maintain a broad audience appeal. The dilemmas involved in representing such women as strong, independent female heroes are reflected in the very public chronicle of the show's production history. From the beginning, the Cagney & Lacey concept was slow to be picked up, having been rejected by several studios. Then, the show gained the dubious distinction of being saved from cancellation with highly publicized comebacks twice in its early years. Other programs had attempted to capitalize on feminism, but this program was attempting to promote it. As such, there were high stakes involved in the show's representation of female-driven, feminist-friendly themes. As Douglas notes, television was "a highly contested terrain in the struggle not just between feminism and antifeminism but over what type of feminism was going to become accepted into the mainstream" (*Where the Girls Are* 202), and the type of feminism to be accepted tied in directly to the empowered female identity a show constructed. Recognizing this struggle is imperative to understanding more about the mixed messages mass media portray about being a strong, independent woman in American popular culture and the way the FFF navigates these messages.

Cagney & Lacey, with its premise of women bucking a sexist justice system—and its commitment to showcasing women's vulnerabilities (including sexual harassment in the workplace and date rape) and their strengths (as crime-fighters and also as women overcoming numerous obstacles)—provided a primer for the FFF narratives that would follow. In fact, it was the first primetime show, of which I am aware, in which a female protagonist gets beaten (Lacey, in "Beyond the Golden Door" 01.03), shot (Cagney in "Partners" 03.06 and Lacey in "Happiness Is a Warm Gun" 06.20), or date-raped (Cagney in "Don't I Know You?" 07.09).

Additionally, the show offers multi-dimensional female heroes who are imperfect, who make mistakes, and who are often deeply troubled. Neither of the protagonists is a paragon of virtue like heroines of the past, nor are they perfect, one-dimensional heroes who triumph without struggle. Cagney, dealing with the stresses of losing her father, becomes an alcoholic later in the series. Lacey, the self-described "mother-wife-cop" (01.01), even has a nervous breakdown at one point and flees the city because she's overwhelmed by efforts to balance her work and family ("Burnout" 02.17). Still, both women remain heroes, and their imperfections only increased their popularity with their dedicated fan base, populated by many women who shared, and were inspired by, their flaws.

This chapter will provide more detail about these FFF themes in the following sections. For now, it's important to focus on the show's influence on American mass culture in the type of new female identity it promoted, which emerged from both its status as a feminist-derived popular television show and its construction of not one, but two, survivor protagonists.

Certain other narrative elements in *Cagney & Lacey* have been acknowledged to be an important part of its feminist-friendly message. For example, the show highlighted the friendship between the two female heroes. It also emphasized the agency they expressed in their personal and professional lives, indicated by the narratives' emphases on the decision-making processes behind the resolution of their personal and ethical dilemmas. These elements have been seen to play central roles in the show's deliberate focus on affirmative expressions of female empowerment. The female heroes thus exhibit strength and independence because they make their own choices and take responsibility for themselves (Clark 123).[4]

Emphasizing agency and choice is a necessary component of any empowered-woman and feminist-friendly narrative. Still, the concepts of agency and choice are themselves fraught and cannot be understood outside of the context wherein that agency to choose is exercised. The emphasis on context in determining women's choices—and the way that male domination shapes context—was fundamental to the feminism in *Cagney & Lacey*, as well as to the FFF story lines to follow it. Looking at the particular strategies used to exemplify limited agency and to create obstacles for the FFF heroes clarifies: the limits to seeing choice alone as an expression of empowerment; how disempowerment acts to empower fighting females; and the regressive and progressive readings of empowerment through disempowerment. That's why this analysis of FFF characters orients more around the survivor identity they construct based on tropes of female disempowerment—and around the ways female heroes are shown to be threatened or made vulnerable by gendered power imbalances that then affect their identities and behaviors and/or control their choices.

1990s: Woman-as-Survivor and Mass Media

The popular media—television, newspapers, and journalistic representations of current events—is often critiqued for backlash representations of women that undermine feminist-friendly politics. However, the media also helped cultivate the very perception of the woman as both strong yet vulnerable—a survivor—that has informed the development and continued popularity of the fraught fighting female hero.

Cagney & Lacey facilitated the entrance of the woman-as-survivor into mass culture and was a cultural phenomenon that facilitated the emergence of the FFF. However, there were three other noteworthy contributors to changing perceptions of women from the early 1990s, the very time when FFF characters emerged in greater numbers in popular culture.

First, there was a minor revolution in films in 1991 when three female-driven movies were released. Two of them earned blockbuster status by being in the top five gross earners for the year (*Terminator 2: Judgment Day*, at the number one spot, and *The Silence of the Lambs* at the number five). While not a top earner, the third earned a blockbuster reputation for its portrayal of violent women on the lam in *Thelma and Louise*. The year 1991 was an unprecedented one for female heroes with guns in film, and the protagonists of all three films offered different versions of FFFs representing strong and independent but also vulnerable women as heroes. These movies not only showcased the changing perspective of female heroes but also ushered in a new era of notable female heroes that included not only other FFF heroes but also Buffy, Xena, and GI Jane. Even *Cagney & Lacey* picked up where it left off, returning with four made-for-TV movies between 1994 and 1996, films that explored a whole new set of problems for the aging woman survivor of the justice system.

These three influential films reflect the way "popular films and TV in the 1990s begin to undermine assumptions about female vulnerability by severing the link between vulnerability and powerlessness that earlier forms of cultural production had trained audiences to expect" (Hagelin 10). Hagelin doesn't reference these three movies, only the cultural milieu of the 1990s in general. She does, however, make an excellent case in Chapter Three of *Reel Vulnerability* for the influence of the 1997 film *G.I. Jane* on later representations of abused females, and she believes Ridley Scott's work on *Thelma and Louise* enticed Demi Moore to participate in the film. Relating to the gender transgressions and the controversies sparked by *G.I. Jane*, I would agree, yet these early 1990s films still lay important cultural groundwork. Additionally, the controversies they sparked about transgressive female violence in *Thelma and Louise*, the portrayal of deviant homosexuality in *The Silence of the Lambs*, and about female guns—in this case, protagonist Linda Hamilton's chiseled arms and androgynous physique—in *Terminator 2: Judgment Day* further ensured their cultural impact. Feminist critics rushed to applaud, reject, or problematize these films and debate about whether they represented feminist-friendly interests.[5] The space for fighting females in the American imagination has only continued to expand since.

Second, in 1991, Anita Hill made possibly the best-known accusation of sexual harassment until that time in American history when she testified that Supreme Court nominee Clarence Thomas had repeatedly offended her with unwelcome sexual advances. (Dr. Christine Blasey Ford's 2018 accusation of Justice Brett Kavanaugh proved, unfortunately, equally ineffective in preventing the justice's confirmation).[6] Through Hill's televised testimony, Americans became intimately familiar with the experiences of this young, successful, composed lawyer and debated the possibility that her accusations were true. The outcome of her testimony isn't as important as the fact that her experience was instrumental in spreading the image of the empowered and vulnerable woman, whose very presence implied (to those of us who believed her) that if it could happen to her, it could happen to other women.

In terms of impact, Marcia D. Greenberger, founder and co-president of the National Women's Law Center, explains that in 1991, sexual harassment "was an invisible issue, until Anita testified" (qtd. by Noveck). Jocelyn Noveck herself writes, "Not only did Hill's testimony raise public consciousness about sexual harassment in the workplace [...] and spur other women to make claims, but only months later, the Civil Rights Act of 1991, which addressed issues of employment discrimination, was passed with strong support." Furthermore, in the years between 1992 and 1996, the Equal Employment Opportunity Commission reports that there was a 50 percent increase in claims of sexual harassment, not because of any actual increase in incidences but because of increased reporting of harassment (Walsh).[7] Women took heed and took a stand. The impact of Hill's testimony endures more than twenty years later—as evidenced by the release of the documentary *Anita* (2013)—which not only chronicles the dismal, offensive experiences Hill faced but also her perseverance in standing her ground and trying to salvage her life and reputation after the hearings.

Noting the cultural impact the Hill hearings had, particularly in terms of feminist culture, is not new, and most analyses of this period refer to its reverberating effects. However, there is an aspect of her experience that has not been as clearly noted. That facet lies not just in the allegations of sexual harassment Hill made but in the very way Hill was treated during the hearings. That treatment emphasized her contradictory position as a strong and independent, yet oppressed and outnumbered, woman who was subject to the limitations of a male political and social hierarchy. As Hill notes in a 2014 interview, the "harsh contrast" in the visual of her sitting before an all-white male panel was "like *Mad Men*," and "[i]t was a reflection of their power and privilege" and Hill's distinct lack of both. Hers was an image that seemed to resonate with a portion of the public who rallied behind her (qtd. in Noveck). Hill's treatment during the hearings exposed the "lie" about patriarchy that some fighting female narratives depended upon: that "there was no such thing as patriarchy, but if there was, it was beneficent and would protect women" (Douglas *Enlightened* 298). In that panel, no one was there to protect Hill but Hill herself. She, therefore, embodied both the victim and the agent in her role.

As many other feminist critics have noted, support for the disenfranchised Hill and rejection of the backlash politics of the first Bush administration helped usher in the so-called "Year of the Woman" in 1992—the third noteworthy contributing factor to changing perceptions of women from the early 1990s. Hill's experience before that all-white male panel highlighted the political dominance of men in the Senate, and it moved an unprecedented number of women to run for the available seats in both the Senate and the House of Representatives during that year's election. The mass media regularly invoked the link between these two stories and how the candidates' awareness of the unfair treatment and unequal standing of women forced them to act. Of course, the "Year of the Woman" label was extremely overstated: even though the election did result in the largest influx of women into the Senate to the time, there were still only five to hold a seat. Yes, five.

So, there are two interrelating stories of the engagement between disempowerment and empowerment in this period: first, women's political response to the Hill/Thomas hearing, a story of how disempowerment can't hold strong, independent women down; second, a story of how, even after taking a stand and showing their strength, women's political position remained imbalanced and vulnerable. The fact that this was a momentous event in election history certainly helped more people recognize not only the precarious position women hold in Hollywood and in the workplace but also in the America's political system. While these women represented empowered role models, their token status also represented deep-rooted limitations to women's enfranchisement.

In addition to the impact of these three occurrences, there were other cultural representations during this time that navigated the tricky ground between portrayals of the empowered but vulnerable woman, in effect solidifying the connection between survival and strength. One of the biggest critical engagements came from arguments about whether the have-it-all dream is really possible for women, much less desirable. Chapters Two and Three explored the cultural impact of this dream, but its influence on media constructions of female identity cannot be overstressed. Media discussions about the mommy wars, the second shift, pay disparity, and the glass ceiling all either highlighted or assumed how far women have come—being established as a part of the workforce as successful professionals. However, they also relied on depictions of how far women have to go to achieve parity, even in their very family lives, not to say their work lives. In other words, these stories rely on the assumption of women's empowered position in society, their general strength and independence in being able to become what they want to be, but they also highlight their susceptibility. Overall, the have-it-all dream is one with a fraught underbelly that has been exposed all through the media for the last thirty years.

Today, not only academic scholars but also critics in popular media—writers in *Glamour, Marie Claire,* and *Redbook,* bloggers, singers, CEOs, and even advertisers—have seized upon and/or exploited (depending on your perspective) the refrain that while women can and should have it all, it won't be easy because they are women. These people anxiously identify the unfair standards women face and interrogate the ways in which women remain vulnerable and the reasons why power continues to elude them. Even the very concept of empowerment has been argued to harm women by creating unrealizable standards of perfection that are unique to women, as Spar has argued.

However, people addressing this issue all maintain the assertion that women can, and should, be able to do what they want. They also posit that by no means should women simply identify themselves as victims, even if they are still vulnerable as a sex, because they are more than that. When political campaigns around 2010 and again in 2015 embraced the "war on women" phrase that feminists have been using since the late 1970s, the goal wasn't only to address women's unresolved political, social, and economic disenfranchisement or to help women see how they are still victims of an unequal system; it was also to empower them to do something about it by voting, getting involved in politics, seeking office and leadership positions. This has been the popular tenor of the last thirty years, particularly with the most recent #MeToo social media campaign meant both to reveal the still widespread sexual harassment and assault women experience in the workplace but also to provide a source of strength for the survivors sharing their stories and encouraging each other to speak out against their perpetrators. Thus, it seems that the woman-as-survivor characterizes one perspective of women's position that actually has the broadest appeal, in part because it is so difficult to pin down. That the FFF would emerge out of, and become more prevalent during, this chaos makes sense.

The woman-as-survivor identity is currently predicated on the male-as-dominator identity, which makes it essential to discuss depictions of heterorelations as part of the construction of this identity. Again, as much as popular media is often and rightly considered a tool wielded by patriarchy, it

Four. What Doesn't Kill Her Makes Her Stronger

also consistently reports on and represents oppressions individual women experience, which, when added together, indicate that women's oppression as a sex is a problem. These representations include workplace and intimate examples of injury, exclusion, or manipulation emerging from the current system of gender hierarchies and perpetrated by men. Myriad media fantasies and news accounts incriminate men by identifying them as husbands whose careers come first and who don't share the domestic duties,[8] as fathers who embrace traditional roles once they have children,[9] as bosses who don't hire or promote women,[10] as colleagues and strangers who sexually harass women, as politicians who support legislation that directly harms women,[11] or as sexual harassers, domestic abusers, and rapists. So-called "men's rights advocates" glommed onto perceived media attacks against their sex, initiated by feminism and the "liberal media," based on just these kinds of portrayals to prove how they are oppressed. Their resentment and backlash prove the impact that the repeated man-as-dominator identity has had, even though this identity makes up only one version in a media filled predominantly with other portrayals of male power and awesome-man identities.

In 2017, *The New York Times* reported that claims of sexual harassment had been made against Hollywood heavyweight Harvey Weinstein. He was found guilty in early 2020 and now faces up to 25 years in prison. Before Weinstein, Bill Cosby was accused of drugging and raping approximately 60 women over the span of five decades and was recently found guilty of an aggravated sexual assault he committed in 2004. Other popular and powerful male celebrities have faced similar accusations of long-term sexual harassment, abuse, or misconduct, both before and after Weinstein, including our current infamous pussy-grabbing commander-in-chief, Bill O'Reilly, Charlie Rose, Matt Lauer, Louis C.K., David Copperfield, Kevin Spacey, Michael Douglas, and James Franco.[12]

In response to the unprecedented focus on sexual harassment and misconduct in Hollywood, Alyssa Milano (also a survivor) added a hashtag to the phrase "Me Too" that activist Tarana Burke had coined in 2006 and tweeted a call for women to share their stories of abuse. Milano was also sure to give Burke credit, as did *Time* when the magazine included Burke as part of a group of women who earned the "Person of the Year" award in 2017 for their activism. In addition to the actresses who had been harassed by Weinstein—more than 80, including Ashley Judd, Angelina Jolie, Gwyneth Paltrow, and Carla Delevingne—an astounding number of non-celebrity women also shared their painful experiences all across Twitter and Facebook.

The #MeToo campaign and the celebrity men and women who agreed to wear black at the 2018 Golden Globes to protest sexual harassment in Hollywood show women (and some men) both as the helpless victims of male power and as activists to bring those men to justice. The purpose of this activism, in the words of Alyssa Milano, was to "give people a sense of the magnitude of the problem" (Khomami). It also had the effect of giving the victims agency in seeking change, if not for themselves, then for others in the future.

Exposing women's problems is not a new theme in mass media. For more than three decades, celebrity news headlines and popular daytime talk shows have conveyed stories and images of women who embody both empowerment and vulnerability, strength and weakness, as women who were abused by men long before the more recent scandals—women like Rihanna, Halle Berry, Madonna, Oprah, Lady Gaga, and Drew Barrymore. There's a section on a website entitled *Ranker.com* called "53 Celebrities Who Were Abused" that lists celebrities (the vast majority of whom are women) who have experienced abuse and shared their stories. The introduction states, "Many of them speak of their past, so that other victims can feel empowered to move past their experiences." It is a statement that links their victimization to the agency they exercise in sharing their stories to help others. The creation of Lifetime Network in 1984 (dubbed "Television for Women") and its continuation has contributed much to the popular woman-as-survivor identity. Not only has it been a bastion for daytime talk shows and syndications of often female-driven dramas (including *Cagney & Lacey*), but over the course of its thirty-year tenure, it has also specialized in producing dramas and made-for-television movies that not only feature women who are often survivors of male abuse but also true stories of their abuse that are "ripped from actual news headlines." One of them is the 2014 Lifetime movie *The Assault*, which dramatizes the infamous Steubenville rape case (Hess).

These galvanizing moments have had an impact on a diverse group of women, and rightly so because if there is one arguable area where women converge in terms of shared experience, it is as the primary victims for sexual assault, domestic violence, and political exclusion. We can see the positive impact in the results of the elections of 2018, which was also dubbed by some in the media as the "Year of the Woman." Across America, 117 women won elections "flipping seats and taking names," as Maya Salam describes it for *The New York Times*. There were also more than 250 women on the ballot. Of the women elected, a record 42 are women of color, two are Native American, two are Muslim, and three identify as queer.

Yet, even as women continue to make strides in politics, when it comes to the American cultural imagination about whose stories are worth telling, the representation of the victimization of women in the media tends to focus on the images of women who are still most likely to be associated with a fragile femininity—white, cisgender, heterosexual women—rather than the women who are most likely to be victims—black and other women of color, poor women, and queer individuals. As Susan Green reports, in addition to experiencing racism by being unfairly targeted or excluded in American institutions and traditions, "Black women were two and a half times more likely to be murdered than their white counterparts." Multiple studies have shown that Alaska Native/American Indian women are "2.5 to 3.5 times more likely to experience sexual assault" ("Prevalence Rates"). The Human Rights Commission notes that people from the LGBTQIA+ community "face higher rates of poverty, stigma, marginalization" than their heterosexual counterparts. Their website cites both the CDC's National Intimate Partner and Sexual Violence Survey findings that "46% of bisexual women have been raped, compared to 17 percent of heterosexual women and 13 percent of lesbians." A U.S. Transgender Survey from 2015 that "found that 47% of transgender people are sexually assaulted at some point in their lifetime" ("Sexual Assault and the LGBTQ Community"). These are the aspects of many women's identities and realities that are often excluded from the mass-media representations of women's struggles and their efforts to overcome them so that the effect is a uniform experience of womanhood that doesn't fit all women and again privileges a white or cisgender heteronorm.

Even so, as the experience of Dr. Blasey Ford, occurring 27 years after Hill's stand for justice, reminds us—as all the unconvicted celebrities, politicians, and powerful public figures still enjoying their freedom and (only slightly marred) reputations remind us— no matter the woman's race, ethnicity, sexual orientation, or class, the likelihood of justice for survivors is bleak indeed. For every Andrea Constand—one of 60 women who accused Bill Cosby of assault and whose case led to his conviction—there are millions of women who strive to function in an unjust system so they can be safe in their own homes and communities, protect their children and families, or make a living, much less break the glass ceiling. This reality makes the impact of the woman-as-survivor fantasy all the more alluring.

Representations in popular culture of the uneven path women traverse in a patriarchal society indicate an important realization at the basis of the FFF version of the strong, independent woman archetype: highlighting women's victimization, particularly at the hands of men, does not necessarily make women appear weak or belie women's desire to feel and need to project strength at all times in order to succeed. Doing so is simply part of a growing representation of female protagonists in general,[13] and FFFs in particular, that better reflects the complexity of women's lives (and loves). It's why FFF character types are the most common fighting females on-screen these days. They hit a deep nerve. They reflect the burgeoning dissatisfaction and disillusionment that correlate with assertions of female empowerment, particularly the idea that has shaped all of the fighting female narratives: that women can and will have it all. Much of this dissatisfaction comes from recognition of the fact that empowerment and oppression go hand in hand for many women—that you can't have it all if you can't afford it, don't have time for it, are too battered, exhausted, or depressed to pursue it, or otherwise won't be allowed to get it. This recognition has been aided by representations of both real and fictional women in popular culture in which women's victimization is highlighted in conjunction with stories of their strength and independence.

Fighting for Justice, Fighting the System: Implicating Difference in Fraught Fighting Female Narratives

Oftentimes, the victimization highlighted in FFF narratives emphasizes the female hero's sex difference and thus explicitly critiques the oppositional nature of traditional hetero-gendered power dynamics, a narrative trend that began in the 1980s with *Cagney & Lacey*. There are two common themes of disempowerment in this section that the FFF narratives like *Cagney & Lacey* rely upon to form this identity, including sex discrimination/harassment and sexual assault. These themes reflect the dilemma of representing female power and negotiating tensions between traditional views of hetero-relations and burgeoning expectations for female empowerment, all while still appealing to audiences.

Sexism

Women facing sexism is a theme that shapes the entire *Cagney & Lacey* series, beginning with the very first episode. Christine Cagney[14] and Mary Beth Lacey (Tyne Daley) are the first female detectives in their precinct, and most of their male colleagues are not welcoming. Their lieutenant, Bert Samuels (Al Waxman), complains about them as the latest gimmick, stating that the last year it was "blacks," this year it's women. Later in the same episode, when the first drug-detection dogs are introduced to the precinct, Samuels makes a similar crack about first having to get used to "broads" and now dogs. Comparing female cops to animals further reinforces the kind of disdain the heroes face by entering this department. Throughout the series, Cagney and Lacey also have to contend with machismo and blatant chauvinistic comments from Detective Victor Isbecki (Martin Kove). More than once, victims of crime on the show mention how unusual it is to be helped by a female detective, and in "Better than Equal" (01.06), the final episode of the short first season, one victim—an infamous female critic of the ERA who closely resembles Phyllis Schlafly—outright objects to being protected by female detectives.

Hostility and reminders of their marginalized position define Cagney's and Lacey's circumstances throughout the series, even as they continually prove their detractors wrong, solve case after case, face and survive danger, and save others from danger. Chapter Two includes an analysis of the inclusion of sexism in a narrative as a way to bolster the love-buddy fighting female's authority in the 1980s programs even as it enacts a constant reminder that she is not the master of her own fate. In other words, her authority is always circumscribed. So, Laura Holt's monologue for *Remington Steele* sets the scene for the show to remind viewers every week that with each case she concluded, Holt proved wrong those clients who sought a "decidedly masculine superior"; she is capable and good at her crime-fighting profession. She can overcome the sexism and succeed.

At the same time, because she eventually has to take on a male partner without any say in the matter, her success always reminds viewers that she can't break free from the sexism that has entirely organized her circumstances. She can only work within it. The agency never becomes Laura Holt's—it's always Remington Steele's. Here is where the problem becomes apparent when relying on a woman's ability to choose as an indicator of autonomy. The only choice Holt can make is to work with Steele (thereby accepting limited agency) or close the business (maintaining her authority but then being out of work). That aspect of the narrative doesn't seem very liberating. The difference between the sexism that the fighting females in the love-buddy shows experience and the sexism that FFFs confront is that the latter tend to face more explicit, detrimental, and/or more alienating sexist treatment. In Holt's case, the prejudice she encounters is only rarely enacted in the actual narrative, and it is never hostile. As noted before, the show was a much more lighthearted take on sexual politics. There was certainly feminist-friendly potential there, but the glancing implication of sexism comes off more as throwing a feminist bone to an audience just beginning to take pleasure in the idea of strong women besting outdated ideas than as necessarily interrogating the effects of sexism on the hero.

This is not true of the sexism in *Cagney & Lacey*, sexism with which the series deals in meaty chunks. The two heroes bump up against prejudice time and again, in different forms, ranging from generic, sometimes unconscious-seeming, chauvinism toward female detectives (being overlooked for promotions and certain cases)—to female objectification (the men in the department are fond of using prostitutes for practical jokes against other men and having strippers for birthday, wedding, and retirement celebrations)—to sexual harassment (Cagney brings charges against a fellow officer who demanded sexual favors for professional advancement). Even during the final episode of the television series (before the series of made-for-TV movies that would come in the 1990s), and after the heroes had earned the respect of all in their precinct and even gained rank (Cagney makes sergeant), the heroes still had doubts about their positions as women in the force. They wonder if the reason they were assigned to a life-threatening "crap" detail—as Cagney referred to it—and excluded from knowing about a related, ongoing undercover operation was because of enemies in the department who resented working with women.

Related FFF narratives also interrogate the constraining effects of sexism regularly and/or explicitly, to varying degrees. These narratives include TV programs like *Prime Suspect*,[15] *The Closer* (2005–12), and *Top of the Lake* (2013) and movies like *Blue Steel* (1989), *The Silence of the Lambs* (1991), *Murder by Numbers* (2002), and *Taking Lives* (2004). All of these exhibit forms of sexism that differ from Cagney and Lacey in degree if not in kind, including sexism from reluctant or actively hostile colleagues and old-boy networks. In fact, *Prime Suspect*, much like *Cagney & Lacey*, was a product of a female creator who was inspired by stories of female discrimination.[16] Lynda La Plante devised the series after she learned that only a handful of female Detective Chief Inspectors (DCI) worked in Scotland Yard. She interviewed one of them, DCI Jackie Malton, and found stories about her difficulties and dedication so fascinating that she created character DCI Jane Tennison based on Malton.

As were Cagney and Lacey, Jane Tennison, the female hero in *Prime Suspect*, is introduced as a woman under professional constraints due to sexual discrimination. At the beginning of the first episode, Tennison is passed over to lead a rape/murder investigation that should have been assigned to her as the DCI on duty. When the male DCI who was put in charge of the case dies suddenly of a heart attack, Tennison must maneuver her way into the lead to avoid being passed over again. When she asks the Detective Chief Superintendent for the chance to "prove" herself, he responds by saying it is the wrong time to "thrust women's rights" down his throat. Tennison does get the lead, much to the vocal dismay of her colleagues, and it causes something of a fracas in the department. She generally faces petty complaints and resistant colleagues who make her job harder, like the unbearable Detective Sergeant Bill Otley (Tom Bell). Every step she takes toward advancement through the series is met with male resistance and requires serious political finagling and the occasional overstep into unethical or gray areas. As she gains in rank through the series, eventually reaching Detective Superintendent, she gets assigned to less desirable areas of the city.

In *The Closer*—which critics, the show's creators, and its star have acknowledged as "owing a debt" to *Prime Suspect*—Deputy Chief Brenda Leigh Johnson experiences similar alienation from the squad she's been tasked to lead as the new head of the Major Crimes Division. The squad resents her authority, and they all put in for transfers in protest. Even though the objecting team includes a female detective—and they claim only to object to the replacement of the current head of the division, Captain Taylor (Robert

Gossett)—the squad's treatment of Johnson clearly suggests resistance to her as a woman because her brusque, aggressive manner transgresses traditional gender expectations. From the beginning of the series, she marches in and begins giving orders to a group of men who don't look pleased to follow her demands. She confidently corrects the mistakes of other detectives, sending one home, and asserts her authority over those who question her experience and her right to the position she's earned. She does so without apologizing or asking for permission even from her supervisor because her job is to lead. When one detective tells her not to be a bitch, she curtly replies, "If I liked being called a bitch to my face, I'd still be married" (01.01). Thus, by rejecting her for expressing a less genial, feminine form of authority, they indicate their own prejudices about women in charge.

However, Johnson is feminine in other ways. She often looks feminine in flowery dresses, heels, and bright lipstick, with her curled hair flowing. She often performs femininity when she interrogates suspects, putting on comforting, nurturing airs, or professing ignorance. She also wields politeness and her Southern wiles in difficult work situations, though it's usually clear that she's not entirely sincere, as when she says a drawn-out "thank yeeew" after giving an order to someone who's not pleased to follow it. In general, the ruffles cover a gruff interior that is always present. As Mike Hale describes her, Johnson is "[p]ainted as both a neurotic, narcissistic supercop and a likable, nurturing den mother."

When Captain Taylor argues with Assistant Police Chief Pope (J.K. Simmons) about Johnson's lack of experience in the precinct, Taylor refers to Johnson as "this girl, person, woman, whatever it is we're supposed to call them," emphasizing a touchiness about her sex and about a man's being forced to reckon with it. The two oldest members of the squad, Detective Lieutenants Provenza (G.W. Bailey) and Flynn (Anthony Dennison), openly resent Johnson and being under a woman's authority. They, like Taylor, protest vocally, and lash out throughout the early seasons, acting on their own and against her instructions, often causing problems that Johnson later has to clean up.

However, these two older men function as something like court jesters, and their machismo and old-school ways often make them look foolish. The narrative clearly mocks them, but in essence, they resist the same thing that the rest of the squad resists—a woman in authority who doesn't act like they expect a woman to act. They are only more explicit about it and less quick to fall in line once Johnson proves herself. The narrative additionally includes more insidious illustrations of sexist treatment, as when Johnson puts up with investigations into her sex life and allegations about sleeping her way to the top. Accusations of sexual misconduct make her colleagues question her professionalism, even though they don't affect the reputation of the man involved, who is of higher rank.

Top of the Lake is another miniseries that has been identified as indebted to *Prime Suspect* (Haglund). Detective Robin Griffin (Elisabeth Moss) is treated with similar disdain as a "female detective" from the all-male department to which she's temporarily assigned to investigate a case of a pregnant pre-teen named Tui (Jacqueline Joe). Cop Megan Turner (Jamie Lee Curtis) in *Blue Steel* and FBI agent Clarice Starling (Jodie Foster) in *The Silence of the Lambs* experience subtly pernicious sexual discrimination in films that stress the alienation and isolation the heroes experience for their token female status in a male justice system. In more recent films like *Murder by Numbers* and *Taking Lives*, the FFF cop heroes face explicit but less obtrusive sexism enacted more as character flaws of unenlightened men: their colleagues make sexist cracks about them or other women that maintain a tension between the protagonist and her colleagues. However, these narratives make sense of the alienation the women experience in their professions just as frankly apparent as the narratives of the previous FFF texts.

These programs and films mark decades of FFF chronicles that emphasize the following: the token position of women and the sexist basis of a criminal-justice system that designates men as the primary protectors; the attendant tensions between male and female cops working in this system; and, most relevantly to my argument, the effects that underscoring prejudiced environments and disrespectful male colleagues have on the strong, independent woman image projected by female heroes. Highlighting sexism in the fighting female's "fraughtness" sows the seeds of unsettled gender dynamics into the narrative and underscores tensions between men and women in the workplace deliberately. Put another way, this tension exists not only in service of proving the hero's strength in overcoming it but also specifically in service of imbuing a basis of doubt and mistrust between men and women on screen as a source of female vulnerability. The FFF essentially can't help being an outsider simply because she's a woman. She has no real choice in her marginalization, except to choose to continue despite it. Her marginalization as a woman might be reduced, as in *Prime Suspect*, or it might prove only an annoyance that she brushes off, as in *Murder by Numbers* and *Taking Lives*. However, it remains part of her character's identity throughout, symbolizing her position as, at best, a survivor or at worst as an outcast, as susceptible in ways that male heroes aren't.

The Closer, in contrast, focuses throughout the series on the way men learn to respect Johnson and downplay the sexism as the series progresses, taking us far afield of the alienation inspired by *Prime Suspect*'s finale. Johnson proves herself to her squad in the first episode when they see her in action in the interrogation room and look on her with respect. She eventually even proves herself to Captain Taylor, the most reluctant to accept her. Still, the ending plays up her sense of her exclusion, along with her sense of belonging. She leaves Major Crimes to begin a position with the DA, but she takes the position in response to a reprimand she receives from the department. Her ultimatum is that either they remove the reprimand or she will leave. The reprimand is not removed because it serves Taylor's desire to restructure Major Crimes. Her sex is not implicated in this decision, as she's replaced by another woman. However, Johnson essentially loses the battle for the same reasons she was initially rejected by the squad: her aggressive tactics and her no-holds-barred approach to authority or taking down criminals. These are behaviors commonly attributed to male cops who don't receive anything more than a dressing down or a slap on the wrist.

Each of these narratives makes the sexism the FFF faces one of the first things we learn about her in the opening scenes when she's introduced on-screen. The repetitive nature of this trope makes it seem as if sex-discrimination is an inherent part of being a female detective, even in the shows developed in the last ten years. She and her performance as a hero are accordingly marked by an intrinsically gendered obstacle and by the perceptions of the prejudiced men around her. The prejudiced men are also marked by their chauvinism. Whether or not they change their minds about the hero, whether or not the narrative mocks them, their discriminatory behavior comes off as an unavoidable first response—purely reactionary and automatic. Marking the characters in this way imbues the subsequent representations of hetero professional relations with the power struggles attendant to hierarchical sex divides.

Assault and Violence Against Women

Another theme of female disempowerment in these particular FFF dramas—sexual assault and sex-based violence—reproduces this same kind of sex-based marginalization. The most common form is rape, though this is not the only one. *Cagney & Lacey* includes probably the widest focus, with episodes on rape, child abuse, sexual harassment, and domestic violence. The episode "Fathers and Daughters" (04.05) deals with the murder of a father who had sexually abused his daughter, and "Child Witness" (04.01) features a child who's been abused by her babysitter. In the episode "A Cry for Help" (02.21), Lacey learns that a colleague from her police academy days beats his wife. In the episode "Revenge" (06.09), a husband who abuses his wife ends up murdered, and it turns out he was a suspect for the rape and murder of the sister of Detective Marcus Petrie (Carl Lumbly) fourteen years earlier.

Additionally, there are four specific episodes in *Cagney & Lacey* that include rape. Two revolve around the rape of other women during season two (02.14, 02.16), and two center on the date rape of Cagney in season seven (07.09, 07.19.). (Date rape as a form of assault was relatively new to 1980s media.) Even after years of watching violent crime-based dramas that often included female victims of rape, when I watched this show for my research, I was unprepared to see a cop face her own rape. It's equally surprising that Cagney suffered the rape, as she is clearly portrayed as the tougher, more aggressive, and, frankly, hard-assed of the pair. Cagney's rape was a powerful choice on the part of the show's creative team, certainly an interesting one in terms of understanding the connotations of rape as a threat that only women face and the effects of rape on a fighting female hero. The narrative includes dialogue that specifically links Cagney's victimization to the victimization of the other women she and Lacey help during the series. Cagney does not fight back. She submits out of fear for her life because the rapist said he would kill her if she didn't. She does not pursue the rapist with her gun after the fact. Also, she must defend this choice to her male interrogators and colleagues later and argue, "I did submit because I wanted to stay alive. Damn it, it's my body. He had no right."

It might be tempting to read Cagney's rape as a warning against female promiscuity, as a "punishment" for her refusal to marry or for being an actively sexual single woman—choices she makes throughout the series. Look at *Fatal Attraction* (1987) and the earlier independent-woman cautionary tale *Looking for Mr. Goodbar* (1977). The crazy and/or misguided promiscuous woman who asserts her desires is clearly represented as deviant, and her death in these narratives comes as an almost inevitable conclusion for a woman who doesn't know her place in the traditional hetero-relational scheme.

However, *Cagney & Lacey* takes a much more sympathetic view of Cagney's situation by showing just how negatively victims are often treated in the aftermath of rape and by associating the tendency to blame or not believe the victim with this poor treatment. It's interesting to note that one of the arguments that the rapist and his lawyer mistakenly make about Cagney—that she regretted their one-night stand and decided to call it rape—is one that Cagney assumes about a victim in the episode "Date Rape" from season two. Of course, by the end of that episode, Cagney changes her tune and becomes much more respectful of the victim's situation.

Also, in the season seven episode "Don't I Know You?," the audience doesn't witness Cagney's rape. Considering its primetime schedule, this isn't unusual, but there is no evidence of the attack or any violence even hinted at during the scene. The scene cuts from her date's returning to her apartment with complaints of car trouble to Cagney's calling Lacey early in the morning to come over. This intentional cut can be seen to leave the viewer questioning Cagney's accusation, but only if one doesn't take into consideration that throughout the series, Cagney has had previous one-night experiences and has neither regretted nor lied about them. To think that she would suddenly become ashamed or make accusations would not be in keeping with her character development. Clark also makes a useful point that avoiding any representation of the rape is evidence of the show's "focus on the social and political implications of rape without objectifying a woman" (129).

Essentially, Cagney is the most stereotypical portrayal of the "strong, independent woman" archetype on the show because she is what audiences had generally been schooled by popular media to identify as such—single, aggressive, career-driven, and physically feisty. These qualities make her character's rape experience a distinct rejection of the common representations of the strong, independent woman-as-impervious (like the excessively empowered earlier versions of fighting females like Emma Peel or Wonder Woman). Additionally, her experience defies stereotypes of the rape victim as a prostitute or "loose" woman (who was assumed to be asking for it) or as helpless (who was assumed to be unable to prevent it) that were, and still are, often employed in film and television. Cagney's experience, and the narrative's obvious sympathy with her over the coarse and disrespectful treatment she receives, manages to show how no matter how strong a woman might be, she is still subject to the same vulnerability that most women and women-identified individuals feel at some point in their lives. In so doing, the show capitalizes on the difference between the fraught female and male hero—that a female cop dealing with a rapist sends a more distinctive message about female victimization than a male cop sends by dealing with the same. He might be offended. He might seek revenge for sexual assaults on his loved ones. But his body has not been rendered susceptible with the introduction of a rapist into the criminal narrative. The male hero does not inhabit what Kevin J. Ferguson notes is "the troubling identificatory space between female victims and female detectives" (*Eighties People* 96). The female hero's body, however, is susceptible, but, crucially, her body is allowed to be resilient, to be tough at the same time, to be the same body to catch the perpetrator. Her vulnerability does not reduce the intimations of her strength, but it does set her apart from the male cops.[17] Brown also makes a distinction between the effect of rape and torture on male and female action heroes, noting how "contemporary depictions of torture and rape lay bare the tenuous links assumed in our patriarchal culture between notions of power and powerlessness, masculinity and femininity" (24).

In both *Blue Steel* and *Top of the Lake*, the fighting female heroes are also rape victims. In the former film, Turner's rapist is an obsessive psychopath named Eugene Hunt (Ron Silver), whom she later shoots and kills. The rape occurs before the final showdown and associates her triumph with an element of revenge. *Top of the Lake*'s Detective Griffin also faces down at least one of the four rapists who attacked her when she was a teenager while she was still living in the small town to which she has returned to investigate young Tui's pregnancy. There may also be a possibility that Griffin was raped by Detective Al Parker (David Wenham) the night that he drugged her when she was over for dinner at his house—a night that she doesn't remember, in the same way that Tui and the other girls don't remember. In fact, Griffin figures out what happened to Tui after she associates Tui's lost memory with her own later on in the series.

Both narratives include an additional focus on domestic abuse, as both Turner's and Griffin's mothers suffer abuse from their fathers (a stepfather, in Griffin's case). The narratives in *Murder by Numbers* and *Taking Lives* also address domestic abuse. In *Murder by Numbers,* the abusive ex-husband of Detective Cassie Mayweather (Sandra Bullock) once stabbed her and left her for dead, which we learn through a flashback. In *Taking Lives,* the climactic, violent showdown between FBI profiler Illeana Scott (Angelina Jolie) and the serial killer she's been hunting takes place in a cozy kitchen, with Scott wearing a nightgown and apparently pregnant with the killer's child. When the killer knocks her around and threatens her life, the scene clearly makes reference to scenes of domestic abuse that further associate Scott with vulnerability.

Lisbeth Salander, the hero of the recently popular Stieg Larsson *Girl* trilogy, also had a mother who was abused by her father, and Salander is a rape victim as well.[18] Salander is an unsanctioned detective, unlike the cops and FBI agents in the other FFF narratives mentioned. However, the contribution of this narrative to the FFF hero rape/abuse theme can be seen as significant, considering how popular the novel trilogy and two film versions have been. In fact, the trilogy has been followed up by two more recent additions, written by David Lagercrantz, with one of the additions—*The Girl in the Spider's Web* (2018)—being used as the basis for a new American movie adaptation.[19]

Salander, as we learn in *The Girl with the Dragon Tattoo,* the first installment (and first film), is a ward of the state and an amazing researcher and hacker who helps reporter Mikael Blomkvist[20] track down a serial killer and rapist. Then she helps expose a sex-trafficking ring in the second and third installments. However, Salander is also a deeply disturbed young woman who had a traumatic childhood. She attempted to murder her abusive father, was committed to a mental institution, and, following her release, was placed under legal guardianship.

Sadly, for her, the trauma is not confined to her past. Upon the death of her first legal guardian, a man whom Salander had grown to trust, another guardian is appointed. This man controls her money and her time and sexually assaults her before he'll grant her favors (like giving her access to her own money). In one scene, he forces her to fellate him. In another scene, thinking she was going to set him up by recording him asking her for another sexual favor, he actually handcuffs and brutally rapes her. This scene is by far the most graphic depiction of rape or abuse in any of these FFF narratives.[21] The original Swedish title for the novel *The Girl with the Dragon Tattoo* was

Män som hatar kvinnor, which translates *Men Who Hate Women*—a title that explicitly captures the male domination trope that the story constructs and reflects. The fact that the books and the *Girl* movies have continued after the death of Larsson, the series' original author, indicates how enduring this trope is,[22] as does the on-screen adaptation of the *Jessica Jones* Marvel comic on Netflix.

Jessica Jones is literally one of the strongest of the fraught fighting female protagonists I'll address in this book and by far the strongest woman on-screen to be a rape victim (though Silk Spectre from the 2009 movie adaptation for *The Watchmen* is an equally strong victim of *attempted* rape). Jessica's story is particularly compelling because she already has her powers of super-human strength when she is raped by another powered villain, Kilgrave (David Tennant), who is able to control minds and make people do whatever he says. Jessica's story, for viewers, begins after this happens, and Kilgrave is the first antagonist she faces. Her journey takes place during the first season. What is unique about Jessica's story is that the audience sees less of the physical violation—which is mainly implied through flashbacks and when she verbally recounts memories of the rape—and more of the emotional trauma that surrounds the violation and the fact that he forced her to kill someone while she's under his spell. Still, as essayist Natalie Zutter notes, the series

> us[es] the word "rape" unflinchingly, asserting in nearly every episode what Kilgrave did to Jessica. How could it not? 2015 has been the year of rape in fiction and real life, from watching Columbia University student Emma Sulkowicz carry her mattress around campus to the triumph of *Mad Max: Fury Road*'s Wives using their own chains to escape Immortan Joe—witnessing survivors of repeated sexual assault and slavery take back their control.

Zutter makes an important connection that aligns the character's fantasy role as a woman-as-survivor with women's lived realities as victims, and it does so without identifying the "victim's" personal faults or failings as the reason behind the rape, avoiding any victim-blaming pitfalls. This avoidance is an important aspect of all of the case studies discussed in this section. The fault is kept clearly on the perpetrator. Unfortunately, even when "justice" prevails (which in Jessica's case comes when she breaks Kilgrave's neck at the end of season one), the pain and the after-effects of the assault never go away—the victim continues to carry the weight around with them like, well, a heavy mattress. The real darkness behind this Netflix comic adaptation of Jessica's story is that her position as a super strong and definitely independent woman could not spare her. The implication is that *every* woman is a potential victim, that there is no level of strength that can protect a woman from violation because there is likely some man who is stronger and susceptible to victimizing women in an evil power play.

In other storylines, the FFFs aren't directly victimized by sexual assault or gendered violence, but they act to protect other female victims of sex-based crimes, which in some cases associates them with a parallel victim position. In *Prime Suspect*, Tennison puts away a rapist-murderer during the first season but must revisit the case in season four when similar crimes begin occurring. (These turn out to be the copycat crimes by a woman-hating prison guard who was influenced by the criminal caught in season one). In the course of her interrogations, Tennison meets with prostitutes to ask about the victims. She is always very respectful and sympathetic in her talks with them. Such meetings happen twice, and both times, even though she is not undercover, a potential "John" seeking her company mistakes her for a prostitute. In this way, the scenes associate her with the victimized group, a point Deborah Jermyn also argues and backs up with the observation that Tennison "is recurrently framed against pictures of [the victims'] corpses" (64). The beginning of the first episode in season two also addresses rape. Tennison appears to be interrogating a suspect accused of rape. However, she's actually leading a demonstration for other cops. Tennison concludes the session by addressing myths about why women are raped and discussing the dismal number of rape cases that are reported in comparison with the actual number of rapes that occur. Then, it turns out that Tennison is having an affair with the officer who portrayed the rapist in the demo.

In *The Closer*, Johnson faces several rape and domestic violence cases. In "Fantasy Date," a man who responds to a personal ad from a woman seeking to act out a rape fantasy mistakes Johnson for the woman. She's punched in the face before she responds with a head butt and a gun to the man's stomach (01.01). In the episode "Cherry Bomb" (04.03), Johnson charges a man not only for the rape of a young suicide victim but for the rape of other women whom he and his friends had assaulted as part of an atrocious "cherry-picking" game. In the tense season-five finale, Captain Raydor (Mary McDonnell) approaches Johnson to help with a potential domestic abuse case of a female police officer who goes astray; the officer shoots her abusive husband.

Johnson's most important case, and the one in which she herself becomes the potential victim, begins when she meets a serial rapist-murderer nemesis in season four. He is a lawyer named Philip Stroh (Billy Burke), and for the show's final three seasons he regularly appears to taunt Johnson and eventually has her reprimanded for harassment when she refuses to stop pursuing him because she's (rightly) convinced he's the culprit. Eventually, Stroh does attack Johnson in her own home during the series finale. She's tipped off when she returns home and finds indicators that match the previous crime scenes of Stroh's murdered rape victims—in other words, Stroh has set her up to receive the same fate, creating a sense of her possible violation and victimization. However, she ends up shooting him, through her purse, no less, and saving herself and a young witness she had brought home with her.

While the crimes Starling investigates in *The Silence of the Lambs* don't involve rape, they do involve sex-based violence. A serial murderer nicknamed Buffalo Bill targets women in order to create a woman-suit from their skin. The way he violates their bodies is not sexual, but it is sex-based. They are targets because they are women, and he wants to be a woman. Due to a diagnosis of psychological instability, Bill can't get sex-reassignment surgery. Starling faces the culprit alone in his hidden lair (the lair that remained undetected by her male colleagues). The camera positions Starling as a possible victim of this predator, who stalked other women, by having him watch and follow her wearing night-vision goggles. She stumbles around, blind in the dark, while we hear his breathing and feel the violent predatory implications of his pursuit until she fires into the dark and takes him down.

The overlap of sexism and sex-based violence, in which the threat exists for the FFF even on the job, indicates how a woman's vulnerability doesn't necessarily change when she takes a non-traditional role, like that of a cop; it also promotes a sense that the strength to survive, to overcome the victimization that follows women, as women, is a must for all women. Implicating sexism and sexual assault in obstacles the FFF faces personally and/or professionally thus not only sets the female hero apart from the male but also adds another dimension to their fraught hetero-relations.

Basically, half of the aforementioned FFF characters are actual victims of abuse by men, and they all fight against women's abuse by men. So, male colleagues—the men women are supposed to be able to trust with their lives as fellow cops and agents—pose potential threats at the workplace, rendering them psychologically vulnerable to hostility and the effects of limited agency. Variously, male criminals pose physical threats and render the women's bodies vulnerable. Both of these male character positions—the sexist and the rapist—mark them as women's enemies who share one commonality—their maleness. Now to be clear, the narratives don't conflate the sexist cops with the abusive criminals. Rather, they combine to create a sense that the isolated female hero exists within a generally hostile male environment in which "[m]isogyny lies in the mundane" (Jermyn 63). Regarding *Prime Suspect,* Jermyn makes this statement specifically to conflate the cops with the rapist-murderer George Marlow (John Bowe), saying that the "difference" in the sexism exhibited by the officers and the "spectacular excess of George's crimes [...] is one of degree rather than nature" (63). In other words, these narratives can be seen reflecting a women-against-men-who-are-against-women approach to sexual politics.

These FFF themes that associate the hero with victimization at the hands of men clearly indicate feminist-friendly influences on the narrative in terms of presenting women as objects of male domination through physical and sexual violence and as subjects who undermine that domination. What makes the themes noteworthy in terms of discussions about the strong, independent woman archetype is that such themes rely upon representations of men and women that are often assumed to be off-putting for audiences, for different reasons. In the 1980s, studio executives for *Cagney & Lacey* thought the show's viewers wouldn't respond to the feminist issues it addressed. The series was under constant threat of cancellation—despite fan response, ratings, and awards—because it was always transgressive. Yet it found a foothold with audiences who sought complex female heroes who had more complicated lives.[23]

Since the 1990s, in addition to lingering concerns about explicit feminism executives might still have, audiences have also been assumed to believe that feminism has served its purpose, meaning that issues like sex-discrimination are supposedly passé, relics of a bygone era. To show a contemporary woman dealing with it is generally considered a drag and also unnecessary since we are all supposedly more enlightened about women. Some viewers do hold this view. For example, Melissa Silverstein believes the 2011 American version of *Prime Suspect* wasn't picked up because "in 2011 too much time had passed and the aggressive male behavior in the pilot towards Maria Bello who played the American version Jane Timoney just didn't work. It was too much. Way too over the top." I will follow up on this basis for disagreement in the next chapter.

Thus, there is a surprising replay of the sexual assault theme (including in other narratives like long-running *Law and Order SVU* and its varied permutations), which comes dangerously close to the dreaded and controversial representation of America as a "rape culture." Essentially, sexism and assault FFF themes predominantly present women as victims of men and highlight male misogyny and prejudice. Neither of these is assumed to sit well with the majority of the popular-culture population, and both have been argued to alienate film and television viewers. Men may be uncomfortable identifying with the perpetrator, and women may be uncomfortable identifying with helplessness or perceiving that there might be a cultural conspiracy to hurt them. As these narratives locate these repetitive themes in crime-fighting dramas—in which the hero eventually does catch the culprit, face her trauma, or get revenge—they can also be seen as cathartic. They displace the threats from real life onto on-screen life, where they can be resolved. Yet, in order to do so, the stories still constantly invoke the threats.

One could assume that the presence of sexism and sexual assault establishes an alibi for the FFF's transgressive violence and aggression or establishes a "reason" for her to become a fighter. This alibi might particularly apply FFFs who faced trauma before their narratives begin, like Lisbeth Salander and Detective Griffin, or Megan Turner, who grew up watching her father abuse her mother. Similar judgments have been cast on the "final girl" heroine in slasher films as well as rape-revenge heroines in general. After all, combatting the violence of sexual assault against women has become what Jacinda Read calls "perhaps *the* quintessential feminist issue" that would justify the credibility of the violent actions of even the most typical female, i.e., a non-heroic woman (6, emphasis in the original).

However, Jessica Jones and the remainder of the FFFs discussed herein experience their victimization on the job, after they have made their decisions to be crime-fighters. More importantly, the "final girl" generally fights for herself. The FFFs I discuss have chosen the life of a crime-fighter. They have chosen to work through their vulnerabilities not just to save themselves but also to save others, a choice that Brown notes in his discussion of Salander's character "raises the revenge narrative to the level of feminist politics" (52).

Vulnerability and victimhood are only fractions of the tale the FFF tells, and both function in service of assuring her strength as a protector and hero. She is not a drag; the instances of victimization are the drag, and viewers can see beyond those moments to embrace her overall identity while being inspired by her ability to survive. That is and has been the basis of her appeal, and it indicates a willingness to engage in much more complex thinking about female characters, at least in certain areas of American popular culture over the last few decades.

You Made Me This Way: Domination and the Fraught Fighting Female

The stories in the FFF narratives examined thus far explicitly construct the hero's identity as a survivor of sex-based violence. However, other FFF fantasies construct a survivor identity that highlights the conjunction of female vulnerability and heroism by emphasizing her limited agency under more implicit forms of male domination that deny her consent in other ways. Instead of the shared tropes of sex-discrimination and sexual assault, these FFF narratives emphasize paternalistic authority and male-partner betrayals. These forms of domination further clarify the obstacles that define the character's strength and independence, what those obstacles symbolize in their hetero relations, and the conflicting messages they send about female empowerment through a survivor identity.

Paternalism

The FFF narratives that are the focus in this section include four Nikita stories: the original film *La Femme Nikita* (1990), its American remake *Point of No Return* (1993), the USA Network television series *La Femme Nikita*

(1997–2001), and the CW Network series *Nikita* (2010–13). The ABC network series *Alias* (2001–06) and the movie *Salt* (2010) also fit this category.

All of these FFF narratives share a similar storyline: The hero is cultivated (or brainwashed) as a secret agent—either unwittingly or unwillingly. Her compliance is ensured by the threat of death over both herself and her loved ones. During the course of the narrative, she eventually chooses either to escape or to fight back against the organization that threatens her freedom, her life, and the lives of others. One of the two sources of tension for these FFFs is some form of paternalistic authority that limits her autonomy, forces her to make painful choices, and threatens to harm, or actually harms, her loved ones.

In a way, all of these stories can be seen as variations on a theme established by writer and director Luc Besson in the original film, *La Femme Nikita*. The hero Nikita (Anne Parrilaud) starts out as a violent young junkie who kills a cop during a botched robbery and ends up in prison. A kind of black-ops government agency called The Centre fakes her death in order to recruit her. She has to choose whether to be trained by and work for them as an assassin. If not, she will be killed. She initially tries to escape, and she gets shot in the leg for her troubles. Following this, she reluctantly chooses the life of an assassin.

In the course of her instruction and under the tutelage of various trainers, including the chic and cold Amande (Jeanne Moreau), Nikita becomes a deadly, sophisticated beauty. However, despite being a quick study and having a natural ability for the work (a point that is emphasized not only in all four Nikita versions but also in *Alias* and *Salt*), Nikita hates killing and longs for freedom. One purveyor of paternalistic authority in the original film is a man named Bob (Tchéky Karyo), the man who introduces Nikita to The Centre and who shoots her for trying to escape. There is also a nameless older man to whom Bob reports who is the one who decides if she lives or dies. Finally, there is a cleaner named Victor (Jean Reno) who takes over the first mission Nikita runs on her own.

With a few differences here and there, the general storyline holds for the remaining three Nikita narratives, with some slight differences regarding Nikita's origin story. Also, both of the television series go into more depth about her past and her experiences in the training. For example, in the television *La Femme Nikita*, Nikita isn't a junkie-murderer: she's framed for the murder of another man who isn't a cop. Also, in this show, the cleaner is not one man but a man and a woman who remain nameless throughout the series. And in *Nikita*, there are many cleaners, men and women.

No matter the version, all Nikita narratives put a man in charge of Nikita, a division of the organization, and in later stories, the organization as a whole that essentially kidnaps and trains criminals to become assassins, like Nikita. In *Point of No Return*, Nikita is now called Maggie Hayworth (Bridget Fonda), code-named Nina, and her original contact is also a man named Bob (Gabriel Byrne) who shoots her in the leg. There is also a cleaner named Victor (Harvey Keitel), and the nameless head of the division is now called Kaufman (Miguel Ferrer). He, like his original, has little patience with Nikita's rebelliousness and is ready to "cancel" her.

The films, which focus more on Nikita, never really introduce or develop anything about the organization in which she works. However, the television programs, which are able to cultivate the Nikita myth with much more depth, are also able to include much more detail about the organization and its workings and, thereby, the tenor of male domination. In the television version of *La Femme Nikita,* Nikita has a trainer/supervisor named Michael Samuelle (Roy Dupuis); the division of The Center in which she works is called Section One under the command of Operations (Eugene Robert Glazer); and the head of The Center is Mr. Jones (Edward Woodward). In the television series *Nikita,* her trainer/supervisor is Michael Bishop (Shane West), and the organization she works for, called Division, is under the charge of Percy Rose (Xander Berkeley). Division, under Percy, eventually starts working for Phillip Jones (David S. Lee), the head of the group The Invisible Hand (a.k.a., The Shop). When the rogue Nikita defeats Percy and the American government takes over Division, Nikita is then under her ally Ryan Fletcher (Noah Bean). All of these Center permutations imply a male chain-of-command that essentially controls what happens to Nikita (and in later stories, her friends and colleagues), though the 2010 Nikita complicates this male hierarchy later in the series when it introduces a female president.

Alias includes a similar organizing structure and has actually been identified by fans as a knockoff of the *La Femme Nikita* franchise.[24] However, there are several organizations (both criminal and not) the FFF hero, Sydney Bristow (Jennifer Garner) must help or fight. There are also some other differences. For example, Syd was recruited fresh out of college to work for the clandestine government agency, SD-6. She was not forced or threatened with death (at least, not at the beginning of her career). When she learns that SD-6 is, in fact, a criminal organization, she chooses to become a double agent working for the CIA to take down SD-6 and the organization under which it functions, The Alliance of Twelve. At the CIA, she works under a male handler, named Michael Vaughn (Michael Vartan). This show is full of male-dominated splinter-cell groups, both legal and illegal, including Authorized Personnel Only (APO), a CIA black-ops group run mainly by different men, Prophet Five (a group like the Alliance of Twelve) and its divisions called The Shed (cells like SD-6), which also feigned an association with the CIA to recruit operatives. All of her mentors and superiors, then, are men. There are many threads throughout these groups that generally weave together to form a clear picture not only of male domination but also male corruption.

Finally, in *Salt*, the FFF Evelyn Salt (Angelina Jolie) works as an agent for the CIA. However, she turns out to be a sleeper agent who was taken from her family as a child, brainwashed, and raised to be a soldier and assassin for Oleg Vasilyevich Orlov (Daniel Olbrychski). Oleg is not a member of any specific terrorist group; he is a rogue agent with his own mission. Flashbacks show Salt as a young girl being "raised" by Oleg in an orphanage-type home environment receiving training, listening to propaganda, and, effectively, being brainwashed. Every night before bed, she and the other child recruits would kiss his ring, making clear the implications of his dominance over her. He represents a specific kind of paternalistic authority that is reflected in several of these FFF spy narratives: the father figure. The father figure is an older man with whom the hero has intimate ties, generally either from growing up around the person, as with Salt and Oleg, or from actual blood ties. The father figure also has questionable or nefarious intentions for the hero/daughter figure.

In the 1997 television show *La Femme Nikita*, Mr. Jones, the leader of The Center, turns out to be Nikita's long-lost father. He had her framed for murder, kidnapped into Section One, and trained to be an assassin because he wanted to groom her to take over The Center in his place. It was not until the final season that Nikita learns this; she spends all of the previous seasons agonizing over why she was framed, planning how she can escape Section One, and attempting to reconcile her morals with her position as an assassin. Jones never asks for her input or gives her a choice to be taken.

Syd, from *Alias*, has two father figures. The first, Jack Bristow (Victor Garber), her actual father, is also her superior at SD-6 and in the CIA. Before she turns on SD-6, she learns that Jack also works for the organization in a much higher position, as Director of Operations, under the head of the cell, Arvin Sloane (Ron Rifkin), who is Syd's other father figure. Arvin and his wife Emily were her temporary guardians when she was a child, and throughout the series, they treat her like the daughter they never had. However, both father figures have a problematic relationship with Syd, and she regularly confronts her lack of trust for both of them.

Like Mr. Jones, both of Syd's father figures presume to know what is best for her and regularly assure her and each other they want only to ensure Syd's safety. Also like Mr. Jones, both of the men take questionable steps to do so. Arvin recruited Syd into SD-6, without Jack's knowledge, because he wanted her to be a part of his work family, so to speak. Jack subjected Syd to an experimental government program called Project Christmas when she was a child that essentially hardwired her to be a spy, which can be seen as a type of brainwashing. Arvin grooms Syd because he thinks she is part of a prediction forecast by Milo Rimbaldi (a fictional prophet who combines elements of Leonardo da Vinci and Nostradamus). To further drive home the point of Arvin's depraved sense of paternalism, he uses his own actual daughter (whom he learns about later in the series) to fulfill Rimbaldi's prophecies. Arvin orders the death of Syd's fiancé, and Jack was aware of this order. Arvin also assigns an agent to kill Syd in season one when he thinks she has become a threat to the organization. However, she is eventually able to convince him that she is loyal, mainly through emotional appeals. Both of these father figures lie to Syd multiple times, whether they state it's for her own good because she's not ready or to carry out other plans they have determined take precedence.

By the end of the series, the full justification for Syd's distrust of Arvin becomes apparent, as the audience learns that all along, no matter how much he had appeared to change, how much he professed his dedication to Syd and his own daughter, he was always working to fulfill his plans to achieve immortality using the Rimbaldi device at any cost. He is a corrupt father figure, undoubtedly—one who might struggle emotionally and have redeeming moments, but ultimately one who uses his power and his sense of entitlement for his own goals. Jack, on the other hand, is presented by the final events as being validated in his fatherhood, as proving that he just wants the best for his daughter—when he gives his life to end Arvin's. Thus, it would seem that all of Syd's doubts about him prove incorrect. However, we cannot forget a very important part of the narrative that still places Jack firmly on the side of paternalistic authority that is implicated in Syd's "fraughtness," even if he works to redeem himself (a point to which this account will return): Syd's brainwashing as a child, based on Jack's decision to have her participate in "Project Christmas," a government operation intended to raise the perfect spy using child subjects, one that the government eventually disbands for ethical issues.

The brainwashing incident epitomizes the way the narrative implicates *all* forms of paternalistic authority, including the benevolent, in the struggles the FFF hero endures and the limits to her agency that come through male domination. When Syd learns of her brainwashing under Jack, she becomes rightfully incensed, and the knowledge drives one of many wedges between them. She is angry because he violates her agency; she feels she had no choice but to pursue her life as a spy, a life that has caused her only heartache. Both her fiancé and her best friend die, while another close friend has his life threatened and has to take on a new identity and disappear from her life. She suffers from isolation and a lack of confidantes and from not knowing whom to trust across much of the series. In season three, the story implies that her childhood brainwashing—again, authorized by her father—prevented Syd from being successfully brainwashed by The Covenant when she was kidnapped. So, it could seem like all of her pain was justified, that it served to make her stronger and actually protect her autonomy from being undermined by an enemy. However, had she not been programmed as a child, she might not have chosen the career in which she was then subject to brainwashing by The Covenant. So, there are legitimate and clear implications that this brainwashing is most certainly a violation, and from one who supposedly loves her more than anyone. It's a violation that prevents the hero from being able to choose the life she wants to live, just like the glorified abduction of the other FFF spy heroines that the men in charge justify as a valid means to their idea of the just end.

Paternalistic authority, then, is exposed in the male-dominated terrorist and criminal organizations the hero fights against, in the male-dominated crime-fighting organizations she fights for, and in authoritative father figures. Each of these representations of authority in some way fails, injures, or betrays the FFF in ways that define her as a crime-fighter. While the narratives clearly portray the criminal organizations as evil, the same can't always be said for the crime-fighting organizations and father figures. Both tend to relate to the FFF in terms of protection, opportunity, and support. A recurrent refrain in the Nikita storylines is that The Center/Division groups give her a second chance, that without their intervention, she would be dead or rotting in jail, that now she has an opportunity to do some good in a society that had otherwise deemed her unfit or a threat. The loss of her personal freedom is necessary for her opportunity. She's been protected, and she's being taught how to protect.

Of course, Jack and Arvin supposedly want only what's best for Syd, both claiming their actions are for her own protection. This urge toward protection of the fighting female, who proves over and over that she is capable of taking care of herself or that she doesn't want what they offer as protection, thus seems outdated and unnecessary, at times causing more problems than it solves. We clearly see the protection impulse of the paternalistic authority figures for what it partly is—a desire to control the hero. At best, the questionable protective impulses over the strong woman become a form of what Hagelin refers to as "insidious condescension" because it reflects sentimental versions of male/female relationships that are less reflective of today's empowered women (89).[25] At worst, it's a complete violation.

The paternalism representations also add up to negatively portray the sexual politics that still inform a mostly corrupt old-boys network and that make up assumptions about male authority in general that uses physical force, emotional manipulation, and deception to control an empowered woman. Now, it would be easy to claim that these FFFs deal with the same kinds of villainous organizations and male bureaucracies that male characters have faced for some time. After all, in a world of war, espionage, and power-hungry violence, men are the primary perpetrators because they have been the primary participants. So, a certain kind of heroic parity is apparent. However, that same world, because of the involvement of only a small number of female heroes present, is much more vividly symbolic of patriarchy.

To further emphasize this difference, take into consideration the character Evelyn Salt. The character was originally written as Edwin Salt, and "Tom Cruise was supposed to star but pulled out because the film too closely resembled *Mission Impossible*" (Haimoff). Angelina Jolie stepped in. Had it been a man, I could not make the same argument, and different genre or action paradigms that emerged from assumptions of a male hero would prove more relevant. While the story was supposedly revised specifically not to emphasize her femaleness and to make it realistic for a female fighter up against much larger male adversaries, the character's sex does come with its own unique patriarchal baggage. As the director Phillip Noyce explained, there was "huge sequence" in the original script in which Edwin Salt was supposed to save his wife, who's in danger. This scene had to be revised because it seemed to "castrate" the husband character a little, so he "was made tough enough that he didn't need saving" (qtd. in Woerner). The husband's character ends up being killed in the final take. Even in a film in which the director agreed to a sex change to the original role and had a star and female crewmembers advocating to ensure the character's badass cred (Woerner), the man's reputation for strength had to be considered when a woman's reputation in the same scene probably wouldn't have been. What better way to characterize the gendered tensions a woman brings to the action role. Paternal guidance over a female character, thus, has to be considered as a definite gendered dynamic in the way these men dominate the FFF hero that epitomizes a critical fantasy problematizing patriarchal institutions and assumptions.

Betrayal

As if the constant threat and betrayal by the so-called men in charge weren't enough, some of the narratives increase the hetero-relation tensions for the FFF hero by introducing partners who betray her (or seem to betray her) or who are her enemies at some point. In *Mr. and Mrs. Smith*, there is a similar question when it's still unclear to Jane and John are trying to kill each other. Still, the question of betrayal is on the head of both characters (in emphasizing their similarity as love warriors). In these FFF stories, the male partners are the ones who are the potential betrayers.

Television's 1997 *La Femme Nikita* probably makes the most explicit use of this theme. Nikita's trainer, supervisor, and eventual partner Michael Samuelle is as problematic as they come. He plays a skilled lothario who uses his ability to woo women to gain their trust and then, eventually, betray them. He does this in a long-term undercover case (where he marries a woman and even fathers a child with her for his cover), in several short-term operations, and with Nikita herself. They end up sleeping with each other and having something of an affair, until Nikita learns that he was ordered to do so to gauge her loyalty and keep an eye on her. This happens not once, not twice, but several times throughout the early years of the series. The question for audiences is not the typical will-they-won't-they get together but rather is-he-isn't-he lying again? Does Michael mean it this time? His betrayals are real and repeated and cause a great deal of emotional stress for Nikita, who already feels isolated and angry about being an unwilling assassin.

In the 2010 television series *Nikita*, Nikita (Maggie Q) also ends up in a relationship with her handler, Michael Bishop. However, for the first part of the series, Bishop is explicitly tasked to take her out as an enemy and traitor. This latest version of the Nikita myth begins three years after Nikita has escaped Division. Nikita has made it her mission to take down Division and rescue the other recruits. During most of the first season, Bishop is her enemy. However, in flashbacks to the time when Nikita was still working in Division, we see that they have feelings for each other—though they don't act on them at the time. When she leaves, he follows orders from Percy and continues functioning under Division rules. Despite his feelings, he is willing to take her down. Eventually, however, Bishop's feelings for Nikita—and what he learns about Division going rogue and working against the U.S. government—turn him into an ally.

In *Salt*, Evelyn Salt's CIA partner Agent Ted Winter (Liev Schreiber) turns out to be, like she is, a sleeper agent whom Oleg tasks to aid Salt in taking down the Russian president and creating a nuclear standoff between the U.S., Russia, and the Middle East. Winter's betrayal lies not only in keeping his sleeper identity a secret from Salt—she was unaware that he had been one of Oleg's minions, too—but also in his being the one to recommend that Oleg not only blow Salt's cover with the CIA but also to kill her husband, Michael Krause (August Diehl). When Winter finds out that she has betrayed Oleg and the other sleeper agents, he says he will make her a patsy for the destruction about to ensue and becomes her obvious enemy.

Alias does not include partner betrayal so much as it plays on the drama of relationship misrepresentation and deception that characterizes either the other FFF narrative partner betrayals or themes of paternalistic authority. When Syd and her handler, Michael Vaughn, finally declare their love for each other and make plans to marry at the end of season four, he reveals that he is not the person she thought he was. Before he can explain, the car they're driving is hit, and Vaughn gets abducted (though Syd believes he is dead). When season five opens, Syd and the rest of the APO question Vaughn's loyalty when they learn his real name is André Micheaux and that he's been working with a rogue and criminal named Renée Rienne to learn about his father's death. Syd was unaware of any of this. Vaughn's deception is decidedly less dangerous or emotionally abusive than that of Michael Samuelle in the 1997 *La Femme Nikita*. However, considering that Vaughn is a character with which Syd had the longest, most open, and supportive relationship on the show, the fact that even he is dishonest seems to contribute to an overall perception of the ease with which male allies are implicated as untrustworthy in FFF narratives.

Jessica Jones has a few partners who help her throughout the series, including the recovering addict Malcolm Ducasse (Eka Darville) and her adopted sister, Trish Walker (Rachael Taylor). However, Jess doesn't meet her partner in romance and crime-fighting until season three, when she works to get justice for the victims of the serial killer Gregory Sallinger (Jeremy Bobb). From the start, she doesn't trust Erik Gelden (Benjamin Walker)—in part because he's a lot like her: a mess of a human being looking to use booze and casual sex to attenuate the pain of living. It turns out that he has the ability to sense how evil someone is—the more evil they are, the more pain it causes him to be around them. When we meet him, he has been making a living by blackmailing the people who cause him the most pain—all men. This is another reason for Jess's mistrust. Erik doesn't know what they did, only that it was bad, and he bluffs his way through the extortion. When he and Jess start working together, he finds the potential perps, and Jess uses her detective skills to find out their evildoing.

There is only one scene in which Jess believes Erik has actually betrayed her, when she sees him talking to Salinger on the street. However, she soon learns that it was a coincidence and nothing to worry about. Except she continues to worry about Erik, all the way until the end of the season, which is also, unfortunately, the end of the series. After Jess has wrapped everything up, Erik shows up with first aid and Kung Pao chicken, along with a newspaper. The front-page headline says, "Bona Fide hero" above Jess' picture.

Erik tells Jess, "You earned it."

And she says, "Yeah, I did."

He thinks it's cool that she's a hero, and he says, "It would be nice to help, though. I mean it, it wouldn't suck [...] working together."

She says, "You're a good man, but I don't trust you." However, she does trust Erik enough to connect to her police officer ally, Detective Costa, so Erik can now pass on the tips about the evildoers to Costa.

Pinpointing explicit feminist implications in the themes highlighting the FFF's vulnerability is not as straightforward as analyzing the FFFs who faced sexism and sex-based violence. When other feminist critics evaluate certain of these narratives in this section, they tend to focus on the ways these spy heroes represent women's empowerment, particularly with regard to gender-blending tactics and with regard to their fighting abilities, as Joe Goodwill does. Conversely, critics like Tung also focus on how these shows contribute to women's disempowerment, usually in the way they reinforce hierarchical gender divisions that assume women's subordinate position, despite any viewing pleasures they might offer that are based on the assumption of their empowerment. Other concerns are the ways some of the women rely heavily on male authority, as Schubart notes (in her chapter on "Daddy's Action Girl"). Patricia Mellencamp and Inness read the narratives as reasserting femininity as desirable over strength, and critics like Douglas indicate that these narratives continue to foster female objectification by tempering the violent transgressions with tiny costumes and a focus on the fighting female's beauty (*Enlightened Sexism*). Brown adds to this conversation by observing the problem "torture chic in popular culture" poses for action heroines, where scenes of pain and violation "are likely to eroticize them as much, or more than, to validate their strength" (33).

These critics make valid points, particularly Douglas and Brown, though the other claims are somewhat incomplete. They have not fully recognized that these female heroes are themselves disempowered in their interactions with men specifically but are not portrayed as simply weak. They have not realized how the narratives affirm this disempowerment as part of the heroes' obstacles in a way that sets them apart from male heroes—and how, through the thematic repetition, these shows make feminist-friendly assertions that problematize male domination and implicate male behaviors in female oppression.

Consequently, despite differences in the ways they address explicit or implicit male domination, both types of FFF narratives send similar messages: When women are involved in a man's world, they become more prone to violation. When women work to protect other women from men, they run the risk of being violated or threatened with violation. Also, men in power may not be trustworthy because they may attempt to control women and use other men to do it. In general, associating with men is inevitable, but it may hold specific dangers for women, and it requires vigilance. So while the actual sexism and sexual assaults present in the previous FFF narratives aren't included in these narratives, the sense of men violating women often is—not only violations by the boss or a superior but also by the father figure, the lover, the partner. There is a sense that these women have difficulty finding refuge in any of their hetero-relations. This lack of refuge in men emphasizes a refuge in the strength of the empowered woman who fights to overcome the obstacles she faces, even if that strength is presented in contradictory ways.

Not All Men

What audiences are left with in terms of the repetition of male threats and abuses in the FFF narratives is similar to what Clover sees in the "final girl" narratives: a number of "individual acts of domination add[ing] up to pervasive structural misogyny" (144). To be clear, making men the bad guys isn't the feminist-friendly part—that would assert more of a one-dimensional man-hating intention to the FFF narrative that has nothing to do with the character or most versions of feminism. The narratives identify specific male behaviors as the problem, behaviors that not all men adopt (and some women do). Still, the fact that gendered power dynamics that are oppressive to women, and enacted by men, are so deeply embedded in these two FFF storylines, despite their differences, shows just how difficult it is to imagine the FFF without hetero-relation tensions as part of her difficulties and just how gendered her character's heroism still is, despite the inroads toward parity that she also represents. In light of this, there seems little room left to imagine feminist-friendly hetero-intimacy in these narratives.

On the surface, the majority of the FFF texts don't seem to offer a very optimistic view of the FFF's intimate life. The most common ending for the FFF paints an ambiguous picture of the life of an empowered woman. DSI Tennison is alone, retired, and isolated from her family; the series ends on a shot of her walking down a street by herself in a vision that critics have noted is particularly bleak (Jermyn 108). A shot of Maggie from behind, walking away from her home and toward a life on the run, ends *Point of No Return*. First, a shot of a teary-faced Nikita standing alone at the train station, watching Michael Samuelle's train leave, and then a shot of a steely-faced Nikita sitting isolated at her desk at Division One ends the 1997 *La Femme Nikita* series. *Blue Steel* ends with Turner sitting alone in her car, a close-up on her tired and worn-looking face after she's finally bested Hunt by gunning him down in a shootout. *The Silence of the Lambs* closes on a dismayed Starling, who is left with the knowledge that a psychopathic killer has been turned loose into the world again. A final shot of Scott alone in her isolated house concludes *Taking Lives*, as a shot of Mayweather walking down a court hall alone to face her past concludes *Murder by Numbers*. The last shot of *Salt* is of her jumping out of a helicopter and running off into the woods alone, on the run, to continue seeking justice. Lisbeth Salander drives off by herself into the night, presumably hurt after watching Blomkvist drive off with another woman (in the American version). At the end of the series, Jessica Jones is alone at a train station—she had planned to leave the country but changes her mind as she remembers Kilgrave's voice and, ostensibly, her potential as a hero to save others. Jess faces the camera straight forward, looking somewhat satisfied and strong in her stance, her chin thrusting out slightly and her lips close to smiling but not quite. She walks out of the station alone as the song "Keep on Livin'" by the Riot Grrrl band Le Tigre plays, with the gravelly, loud, rebellious voice reminding us of what will be Jess's survival.

Each of these FFF endings leaves a very clear reminder of each FFF hero's susceptibility and segregation in the wake of their triumphs. They all started the narrative isolated, they often fight alone, and even though they all succeed, they all end in seclusion. However, just because there is little optimism and a lot of ambiguity in the endings doesn't mean that a non-couple-oriented ending must be read pessimistically. These endings can be read as transgressive or regressive, depending on an audience member's perspectives on empowered female characters. Certainly, having the FFF end up alone can be read as an "absence of social connections," as Cavender and Jurik note in relation to DSI Tennison, that is "consistent with the type of postfeminist discourse that raises anxieties concerning women's ability to have both a meaningful career and a fulfilling personal life" (121). In this case, the fantasy is that the hero will indeed have to choose one or the other, that this is a burden of her strength and independence. This choice does not necessarily disprove her empowerment and representation as a hero in general, but it does reinforce a stereotypical threat for women in particular. Women can be dedicated to careers, can really succeed, and can even protect the world from criminals and evildoers, but if they do it, they will probably end up doing it alone (whether they want to or not). Considering that the majority of the single FFF heroes above do at some time or another in the narrative have or attempt meaningful hetero-intimacies—and that ending these intimacies causes them a great deal of pain—the assumption is that being without friends and/or loved ones is not their preferred ending. The uncoupled FFFs represent the women who might want it all but just can't get it because having it all is a fiction for such transgressive women. For the viewer who agrees with this viewpoint, this can be appealing because such an ending does not threaten the more traditional expectations of gender roles that the strong, independent woman archetype problematizes. In other words, one could argue that there is no room for feminist-friendly hetero-romance possible in most of these fantasies: the hero's adherence to a strong, independent ideal can only go so far before it leads to alienation.

Another aspect of the FFF's character that supports this pessimistic reading of her as punished for her transgressions as a woman capable of violence, of fighting crime, is that many of the FFFs suffer from a variety of mental vulnerabilities or psychological issues from the traumas they face. Both Tennison and Cagney suffer from drinking problems that affect their personal lives, and Jessica Jones becomes a functional alcoholic who constantly drinks to keep the pain away, even after she's lost her spleen in season three and been warned by a doctor to change her habits. Jones, along with Mayweather and Salander, is anti-social, at best, and clearly suffers from post-traumatic emotional crises. Syd and Salt lose a fiancé and a husband, respectively, because of their jobs and must carry the guilt along with the grieving. Lacey, as mentioned, has a nervous breakdown. Many of the FFFs

Four. What Doesn't Kill Her Makes Her Stronger 163

have nightmares—especially those who have been subject to brainwashing or sexual assault—or panic attacks. Even the milder issues Johnson deals with that seem more like personality quirks—her complicated relationship with food (her obvious love for and fear of sweets), her anxieties about aging, and her lack of housekeeping—connote more complex problems like self-policing and feelings of inadequacy.

These characters are all, at some point, troubled, anxious, depressed, problems that often interfere with their abilities to have successful relationships. Over the course of three different seasons, Tennison has three failed affairs. Unlike the proud-to-be-single Cagney, Tennison does not choose to end them. Both Turner in *Blue Steel* and Scott in *Taking Lives* are attracted to criminals who almost kill them. Mayweather, from *Murder by Numbers*, almost killed by an abusive husband before the movie begins, can only have a series of shallow sexual affairs and fears intimacy. Salander's character in *The Girl with the Dragon Tattoo* attempts to be dominant in her sexual encounters with women and men and treat them coldly after sex (until her feelings for Blomkvist grow, again in the American version). *Top of the Lake*'s Griffin has a difficult back-and-forth with her love interest, whom she has trouble trusting because he was a helpless bystander at the scene of her rape long ago. Jessica Jones adds casual sex to her drinking coping mechanism as a way to escape, not simply because she enjoys casual sex with multiple partners. Because of the difficulties these heroes face, the narratives could be said to be compensating for the woman's heroism and strength not only by making her romances uncertain, temporary, and/or trying but also by harming her emotionally.

However, being an emotional mess can also be said to make the characters more realistic and easy to identify with, as many of the women who enjoy these programs might themselves be troubled. Likewise, the "warning" of a troubled psyche or of the need to choose between success in a career or romance for the single, career-driven woman mentioned above alternatively can be read as a liberating assertion of the hero's independence in one of a few ways. First, ending alone suggests parity with other male lone-wolf heroes. Men have long been presumed to have the strength and independence to bear the burdens of the isolated protector, and now women can be imagined as such. Such an ending was very common for both the classic male detective, like Philip Marlowe, or the classic action hero and spy, like Rambo or Bond. They are also allowed to be anti-heroes or heroes with deep problems, again like Rambo, or like Walter from *Breaking Bad* (2008–13). Being a mess and a hero—being an imperfect woman who at least gets to be great at her job, even if she doesn't find love—is a luxury in the world of women characters, a world in which being likable has long tended to be a required personality trait. We may not like all of the FFF characters Salander, Tennison, Cagney, or Salt, but it's what they do that counts. We watch them because we can sympathize with their losses and troubles and because we want to see them triumph, problems and all, just like with Rambo or Dirty Harry.

Second, ending alone liberates the FFF from the traditional romance narrative and can be seen to "disrupt [...] any compulsory heterosexual resolution of narrative" (Halberstam 254), a view that is most associated with a feminist-friendly perspective, as noted in Chapter One. Whether the heroine has a man in her life can be seen as irrelevant, meaning that being alone transgresses traditional expectations for her as a female character, which, in and of itself, can be inspiring for viewers who seek their own such alternatives. On a related note, ending alone can liberate the FFF hero from stereotypical heteronormative readings either in favor of homo-relational intimacies or in the possibility of imagining such intimacies outside the narrative. This is true not only of narratives that explicitly make this connection with dual-protagonist FFF heroes—like *Cagney & Lacey* or its 21st-century counterparts, *Rizzoli and Isles* (2010–16) and the movie *The Heat* from 2013—but also of lone-wolf FFF heroes who have few intimate hetero-relations in the narrative, like Clarice Starling, whose story Gates references in relation to lesbian viewing pleasures in *The Silence of the Lambs* (274). In fact, one of the most common critiques of the American version of *The Girl with the Dragon Tattoo* is that Salander's homosexual relationships end up trumped by a more typically heteronormative romantic imagining of her relationship with Blomkvist ("Softening and Sexualizing Lisbeth Salander"). Ironic as it may seem, it's possible to read the American interpretation as incorporating Salander's bisexuality not only as a shorthand for her strength, as "homosexuality is often attached to displays of toughness in women" as Inness notes (9), but also for her desirability, as bisexual orientation in women is often mistaken as a ruse put on for the pleasure of men. Still, the response from critics of the American version exemplifies the view of those who find the non-heteronormative endings more open and, therefore, more emancipating for woman-identified viewers.

As for the FFFs who do end up with men, even if the men are not involved with or alluded to in the ending, the narratives allow more imaginative wiggle room in terms of the feminist-friendly hetero-intimacy fantasy. Take, for example, two of the four FFF characters who do end up as part of a happy couple, Lacey and Johnson. Both have happy, generally healthy personal relationships that are presented throughout the series, even if both relationships have rocky patches. These relationships remain intact at the end of the shows, but the shows end depicting the FFF either with her partner (for Lacey) or alone (for Johnson), instead of in a scene with her husband. By not including their husbands in the endings, the narratives reassert that they are female heroes' tales, something that still remains a rarity in terms of female fighters on-screen. In essence, this FFF storyline finds a way to have it all, to show women who get the fulfilling job and the fulfilling personal life, but without resorting to tying the hero's finale to her relationships, again liberating her from the romance narrative without having to preclude romance entirely.

Thus, the ending reiterates the job's importance as a source of meaning for the hero, and in Johnson's case, as her first love—a point asserted by her first words at the beginning of the series (when she enters a crime scene) and her last words at the end of the series (in the elevator): "It looks like love" (07.21). This statement associates the work itself as something she loves and, to some extent, portrays that as a valid feeling for a woman by orienting her narrative around that love, rather than around her romantic partnership. The *Cagney & Lacey* ending also makes this association for both of its heroes, possibly offering even more validation for the lifestyle possibilities for independent women. One hero, Lacey, is married, but Cagney remains single and has done so with intention, wanting to put her career first and having passed up marriage proposals and relationships with nice men to do so because they weren't her priority. Making the final scene for the television series about them foregrounds the friendship and partnership without casting any doubt on their personal lives.

Still, ambiguity remains a part of the endings for both Johnson and Lacey. Both leave under fraught circumstances. As I mentioned previously, in *The Closer*, Johnson has taken a prestigious position in the DA's office, but only because her bosses wouldn't back her up. The story closes on a shot of her alone in an elevator, leaving a job she feels forced to leave, eating her beloved Ding Dongs that were a gift from her squad (but that represent a guilty pleasure food that she would eat primarily when she was stressed). Even the series' framing phrase, "It looks like love," seems ambiguous. It still signals her love for the work she does and the love she comes to share with her squad members, but it also signals a fraught love, one with dangers for the transgressive female. After all, the murder victim Johnson looks at in the first episode's crime scene, when she says the phrase, is a lesbian who was living as a man to hide her identity because of past problems and who was killed by a homophobic woman who had fallen in love with her/him. Johnson says "it looks like love" to explain her verdict that love led to the murder. Johnson's use of the phrase "it looks like love" in the elevator (while looking at the gift of a new purse filled with junk food her squad gives her as a good luck present) thus can be seen as another sad verdict of love leading to loss for another woman.

As for the germinal *Cagney & Lacey*, both stand together in the final shot, but the final scene preceding this picture indicates more frustration and more battles awaiting them. They argue about wanting to do what's right and tell the press about a cover-up in the department over an arms deal gone awry. They have been told, in no uncertain terms, that if they do so, they will not only lose the promotions they just received (to encourage them to keep their mouths shut) but also they will probably lose their jobs. They ask Lieutenant Samuels for advice. He tells them to "put yourselves in a win-win position" by accepting that if they share the story, they will either leave a "legacy" of achieving the promotion they've been warned they won't get or they will at least get a newly painted women's restroom, which they've been campaigning for during most of the series and which he's now offering (07.22). A freshly painted bathroom is nice and all, but it's far from a "win" for these talented cops. This final scene, like *The Closer's*, signifies both triumph and tribulation. Cagney and Lacey have earned the respect of their own squad and become an integral part of the precinct, but rough roads lie ahead. These FFF endings reinforce the narrative trends in all of the shows, trends that both assert the hero's difference as a woman and negate that difference in her position as a crime-fighter to engender a sense of her identity as a survivor and protector, as empowered and vulnerable.

The two FFF narratives in which the endings include the hero and her husband assert more of an egalitarian and optimistic perspective between the hero and her romance partner, similar to the love-buddy and love-warrior fighting female narratives. Such endings negate the hero's difference and de-emphasize her vulnerability as a woman in favor of reasserting her empowerment as part of a hetero-couple.

First, the final scene in *Alias* shows Syd and Vaughn living in a beach house with their two children, years after they saved the world. Syd's old partner Marcus Dixon (Carl Lumbly) shows up, and he's now the deputy director of the CIA. He wants them to lead an op to track down an old nemesis in Paris, saying that his other agents are unavailable for the mission. Vaughn says they can discuss it after dinner, implying that they are interested, and then the couple, their kids, and Dixon all go outside to walk on the beach and watch the sunset. One big, happy family. The ending of the 2010 *Nikita* series ends on a similar upbeat, love-conquers-all note. Nikita and Bishop have eloped and are on a beach in South America. They sit enjoying drinks, while Nikita notices a young boy being harassed by a man saying to the boy that they are at war and they need soldiers. The man wants the boy, who looks scared, to take the gun. Nikita says she knows what she and Bishop can do for their honeymoon, and she gets up to follow the man. Bishop looks surprised, gets up without questioning, and follows. In a final voice-over, as they walk away from the beach, Nikita says, "The real gift isn't freedom. It's what we get to do with it."

The basis for these two endings is predicated on another similarity between the narratives: Both of the husbands start out as the FFF's handler, become her partner, and are rendered vulnerable and victimized within the narrative. Vaughn lost his father as a child but was led to believe his father is still alive, causing him to go rogue from the team, deceive Syd, and even injure Dixon. Unfortunately, his father actually is dead; Vaughn was himself deceived to aid one of the criminal organizations. Additionally, Vaughn is himself betrayed by the woman he married in season two (when Syd was missing and presumed dead for two years). His wife turns out to be a double agent who uses and deceives him, leaving him heartbroken and a mess.

Likewise, Bishop, in *Nikita*, turns out to be an unwitting pawn for Percy's deceptions and criminal intent—meaning that the times Bishop sought out and fought against Nikita for Division, he was doing so under false pretenses. His enemy position is thus rendered moot when he learns of Percy's schemes and joins Nikita in her rogue mission to take down Division and free all of the other agents. During flashbacks, we learn that Bishop entered Division because he lost his wife and daughter—Percy encouraged him to join, saving Michael from overdosing on morphine in his grief. Later in the series, Bishop ends up gravely injured and loses his hand during a mission—Nikita has to chop it off to save his life from an imminent explosion. He struggles for the better part of a season to come to terms with his physical disability, becoming emotionally unstable and insecure. As the narratives render both men vulnerable, they offer what I refer to as redemptive parallels that equalize the men with the FFF heroes and render any betrayals on the men's part if not harmless then, at final count, at least not threatening, dominating, or paternal. The narratives encourage the audience to question the men's loyalties and to believe in the likelihood of their betrayals. Ultimately, however, they offer reparations for any wrongdoings they commit in order to create space for their intimacy with the FFFs.

Another clear example of the redemptive parallel is in *Jessica Jones*. As I've mentioned, she still ends up alone in the end, but it's in a more optimistic way than happens with the other fighting females who are alone at the end of the narrative—a near smile rests on her face as she resolutely faces her future in fighting crime. This optimism is what makes her case interesting and further proves the importance of the theme in establishing character equality. It's entirely possible that, because she has decided to stay and continue her work, she could end up back with her old allies Malcolm, Detective Costa, and maybe Erik. Psychologically, Erik suffers the kind of damage that makes him as vulnerable as Vaughn and Bishop. One of the first times he used his power was when he learned that his father had been sexually abusing his younger sister. He forced his father to confess, and his dad went to jail. Because of this, his mom overdosed on pills and died, and his sister ran away, began using drugs, and became a prostitute. Erik blames himself and his powers, and his self-loathing leads to a downward spiral of drinking, gambling, and blackmailing. Erik is also more vulnerable than Vaughn or Bishop because he has no combat training, weapons skills, or other powers that would help him in a fight; normally, he is more likely to flee than to stay.

The redemptive parallel symbolizes a trend of male conversion in certain of the FFF narratives that suggests a creative negotiation to undermine the negative portrayal of men and create hetero allies, if not always intimates, who contrast from the male dominators. As stated at the beginning of the chapter, for every male enemy the FFF faces, there is a male ally—even if that alliance is somewhat ambiguous. The redemptive parallel also reflects the problematic trend of effacing what Chapter Three argues is a naturalization of sex conflict—a female-versus-male inclination—inherent to hetero-romance narratives that even the more feminist-friendly, gender-bending fighting female romances replicate. Yet, it also suggests another interesting trend as a theme that asserts vulnerability in strong men as an equalizing factor, which further reinforces the possibility that women can still be perceived as empowered even when they are not all-powerful. The inclusion of strong, vulnerable men in the FFF stories makes the strongest claim against reading the extreme focus on male domination as just another feminist attempt to degrade men, for it creates narrative opportunities to counteract the man-hating stereotype associated with feminist-friendly characters. It allows for room to recognize that not all men are bad and also the space to assert that the men who work well with the female characters are simply the ones who support them, respect them, and trust them.

In other words, the redemptive parallel offers a version of male identity that is not only non-dominating but also is often powerless on its own, without the support of the FFF as a partner. After all, without the help of Syd, Nikita, and Jessica, Vaughn, Bishop, and Erik (respectively) may not have emerged from their personal traumas intact. Part of this help involved emotional interrogation and self-analysis of the kind that is not necessarily apparent in the average male heroic tale, in which much of the narrative focuses on overcoming problems through action. Hagelin addresses the trend toward increasing "resistant vulnerabilities" in female characters that have started to replace "sentimental vulnerabilities" in which women either embody the susceptible victim or the male's vulnerabilities are transferred to a female or feminine body. As part of this trend toward resistant vulnerabilities, these FFF narratives offer alternative, transgressive masculinities as much as they encourage an alternative femininity that emphasizes strength and independence. Douglas makes a similar conclusion about competing masculinities offered by certain "warrior women" narratives, which includes *Alias* and *La Femme Nikita*, stating that they proclaim patriarchy as "destructive, inhumane, heartless" and promote "men touched by feminism" who reflect "hope for a new, improved masculinity" (98).[26] The feminist-friendly male and the transgressive masculinities that fighting female romance narratives construct will be analyzed in further detail in Chapter Five.

The Potential in the Survivor Identity

Providing a fantasy through which to navigate femininity and feminism by putting them in concert rather than in conflict, ultimately, is the pleasure that these FFF narratives afford. This fantasy is the function of the woman-as-survivor identity that combines empowerment and vulnerability, making room for the FFF to perform the role of protector *and* victim, which defies narrative tactics that keep the identities separate. One of the tactics used in earlier versions of fighting females, particularly during the 1960s and '70s and in the superhero versions of fighting females today, is overemphasizing the fighting female's abilities by creating a sense of her as an indestructible protector. This overemphasis occurred in television shows like *The Avengers*, *The Bionic Woman*, and *Wonder Woman*, and it's the case with Supergirl and Captain Marvel. (Even Captain Marvel faced some sexism—since her origin took place in the 1990s and rightfully reflected some Riot Grrrl anti-patriarchy rage, though Marvel just overlooks it like the ladies in *Taking Lives* and *Murder by Numbers*.) The overemphasis also happened in certain Blaxploitation films with heroines, like the two *Cleopatra Jones* sagas (1973 and 1975) and *T.N.T. Jackson* (1974). All of these characters are so completely powerful that their fluency as protectors was the predominant impression they gave.

Conversely, underemphasizing her fighting abilities—by giving women superficial positions as crime-fighters that made them convenient targets and victims to be protected by men—happened in *Honey West* (1965–66), *Get Smart* (1965–70), *The Girl from U.N.C.L.E.* (1966–67), *Police Woman*, *McMillan & Wife* (1971–77), *Hart to Hart* (1979–84), and *Scarecrow and Mrs. King* (1983–87). These women were basically narrative objects who almost completely depended and relied upon male partners and bosses to do the actual protecting—hence perpetuating assumptions for feminist critics about the problem that male partners pose for independent fighting females in the first place.

Instead of merely capitalizing on assumptions of women's vulnerability by underemphasizing their empowerment or capitalizing on assumptions of women's strength and independence by overemphasizing her empowerment, FFF storylines reflect the woman character's complex, contradictory identity. Of course, in the end, the woman is victorious. More than that, she triumphs over patriarchal enemies and directs her power at the males who perpetrate sexist acts against women, contributing to the on-screen threat of what Halberstam calls "imagined violence"—a "fantasy of unsanctioned eruptions of aggression from the wrong people, of the wrong skin, the wrong sexuality, the wrong gender" who are usually on the receiving end of the aggression (263). Positioning men, in particular white men who attempt to dominate and victimize, on the receiving end of women's violence thus "transforms the symbolic function of the feminine within popular narratives and simultaneously challenges the hegemonic insistence upping the linking of might and right under the sign of masculinity" (251). The FFF might be a victim herself, but that doesn't mean she won't arm herself and fight back, and the more images of her doing so throughout mass media, the more "productive fear" (259) her character generates in audience members who do or could identify with the perpetrators. The goal of such a fantasy is to create a kind of "think twice" for those who would take power by force.

While the representation of the FFF's victory—often accomplished alone—is compelling and necessary, it is not without its problems. Namely, it may be part of a trend of naturalizing women's susceptibility in such a way that a survivor identity becomes inextricable from expressions of empowerment. In other words, the proof of her strength can only be assured by what she must overcome to express it. Such themes can be considered a problem in that they redirect focus away from changing society (to remove the obstacles) to simply encouraging individual women to act on their own (to overcome those obstacles).

From the perspective of this study, naturalizing women's susceptibility is not as important a concern when one considers the transgressive assertion that a woman's strength and independence can work in concert with her vulnerability and limited agency in an American society where male political and economic dominance remains the reality and a primary cultural narrative. In fact, it may be a necessary step toward the sex parity that many feminists pursue because it constructs a female identity that avoids the trap of either/or thinking: either a woman is vulnerable and therefore weak, or she is strong and therefore invulnerable. Many women struggle to avoid this kind of trap when thinking about their own lives and experiences, in which they have occupied the positions of both the victim and the agent.

Psychologist Lynn M. Phillips interrogates these struggles in the book *Flirting with Danger*. Her inspiration for the study came from watching her female students stumble along the fine line between pleasure and danger, agency and victimization, as they tried to understand their own identity and experiences as women in a postfeminist era. Using research and a variety of interviews with a diverse group of young women who were around their 20s in the 1990s, Phillips characterizes a tendency in young women to refuse to see themselves as weak or as casualties of a sexist system or abusive male behavior; even after a rape, they insist on their agency. These young women are able and willing to recognize when other women have been victimized by abuse, but when it comes to them, they downplay the trauma or overemphasize their responsibility for what happened and thus avoid claiming their own victimization. Phillips believes this cognitive dissonance occurs because "[s]educed by the excitement of 'straddling those fine lines' and 'playing around the edge,' young women may enter into situations that put them at risk, thinking, erroneously, that they have the ultimate power over men" (9). When the risk proves real, the girls blame themselves rather than the perpetrator. However, the way they blame themselves is key: they do not claim that they were too weak to do anything but rather that it was their responsibility to know better, thus claiming that they did not take the proper advantage of their agency, their ability to choose.

A character like the FFF can certainly be seen as contributing to this belief that young women may have the ultimate power—after all, each one ultimately does succeed in taking down the villain. However, the shows are very clear about where the blame goes—either deviant men or men exhibiting toxic gender stereotypes about masculinity, both of which express in terms of dominating values and behaviors that are the source of the obstacles the FFF faces. Again, we must return to problematic hetero-relations as integral to the FFF's function as the strong, independent woman archetype in that these relations continue to be a source of conflict for women. Even when such relationships do not endanger women physically, they can endanger them emotionally. Psychotherapist Leslie C. Bell notes another version of young women's cognitive dissonance that occurs because they cannot reconcile their independent identities with the dependent positions that either physical/sexual or emotional/relational connections require.

While Bell's book *Hard to Get* doesn't focus on women's victimization as a primary issue as Phillips does, she encounters it as an unexpected result of the "paradox of sexual freedom" that interferes with women's sexual and/or relationship satisfaction. Bell believes their dissatisfaction is a result of the fact that "twenty-something women contend with a societal-level split between independence and vulnerability, with vulnerability as the denigrated category. This split holds that independence, safety, and control are valuable and important to maintain at all costs, and that anything infringing on this radical independence is to be avoided:"—including acknowledging any personal identity that implies they are dependent and have needs, or any experience that implies they aren't in control, experiences in which they are being manipulated or in which they might be in danger (172). From Bell's perspective, these women cannot achieve an integrated identity because they can't embrace both their strengths and their vulnerabilities. They can only be one or the other: independent or dependent, self-reliant or needy, sexually desiring, assertive, and emotionally closed or sexually passive and emotionally vulnerable. An unanticipated result of this split is the same contradictory mental state Phillips notes, in which the women Bell interviews often don't recognize their experiences as abuse or realize it only later, after further reflection or prompting from Bell (55, 98), even though

25 percent of the women interviewed described situations of rape or abuse (182).

The phenomenon Bell and Phillips note in the cognitive dissonance of the women they interview clearly indicates a victim/agent divide in women's expectations about a strong, independent woman identity. Phillips concludes that young women's misapprehension of their power and their culpability is a result of their having grown up with mixed messages about sexuality, agency, and victimization, and about their relationships with men. They have difficulty navigating these mixed messages because they lack the insights about women's problematic status that feminists often have. She explains, "Whereas feminist scholars may speak of male domination and women's victimization as rather obvious phenomena, younger women, raised to believe in their own independence, invulnerability, and sexual entitlement, may not so readily embrace such concepts, even as they are raped, harassed, and battered by men" (10–11).[27] Again, while Bell is more focused on women's embracing of their desires in open ways than on understanding how women are victimized, she also notes young women "lack guidance." She notes that they "could benefit from additional help to develop productive strategies"—to negotiate the expectations to "be radically independent" (174) without neglecting their vulnerabilities and needs. Such guidance, Bell maintains, would help them reconcile their conflicting identities and desires (171); cultural images and examples, Bell notes, don't provide this guidance. Essentially, these young girls don't have the tools to reconcile lingering oppressive gender ideologies that lead to the victimization they experience with the agency they are expected to assert. This creates a psychological conflict and a disjunction between their identity and their reality.

Both authors blame mixed messages in the media that idealize women's agency, messages that sell them unproblematic models of women's power, while simultaneously vilifying the victim position and promoting a fear of appearing weak or passive. Peggy Orenstein believes such models promote an "empowerment mystique" that suggests an "amorphous, untethered huzzah of 'Go, team woman!'" Orenstein rightly believes the empowerment mystique capitalizes on young women's desires to see themselves as strong or, more importantly, not to see themselves as weak. This would support Bell and Phillips' assertions that when young women do experience victimization, it becomes shameful to them because they don't know how to merge the two.

The FFF narrative, while problematic because of mixed messages about her, does at least offer an alternative that can be seen to combat the victim/agent divide by constructing the woman-as-survivor identity. The character can still be celebrated on many levels because she's the hero: she takes down the villain(s). That appeal is clear. However, she also appeals because she faces and overcomes male domination in a way that allows her to embody feminist-friendly femininity, to eradicate the divide. Even more so, the FFF appeals to us as an often emotionally unstable or imperfect woman who still has enough reserves of strength to do the work required of her and to seek to right the wrongs done against others. We can't underestimate the power of seeing a mess of a woman—one who struggles with work-life balance, suffers emotionally from her trauma, or even strains just not to eat the tempting donut—be a hero. Through these appeals, the FFF both reflects and constructs a complex, non-dualistic identity that coordinates with what some critics identify as progressive possibilities lurking within the ambiguous positions that female characters might inhabit. Douglas refers to the ambiguity arising from contradictory female experience as both "what it means to be an American woman" and "what it means to be a feminist" (*Enlightened* 20).[28] In this way, the FFF coordinates with what other critics identify as progressive possibilities lurking within the ambiguous positions that female characters might inhabit, like those texts Stéphanie Genz identifies that address the "postfeminist woman" (PFW) or that Bell refers to as the "Desiring Woman" psychological ideal.

For Genz, the "postfeminist woman"

> inhabits a nondualistic space that holds together these varied and often oppositional stances and thus, she provides multiple opportunities for female identification. The PFW wants to "have it all" as she refuses to dichotomize and choose between her public and private, feminist and feminine identities. She rearticulates and blurs the binary distinctions between feminism and femininity, between professionalism and domesticity, refuting monolithic and homogeneous definitions of postfeminist subjectivity ["Singled Out" 98].

For Bell, the "Desiring Woman" reconciles the split between independence and dependence that causes conflicts for young women because "being a Desiring Woman also involves tolerating vulnerability, uncertainty, and lack of control that inevitably come with desire." Bell writes, "Getting what we want from sex and relationships requires accepting and tolerating seemingly contradictory parts of ourselves" (173).

Like the "postfeminist woman" and the "Desiring Woman," the woman-as-survivor identity doesn't reject ideals of the strong, independent woman. It does, however, attempt to eradicate the mystique surrounding that empowerment, the diffuse pro-woman ideal that leaves little room for the realities of external oppression and internal struggles many women face. The survivor identity ultimately supersedes, but does not erase, the victimization and its effects on the hero. Also, removing narrow conceptions of what it takes to be a victim or a hero leaves more room for agency, for not disparaging the woman who takes risks, who makes herself vulnerable, and thus, seems the perfect way to categorize the FFF. In other words, there is little mistaking that these women characters are susceptible to being a victim—no matter how strong they are and no matter whether or not they have put themselves in a position to be victimized—and our sympathy and hopes still lie with them. Finally, by asserting ways that men can and should help women survive, through the representation of nurturing hetero-intimacies[29] as well as more egalitarian hetero-partnerships that question more traditional heteronormative constructions of masculinity, the FFF storyline removes the problem of emphasizing individual responsibility and action in the fight against inequality. Even when the FFF doesn't end up achieving successful hetero-intimacy, she still presents an identity that encourages the audience to accept and "understand that the contradictions in women's stories do not cancel each other out but rather reveal the intricate textures and the nuances of women's hetero-relational lives" (Phillips 32). These are the kind of nuances that remind us that while the heteronorm in 21st-century America continues to dominate representations of intimacy and romance, the tenets of that norm are breaking down in certain representations.

Five

Women Leaders and the Men Who Love Them

This study has explored mass media depictions of three new female identities enacted by different fighting females who embody a "strong, independent woman" archetype: the love-buddy, the love-warrior, and the survivor. Each of these identities emerges from a narrative that negotiates tensions for women between intimacy and autonomy by representing and addressing the empowered protagonist's heterosexual relationship successes and failures. In these popular-culture narratives, we can find, on the one hand, an optimistic "fantasy" about the possibilities of love relationships in which female strength and independence co-exist with intimacy and male support, as in *Mr. and Mrs. Smith* or *Castle* and *Bones*. On the other hand, there remains space for some continuing, very realistic worries about the threats posed by hetero-relations based on patriarchal gender imbalances and old patterns of dependency and domination, as seen in the fraught fighting female narratives, like *Alias* and the Nikita stories.

Still, certain fighting female romance narratives expand representations of femininity. Being tough, autonomous, intelligent, aggressive, and rational is now more compatible with being vulnerable, emotional, and interdependent, at least in some arenas of popular culture. We see this expansion most clearly in characters that can be violent protectors—thus transgressing typical gender boundaries—but also lovers, wives, and mothers. Such characters promote the idea that women can liberate themselves—from would-be enemies and obstacles—but they can also be liberated through egalitarian intimacies that enact feminist-friendly romance. However, some fighting female romance narratives have also helped expand representations of masculinity. Female heroes prove more and more that they don't need men to protect or save them. For any feminist-friendly romance fantasy to work, the men who love them must prove they can be compatible with such fierce, powerful, and unafraid agents.

To some extent, male characters in fighting female narratives have been analyzed in each chapter. Chapters Two and Three detail aspects of the love-buddy and love-warrior male co-leads who enhance (or degrade) evidence of the fighting female's empowerment. Many, though not all, of the examples analyzed assert a sensitive, enlightened male partner who can work in concert with a strong, independent female. The previous chapter on fraught fighting females explored the construction of the male-as-enemy but also briefly addressed how the redemptive parallel narrative tactic allows for a vulnerable male partner to emerge as a new masculine position that is compatible with the woman-as-survivor hero.

This chapter looks at another male role that occurs more frequently in 21st-century fighting female narratives—the accompanying man—and that indicates more progressive alternatives for hetero-intimacies that now range from platonic to romantic. The chapter continues by linking these alternative roles to an emerging new female identity of the young woman as leader and concludes by analyzing the fantasy of romance and leadership.

The Times Are Changing and So Are Men

> *"If they keep up the sexism thing, it will get old."*—sieglinde, 2011

In 2011, NBC created an American reboot of *Prime Suspect*. Like her British counterpart, Detective Jane Timoney, played by the critically lauded Maria Bello, must deal with the sexist and exclusionist views of "the beef trust" (the name the men in the squad give themselves) in the New York City homicide squad. Also, like Tennison, Timoney is aggressive and comfortable asserting herself when she's treated unfairly, and she's actually more violent than Tennison, running after and tackling perps and more frequently wielding her gun. Unlike DCI Tennison, Timoney has a much more solid home life.

In the pilot, which opens with Timoney on the phone with her boyfriend, Matt Webb (Kenny Johnson), we learn that the most difficult adjustment she has with her relationship is childproofing their home for visits from Matt's son from a past marriage. At the end of the episode, when Timoney again faces acrimony and rejection from the chauvinistic male squad, she returns home and cries in Matt's arms as he comforts her. In later episodes, when Timoney has to cancel plans with Matt for work, he never complains. He simply tells her to "be safe" and that he loves her (01.13). He's even happy to buy her a "big gun" for Christmas with new income he earns from a new construction job (01.10). Overall, Timoney's relationship with Matt is mundane and sits comfortably on the margins of her story. They play cards at home with Timoney's father and Matt's son, Matt makes breakfast for her, and they fool around from time to time. He's not in the crime-fighting business. He's not a tough guy. He's just a man who loves his son and his kick-ass girlfriend. Matt's a clear contrast to Tom, the boyfriend who can't handle Tennison's dedication to work and resents when she cancels plans.

While the developers and writers of the reboot decided to maintain the original atmosphere of good-old-boy misogyny, they created a nice, sensitive, supportive love interest for her, one who can stand by her, one the original Jane never found. These choices indicate the difficulty of characterizing male identity in a postfeminist era in which those identities are expanding along with women's identities. Essentially, the show seems to straddle two eras uneasily: one in which men could more easily be imagined as the enemy who stood between women and progress, in which women had to make more personal sacrifices, and one in which men were more enlightened allies who supported and even aided women's progress, in which women could have it all.

Audience Pleas for Nuance

Numerous critics and audience members found the sexism problematic in the American version—far too explicit for a modern story about a woman cop. Writing for *The New York Post,* Linda Stasi notes, "Twenty years ago, when the original debuted, police departments were sexism central, and, as such, the idea of a woman rising to the top was riveting. [...] But recreating that only-boys-allowed premise in NYC in 2011 is about 15 years too late." Viewer NormStansfield is less generous in his critique. He predicts, "The horsesh*t [sic] narrative about misogynistic male cops discriminating against the lone woman in their midst" would "doom" the show. Echoing other viewers who felt the sexism wasn't appropriate for 2011, NormStansfield continues, "Sorry, but this is neither the 50s, nor downtown Kabul. It's just impossible for anyone living and working in the US today to buy into that premise."

Twenty years ago, the original *Prime Suspect* became a hit with both British and American audiences in part because of the way it addressed institutional sexism. As noted in the previous chapter, the sexism was integral to the show's origins, based on creator and writer Linda La Plante's desire to showcase the very real struggles women detectives faced as an extremely marginalized minority in the London police force. This point was mentioned specifically in major reviews, like those by John J. O'Connor (he mentions it in three reviews between 1992 and 1994) and William Grimes in 1993 in *The New York Times* television section. Grimes points out that the "sexual double standard [...] has struck a chord with women in the audience" and quotes Mirren as saying, "All the women I've talked to say, 'I can't believe how accurate this is as a description of what I face in my professional life.'"

Now, even viewers with feminist perspectives who know that such misogyny exists thought the sexism in the reboot was too much, like Fake TV Critic, who claims "the overt and exaggerated misogyny Timoney faces is borderline offensive" because it feels so "dated" and "unbelievable." It turns out that NormStansfield's prediction, that the pilot doomed the new version, might have had merit, as it was canceled after 13 episodes (and predicted to do so a mere three weeks after the pilot). Writer Melissa Silverstein, who was sorry to see the show go, explains it all ties back to the sexism:

> The problem with the show started at the pilot. Remember the first *Prime Suspect* took place in 1991. That's 20 years ago. What else happened 20 years ago? Anita Hill. Sexual harassment, while happening all over the place, was given a name and a face by Ms. Hill and when we saw how Mirren's Jane Tennison was treated by her male colleagues we got it. But in 2011 too much time had passed and the aggressive male behavior in the pilot towards Maria Bello who played the American version, Jane Timoney just didn't work. It was too much. Way too over the top.

The discomfort with the sexism in the most recent version could easily be explained as evidence that postfeminist American culture mistakenly subscribes to the assumption that women are liberated, for good or bad, and sexism has ended. And that is certainly the case for some groups. But there's more to the criticisms lobbied by critics and viewers. The problem many had with the misogyny wasn't so much that it was present as much as that it was heavy-handed, not subtle enough. Twenty years ago, showing a woman dealing with a bunch of sexist blowhards felt more realistic, but today, audiences have a harder time accepting the in-your-face woman-hating. *The New York Times* reviewer Alessandra Stanley nails the difference with her point, "[T]he overt hostility and crude sexism Jane encounters from her all-male squad seem a little dated. Today's finest may still harbor reservations about women on the force, but if so, they have been sensitivity-trained to hide it better." With exceptions, like NormStansfield, there are still viewers and critics who accept that misogyny continues to exist. Still, in a popular culture with at least forty years of feminist awareness behind it, it's more subtle, pernicious, and often harder to pinpoint. Or else, evidence of sexism is more irreverent and taken less seriously these days, a point that Douglas makes in *Enlightened Sexism*: the cushion of women's "progress because of feminism" makes evidence of sexism amusing, non-threatening (9). The gritty depiction the 2011 *Prime Suspect* affords it just doesn't fit.

Referring back to *The Closer*, which was inspired in some part by *Prime Suspect*, and which was addressed in the previous chapter, will further demonstrate the contrast. Deputy Chief Brenda Leigh Johnson encountered sexism when she was appointed to head the new Major Crimes Division of the LAPD. However, the only explicit sexists were two detectives who were over sixty (Flynn and Provenza), and they were regularly mocked by the narrative for their outdated views. No one paid any heed to their openly sexist antics or chauvinist views. The rest of the sexism—the resistance to her authority and feminine demeanor—was implicit. Brenda also had male allies from the beginning, her superior officer, the Assistant Chief who hired her and stood by her, and an old connection from the FBI, who eventually became her husband. Additionally, there was another woman in the squad. Essentially, *The Closer* offered what the new *Prime Suspect* didn't: a more nuanced vision of the workplace and alternative male identities that didn't rely on stereotypical masculinity. A show like *The Closer* indicates the negotiation the fighting female fantasy must make between traditional and newly emerging forms of masculinity that combine more elements of support, nurturing, and interdependence. This is what made *The Closer* seem less disjointed than the 2011 *Prime Suspect*, more of a reflection of the shades of change between the two eras rather than a mashing of them.

Still, the more recent *Prime Suspect* does reflect a noteworthy trend in the way Matt's character was constructed as an accompanying male love interest for a female hero, a trend that is worth analyzing in a study on the relationship between romance and female empowerment in the mass media. Just as popular representations of female identity adjust for expectations of the empowered woman of today, thereby presenting a more complex version of femininity that includes strength and independence, so have representations of men adjusted to offer alternatives of ideal male behaviors and values that fit well with progressive femininities. We can see the movement toward this not only when we compare characters like Tom from the original *Prime Suspect* and the considerably more liberated Matt in the reboot but also when we compare the men in both shows with those in *The Closer*. As a fraught fighting female narrative, *The Closer* certainly kept female victimization at the hands of men at the forefront. However, it also gives more credit to the male allies and offers several varied male roles in ways that reflect more common representations of alternative masculinity in 21st-century fighting female narratives.

The Closer provides a suitable example of the emerging progressive masculinities not only through their variety but also through the role her love interest plays. At times, Special Agent Fritz Howard (Jon Tenney) works as a crime-fighting sidekick when Brenda needs his FBI expertise or connections, but throughout, he generally remains on the margins of the story, often appearing only briefly and often at home, in support of her role as the hero. The key word here is *support*, and it is what sets him and his characterization of masculinity apart from the partner narratives for love-buddy and romaction fighting females. Like John Smith from *Mr. and Mrs. Smith* or Seeley Booth from *Bones*, Fritz is definitely an enlightened male, but unlike them, he is only one part of the hero's story. He gives depth to Brenda's character because he is part of her personal life, but the story could still go on without him. Such male characters are rare in the mass media. In *Cagney & Lacey*, Harvey Lacey (John Karlen) did the same for Mary Beth—when he was unemployed, he was the main caretaker of the children and home. He cooked and cleaned. He listened to her and gave her advice. But Harvey also suffered from insecurities about his masculinities, which the series made clear in the second episode when he was embarrassed that his wife stood up against a bullying male neighbor. Additionally, Harvey fretted about his abilities as a provider for the family, a recurrent theme throughout the show. Still, Harvey was arguably the first of his kind in a cop show or any fighting female narrative for that matter. That was the 1980s, though, and *Cagney & Lacey* tread a very delicate line, attempting to empower women without appearing to emasculate men.

Fritz is like Harvey, only without the insecurities. He is confident, tough, and capable, but he is also nurturing and vulnerable. He characterizes the ideal stand-by-your-woman man, the kind of supportive partner that CEOs like Sheryl Sandberg and Ursula Burns laud when they talk about how their husbands make it possible for them to do what they do, as mentioned in Chapter Two. Fritz respects Brenda's love for her job. Because of this, he exhibits impressive amounts of patience when her work interferes with their relationship as they progress from dating to, eventually, marriage. For example, in "Show Yourself" (01.04), Fritz and Brenda are supposed to go to dinner, but she convinces him to follow a suspect while she hides in the back seat and tells him what to do. In the next episode, Brenda forgets to cancel their date, but instead of fighting, he takes the news with little friction, and they end up kissing before she heads back to work. She cancels another date with him a few episodes later because she has to work (01.08), and instead of using basketball tickets he has, he decides to wait, pick up Brenda's cat from the vet, and bring her dinner at home. Of course, this is because Fritz is also a professional with his own responsibilities; his ability to accept her behavior is logical because he can see it in terms of his own experiences. The best indicator of this understanding occurs in the days leading up to their wedding in "Double Blind" (04.15). Fritz must work on a big case—he has to run off, he can't make it home for dinner, and he needs Brenda to take care of his visiting sister (as he once did with Brenda's mother). Brenda is happy about this because she can focus on a new murder investigation. As his sister says while officiating the ceremony at the end of the episode, Fritz "never gives up on the people he loves," and Brenda "never gives up on anything." Thus, they are made for each other. Immediately following the ceremony, Fritz has to run back to work, so Brenda does, too.

Fritz not only respects Brenda's work life but also accepts her authority in her position and sometimes lets it dictate his behavior as a professional. Several times he finds information for her under the radar that helps her cases, even though it could get him in trouble, because he wants to help her seek justice. He never complains that her work gets in the way of their relationship—in fact, he explicitly refuses to let it do so. On one of the first cases where they are actually assigned to work together, "L.A. Woman" (01.11), they clash over the case because Brenda wants a woman from Iran to end up in jail for murdering her husband—but the FBI wants to give the woman to the CIA and send her to Iran as an asset, and Fritz has to comply. As the episode ends, Brenda attempts to evade Fritz's touch because she's mad at him. He grabs her coat and hands it to her while saying, "You know what would make me upset? Is if this whole working together thing screwed up our whole other thing." She takes the coat and says, "Fine, let's go to dinner." He is, in a sense, the one in charge of nurturing the relationship, the emotional work, which has been a trend with several of the male characters included in this study.

All through the series, Fritz not only shows patience and a willingness to support her position as a very busy deputy chief but also solidly affirms his commitment to her and his desire for the relationship to progress. He is the one to suggest they move in together (02.01). He is also the one who helps her realize that she needs to extricate herself completely from her past relationship with Pope (which happened before the show began). Sure, Fritz is jealous and bothered by her "lack of clarity" (02.12), but he also wants *her* to know where she stands since she seems to be waffling, and he says as much when he tells her she needs to clarify. He ends up sleeping on the couch that night, and she both talks to Pope and gets rid of memorabilia from their relationship. She leaves a note for Fritz that says, "I LOVE YOU. PS, Can you cancel my credit cards for me today?" (She had lost her purse.) She responds to his need, showing that she respects his request; at the same time, she asserts something that she needs. This action reminds us that she can rely on his assistance outside of work so she can do her work. This note exemplifies just how much their relationship exists outside of traditional relationship norms, in which Fritz occupies a position that verges into realms of traditional femininity, as much as Brenda's verges into realms of traditional masculinity. That's not to say that they switch positions—instead, they both blend. They are both made for each other—they are both the same and different.

This theme crops up in a few characters within each fighting female identity that's been outlined, but it's necessary to remember that Fritz is a supporting character, not a co-star. There are even episodes where he is barely apparent. One of the most useful elements of analyzing the supplementary male love interest identity in the fighting female romance narratives is that it shows how much the feminist-friendly love fantasy relies on both men and women to more fluidly inhabit roles and transgress gender boundaries—that that is the basis of a healthy intimacy where female empowerment can blossom. That certainly promotes an optimistic view for the possibilities of liberated romance, a view that *Woman of the Year* (1942), *Adam's Rib* (1949), and other films of the late 1930s and early 1940s depicted, only without a fighting female protagonist. In other words, the attempts at depicting a liberated romance are not entirely new. Today's examples reconfigure an ideal that the 1950s and 1960s domestic romances swept away. Only now, the liberated romance less frequently shows the male protagonist developing a progressive consciousness to accommodate the woman's empowerment and the attendant role upheavals. His acceptance is usually fully intact.

Signs of Progress

The existence and success of a show like *The Closer*—which was in its sixth season when the American *Prime Suspect* premiered—and other crime-fighting narratives with women at the helm may have even contributed to some people's perceptions that men and women have come too far in this postfeminist era to return to stark depictions of misogyny. In general, fighting female romance narratives have had a major impact on the development of male identities. Abele makes a related assertion about male identities changing in American action films, which was dealt with in Chapter Three. In the 1970s, when crime-fighting shows like *McMillan & Wife* or *Hart to Hart* emerged, the wife sidekick oriented around her husband, who did all of the action and usually ended up having to save the wife. These were the kinds of stories that prompted the outrage of feminist-oriented critics. When the female character started to get in on the action, writers had to conceive of male identities that would fit the change. It's one thing simply to turn all of the male characters into ineffectual wimps or bad guys, or have the female hero fight women, or keep the hero's identity a secret, as happened for lone-wolf fighting females like Wonder Woman, the Bionic Woman, Lt. Ripley, Foxy Brown, and Cleopatra Jones. In those days, the woman's strength and independence, her physical power and ability to take care of herself, were more generally accepted as emasculating behavior. Her hetero-relations compensated for that. It's another thing entirely to have a male character who could be secondary to the female hero, either in crime-fighting skills or in terms of being only part of her personal, and not her professional, life. The change indicates that in certain constructions, and for some audiences, at least, female power doesn't have to be developed at the cost of male power.

Thanks to early supportive male characters like Remington Steele, David Addison, and Harvey Lacey, it's now possible to imagine Fritz Howard and Rick Castle and Chuck Bartowski, rakishly attractive fellows with skills of their own and enough security and enlightenment to offer believable male love interests. The best offer balance and parity with their fighting female and manage to perform an inclusive masculinity that allows them to be more dependent than traditional masculinity maintains while still being portrayed as desirable romance partners (much as today's fighting females are portrayed as desirable, not in spite of but often because of characteristics that transgress stereotypical gender boundaries). Moreover, the progression of enlightened male love interests during the last forty years has even helped contribute to hetero-relations in fighting female narratives that don't revolve around romance with the hero but that function nonetheless to support her position.

The number of supporting male cast members who are friends and confidantes of the hero has only risen over the last decade: Kate Beckett has Espo and Ryan in *Castle*; Temperance Brennan has Jack Hodgins (T.J. Thyne) and Sweets in *Bones*, as well as other male squints who come and go throughout the series. Sarah Walker has John Casey and Morgan Grimes in *Chuck*; Sydney Bristow in *Alias* has Will Tippin (Bradley Cooper), Marshall Flinkman (Kevin Weisman), Eric Weiss (Greg Grunberg), and Marcus Dixon (Carl Lumbly). Nikita (in the 2010 version) has Seymour Birkhoff (Aaron Stanford), Owen Elliot (Devon Sawa), and Ryan Fletcher (Noah Bean). Jessica Jones has Malcolm Ducasse, Detective Costa, and Erik, as well as Luke Cage (Mike Colter).

The rise of these male characters comes not at the expense of female characters, who have also actually increased over the last few years in particular, as evidenced in each of the aforementioned series. Now, there are even platonic pairings of men with fighting females in shows not previously addressed, as in *Continuum, Covert Affairs, Rizzoli & Isles, Orphan Black, Elementary, Sleepy Hollow, Grimm* (2011–17), *Quantico* (2013–15), *Agents of S.H.I.E.L.D., Agent Carter, The Flash, Arrow,* and *The Mysteries of Laura* (2014–16).

Some of these shows have women in the lead, some have men, and some have co-leads. However, they all exhibit more varied male identities. Additionally, there are more shows in which male characters work under women who are in charge as the bosses or high-ranking officers. Over the course of *Castle*, Beckett becomes captain of her own precinct. Brenda Leigh Johnson is the deputy chief of the Major Crimes Division. In *Major Crimes* (2012–18), the series that picked up where *The Closer* left off in 2012, Captain Sharon Raydor (Mary McDonnell) runs the division and is the main character.

The impact of this change—the envisioning of a woman as a leader with power over men as a desirable character who may not always have romance in her life (like Captain Raydor) but who isn't portrayed as lacking or lonely because of it—cannot be emphasized enough. The presence of this character proves that there are pockets of popular culture that have truly evolved in terms of plausible authoritative female identities and male identities that can not only co-exist with female power but can also heed that power. There may be problematic aspects, even to the most enlightened seeming female identity or to the relationships that sustain that identity. Still, the narratives provide much to look forward to, not only for imagining the empowered female on-screen but also for envisioning empowering males through new roles and new relational possibilities that don't subject them to traditional masculine ideals.

Future Femininities

One of the elements that contributed, in part, to some of the audience resistance to the American *Prime Suspect* remake is that it didn't reflect the kind of feminist-friendly fantasy contemporary audiences can find believable (whether or not their reasoning about the current realities of sexism coheres with reality). Many people expect more nuanced male identities because the ideas some people have about who men are, what men can be, have changed as their ideas of women have changed.

Another part of the problem is that there is an entirely new generation of viewers, young women and men who were just being born around the time the original *Prime Suspect* premiered in 1991. Some of us who were children or teens in the 1970s and early 1980s grew up along with the fighting female character, which helped certain areas of popular culture subscribe to notions of empowered women and non-traditional hetero-relations. It makes sense that we would be more likely to seek feminist-friendly fantasies that are in keeping with that, fantasies that negotiate the difficulties of being a female-bodied person in a system that has long excluded us—and we saw the proof of women's lack of presence or the lack of their strength and independence. The youngsters of the late 1980s and early 1990s grew into a popular culture in which the fighting female had been around for a while. Her enactments of empowered female identities weren't so new, and her feminist-friendly romance fantasies were not necessarily the norm, but they at least existed.

The feminist-friendly fantasy of the past doesn't necessarily appeal to new viewers, at least not in the same way or for the same reasons. They grew up with Buffy the Vampire Slayer, Xena the Warrior Princess, Mulan, the PowerPuff Girls, and Veronica Mars. They had Riot Grrrls and Spice Girls and Girl Power; they were a generation that matured with more mothers working outside the home than ever before. By the time they became aware of politics and the economy, they had Hillary Clinton, Condoleezza Rice, Michelle Obama, and the Notorious RBG (Ruth Bader Ginsburg) as role models of socially empowered women not to mention athletes Serena and Venus Williams and now Megan Rapinoe, Nancy Kerrigan, and Sheryl Swoopes, who showed how women could be physically powerful as well. The trend only continues in the 21st century, as more female athletes, politicians, CEOs, and celebrities provide more surface evidence that women have "come a long way, baby."

Additionally, new viewers see less evidence of overt sexism and the oppression of women in general; the sexism they grew up with was more "enlightened," to use Susan Douglas' term. It was playful, done with a knowing wink that implied, "We know better now, so let's have fun with it." So, the sexist, evil preacher who was one of Buffy's final adversaries in the show's last season was comically misogynistic, and his sexism was far more harmless than his demonic intentions.

More importantly, children of the 1990s grew up in an era when power feminism became popularized. Authors like Naomi Wolf, Camille Paglia, and Christina Hoff Sommers promoted the idea that women were in and of themselves empowered and capable of overcoming any obstacle on their own merit—that if women were being subjugated, it was because they had the wrong attitude or made the wrong choices. These women eschewed characterizing women as victims in favor of viewing women as masters of their own destinies, and they had more readily available examples of women in power (politically, economically, and socially) to prove their point than ever before. Critics like these no longer claimed female sex as a liability in a patriarchal culture; instead, they championed it as a source of power over men. Unfortunately, they tended to do so at the expense of the victim, who could now be blamed for not owning her strength, and also for "victim feminism," as Hoff Summers called it, which focused on women's victimization as a basis for change. These problematic influences helped usher in a new wave of the postfeminist era. No longer simply a historical marker designating a period following the widespread awareness of the feminist movement and its more public issues, the term *postfeminist* began to apply both to an attitude that takes feminist gains for granted and an idea that feminism has accomplished what it set out to do—give women an equal chance.

The problems that this "postfeminist sensibility," to use Rosalind Gill's terminology, poses aside, it's important to understand that young people who grew up with these role models took their influences to heart. They were encouraged to embrace progressive or even not-so-progressive ideas about female power and often see women's strength and independence as characteristics that are consistent with their femininity. It's not necessarily a feminist-informed femininity for them, as it might seem for older audiences, but just femininity, which has had the result of making the feminist versus feminine opposition less relevant to discussions of contemporary popular culture.

Even young people who would not describe themselves as feminists or necessarily subscribe to feminist gender critiques would find the kind of useless damsel-in-distress position of pseudo-empowered characters like Jennifer Hart from *Hart to Hart* laughable. Many young viewers have been informed by and are drawn to different versions of female power. They seek stories and characters who reflect this strength and independence in ways that speak to their expectations as audience members, for whom the allure of the fighting female, and her representation of female empowerment, is a given. They are, in a sense, a culture primed to be at least feminist allies' but at best future feminists.

After all, for the first time in a long time, and maybe thanks to social media campaigns like #MeToo, more young women are identifying openly as feminists. Writing for *Glamour* magazine, Suzannah Weiss reports that based on a 2,000-person survey, "A full 69 percent of British girls ages 13 to 18 answered 'yes' to the question 'Would you personally define as a feminist?'" A 2016 report from *The Washington Post* and the The Kaiser Family Foundation poll shows "63 percent of women ages 18 to 34 said they considered themselves feminists." And, of course, there are the polls from previous years that have repeatedly shown that even when young women don't call themselves *feminist*, they embrace the principles associated with the term. We can't discount their views, even if we continue to ensure that this view doesn't overshadow women's continued experience of oppression in America and around the globe.

All of these changes surrounding popular culture have made it possible to envision a new empowered female identity: the young woman leader. This girl character can be classified as a young fighting female, a fledgling hero who ranges from teen to college age. She reflects the extent to which the strong, independent woman archetype has become so entrenched in the mass media that even girl characters are depicted as capable of saving themselves and protecting others, including adults. The woman leader narratives introduce girls with great gifts and destinies, and they take us through her journey not only toward accepting the responsibilities that come with being strong and independent but also acting on those responsibilities to make the world a better place.

The New Stories

In 1997, Buffy Summers (Sarah Michelle Gellar), a young blond cheerleader who wielded a mean roundhouse and had a knack for killing vampires and demons, became the first teenage girl to kick some serious ass on the small screen.[1] Not long after the series began, *Buffy the Vampire Slayer (BTVS)* proved a formidable enough hit that it helped The Warner Brothers Television Network, a new venture providing shows for teens and young adults, overcome its ratings struggles and gain a strong foothold on cable programming. Over the next seven seasons, *BTVS* earned a major following with fans of all ages and sexes. It launched one WB spin-off program, *Angel*, comic books, websites, fan fiction, a slew of academic articles, anthologies, and monographs, and even a yearly international conference. Buffy was

Five. Women Leaders and the Men Who Love Them

arguably the first incarnation of the young woman leader—a woman who used her power not only to save the world but also to lead a group of her most trusted allies, men and women, into the fight.

Twenty-one years later, such strong, independent girl characters have only become more popular. Today, there are fairy tale heroines who are reimagined as fighting heroes, leading others to safety and a new, brighter future. Alice Kingsleigh (Mia Wasikowska) in *Alice in Wonderland* (2010) dons armor to fight a dragon and free Underland from the terror inflicted by the pathologically insecure Red Queen and her army. (She fights the Red Queen again in the 2016 sequel *Alice Through the Looking Glass*). Today's Snow White (Kristen Stewart) in *Snow White and the Huntsman* (2012) no longer sits back while her prince fights to save her from evil—she dons her own armor to slay the queen, save her people, and become a benevolent ruler. Female fairy tale villains have gotten rewrites, like the titular character in *Maleficent* (2014, played by Ella Purnell, Isobelle Molloy, and Angelina Jolie), who turns out not to be so evil after all: she actually saves the kingdom and Aurora/Sleeping Beauty (Elle Fanning) from the evil king by fighting his army and restoring order. In the television show *Once Upon a Time* (2011–8), the evil queen makes a similar transformation after a few seasons. Even girls in cartoons are picking up arrows and using magical powers to fight the bad guys, like Anna in *Frozen* (2013) and *Frozen II* (2019)—or Princess Merida in *Brave* (2012), as part of their preparations to become leaders of their people. We also have dystopian revolutionary Beatrice "Tris" Prior (Shailene Woodley), who fights to unite the people of her city by saving them from the tyranny of the militant Erudite faction, in *Divergent* (2014), *Insurgent* (2015), and *Allegiant* (2016).

Last but not least, there's the other dystopian revolutionary Katniss Everdeen (Jennifer Lawrence) from *The Hunger Games* tetralogy (2012–15). This movie franchise is based upon the highly successful novel series by Suzanne Collins. The first three movie installments grossed over a billion dollars; the most recent and final installment opened as number one at the box office and earned, worldwide, over half a billion in less than a month.

The Hunger Games story takes place in the country Panem, which is divided into 12 isolated districts that serve the Capitol. Essentially, the people who live in the Capitol are the wealthy elite who are responsible, apparently, for keeping the peace. One of the ways they do this is by having each of the 12 districts provide a "tribute" in the form of one citizen who will fight to the death in the Hunger Games. The winner goes on to enjoy a modicum of comfort and fame. Katniss Everdeen becomes a tribute, and the movie follows her trials. Katniss is not only a fighter but also a champion, one chosen by the rebels of Panem to lead them into a revolution against the Capitol. She also has to sort out her feelings for two different love interests throughout the stories, Gale Hawthorne (Liam Hemsworth) and Peeta Mellark (Josh Hutcherson).

Katniss and her story are perhaps the most appropriate examples to address in terms of emerging femininities and masculinities in 21st-century fighting female narratives because of her immense popularity. Her character possesses a fluidity that fulfills both a postfeminist sensibility and represents a feminist-friendly empowerment emerging from a postfeminist period. This is why her story has immense cross-generational appeal and why *Catching Fire*, the second *The Hunger Games* movie, was the first blockbuster film with a female lead since *The Exorcist* in 1973 to reach number one for the year it was released (Han). This rest of this chapter will provide an overview of the qualities of empowered female identity that Katniss and other young fighting female leaders exhibit, as well as portrayals of new masculinities in relation to that identity.

Changing the Rules of the Game

In many regards, Katniss embodies the historically postfeminist hero whose strength and independence are assured from the beginning of her story. Jeffrey A. Brown's chapter on "Girl Revolutionaries" makes an outstanding argument about the feminism behind the appeal in *The Hunger Games* and the way that it "models the value of collective action" (179). Katniss is a character that seems refreshingly free of the trappings of any single-gender characteristics but also free from the stereotypical "tomboy" position usually assigned to gender-bending women. She combines a very nurturing, protective, peace-loving attitude with a very bold, calculating, and fierce determination and a deadly aim with her bow and arrow. She has an incredibly serious demeanor, and as the films progress, she smiles less and less frequently. She often acts cold and aloof, but she is very loving to her family, and she feels any loss deeply. She wants nothing more than to protect people, both her family and the innocent civilians caught up in the rebellion against the Capitol [sic] of Panem. Yet, she knows the only way to do that is to fight the enemy, and that fight requires being hard and ready to step up.

The first time we meet Katniss she is comforting her young sister, Primrose "Prim" (Willow Shields), who has awakened from a nightmare. Katniss sings a sweet lullaby to send Prim back to sleep. Then, she gets dressed and heads off to hunt to provide for the family. After Katniss volunteers as tribute to replace her sister in the Hunger Games, she grabs her mother and adamantly tells her she can't "tune out" as she did after Katniss' father died. Katniss seems both cold and angry, afraid and vulnerable as she demands her mother take care of Prim since Katniss has been doing it since his death, as caretaker, protector, and provider.

Katniss is beautiful but utterly unconcerned with her looks or being attractive. She spends the majority of the movies completely covered up and

Five. Women Leaders and the Men Who Love Them 189

wearing no makeup, her hair in a simple braid. When she does dress up, it's only because she's forced to as part of her role in the Hunger Games, and even then, the clothing is generally modest, more decorative and frilly than alluring. She has little interest in being likable or playing a role that doesn't reflect what she feels, but again, when it comes time to improve her audience appeal—whether it's to rally the troops to revolt or gain favor with the viewers of the game—she can comply. Effectively, she shows that she can be and act any way she wants or needs to survive, and her gender identity is never really clear. For the majority of the film franchise, it's difficult even to tell who she is attracted to, as she moves between Gale and Peeta in each film, never fawning or playing coy but rather just being herself, a confused young person trying to figure out who she is and what she wants.

As the hero on whom the fate of Panem rests, Katniss is fiercely autonomous. This plays out in three key ways to reflect a postfeminist fantasy of female empowerment. First, like the fraught fighting female, her autonomy is constrained by her circumstances. Unlike the FFF, she faces the challenge of a larger threat to her existence that cannot be directly related to sex- or gender-based subordination; in a word, these threats are more "universal." In her world, being a woman is not problematic. It's her class. Class has become the new equalizer for fighting females, a problem that doesn't make a female hero stand out *as* a female. She is one of many oppressed people, men and women, old and young, and the enemy is wealth and corruption and divisiveness. In facing the challenge, she still fights inequality. She fights for herself and for her society, and her liberation is the liberation of all men and women from the constraints of their origin.

The second way her autonomy plays into the fantasy is in her self-authorization, an empowerment that emerges as she decides things for herself. She has her own opinions, which are guided by a clear moral compass and are not swayed by others. She has allies who support her, both men and women, but none of them proves an authority over her for long. She kills only to survive or to remove an immediate threat. Even after Peeta is tortured and her sister dies, she never takes a life out of revenge or justice because she cannot act outside of her principles. Additionally, she does not seek validation for her opinions. For example, in the final film installments, *Mockingjay Part 1* and *Part 2*, the rebels, led by self-proclaimed President Coin (Julianne Moore), consistently try to convince Katniss that sacrificing innocent people is part of war, that it's a necessary evil. She refuses to believe this and maintains that the only way to win the war is to show that all of the citizens of Panem, in each of the districts, share a common oppression and must be allies in the fight against the tyranny of President Snow (Donald Sutherland). She defies authority and acts outside of the different systems of rules and regulations that constrain her, both in the games and in the rebellion. At the end of the first film, she's willing to commit suicide rather than kill Peeta and win the game according to Snow's rules. At the end of the second film, she shoots an exploding arrow at the dome surrounding the arena to end the game, again rather than killing her opponents. At the end of the final film, in complete defiance of President Coin's orders, Katniss does not execute President Snow. She executes President Coin, who had proven to be just as power-hungry and manipulative as Snow (Katniss leaves Snow's death to the angry citizens).

Finally, for all of her autonomy, Katniss does not reject alliances and aid. She reflects a strong-willed, completely independent person who, at the same time, learns to recognize that she needs others as much as they need her and that cooperation and alliances can be a source of her power as a fighter and a leader. The way she fights combines caring with justice. The way she maintains her relationships and allows those relationships to help her succeed stands out. Often, the fight becomes a way to bring people together, and they are loyal to her because she is loyal to them. She doesn't believe in sacrificing others, showing it's not her choice to make, though she is willing to sacrifice herself—in true heroic fashion. In the final film, President Coin has a plan that will require, effectively, a suicide mission from the rebels in district two. The leader of this district, Commander Paylor (Patina Miller), balks and says she can't send her people to die, and Katniss agrees. Katniss believes that the lives of all civilians and rebels are equally important, that they are all allies, and that they only need to be enlightened on their common goal.

Her adamant refusal to play the war game and her determination to fight according to her principles is what earns her people's respect and gives her the power she uses to lead them. The very first indication of this occurs after Katniss volunteers to replace Prim in the reaping for the games in film one. As Katniss stands stunned on the stage, the crowd in front of her raises three fingers in salute—a gesture that becomes a signal for the rebellion throughout the series. The tribute also signifies the first act of unity between the districts. The second time we see the gesture is after Katniss tries to save Rue (Amandla Stenberg), a very young girl sent to the games who became Katniss' ally. The people of Rue's district, watching Katniss set flowers next to Rue's body, salute with three fingers, and one of the crowd, presumably Rue's father, attacks a peacekeeper (the Capitol's police), instigating a small riot, the first in the revolution. Ultimately, the community empowers Katniss; partnership with and trust in others help her face down the Capitol. She also empowers others as her influence grows—that's what is so important in her speeches to the districts as she helps the rebels in episodes three and four of the series. In a way, her position as the face and voice of the rebellion signifies her position as an activist for change, a point that Brown emphasizes in his analysis, and her activism, at once personal and public, expresses her empowered position as a young woman leader.

"We saved each other."

Love and intimacy are very important aspects of Katniss's story, as her reason for fighting is not just to save the world but also to save the ones she cares about—she is very much motivated by compassion in her fight. She volunteers for the games to save her sister. She demands a raid on the Capitol to save Peeta and the other players who were left behind when she was saved at the end of the second film. The person she chooses to love ends up being the one who is just as compassionate—Peeta. She chooses him over Gale, the boy she grew up with, the boy who helps take care of her family while she's gone, the boy who stands behind her all the way. Both Peeta and Gale offer remarkable new constructions of masculinity that reflect a shift in male/female power dynamics on-screen. Both characters orient around Katniss' empowered young woman leader in a secondary position. They both enable her leadership and respect her strength as well as her autonomy. They are both capable in their own rights. However, they are quite different in certain telling aspects.

Gale is more like Katniss. He comes on intensely, and he has many strengths—combat, hunting, providing for his family. He is dedicated to his loved ones and wants to protect them. Gale is primed to become a rebel against the Capitol. He makes his rebellious stance known in the first film when he tries to convince Katniss to run away with him to escape the reaping for the Hunger Games. When she rejects his offer to stay with her family, he stays, too. Once war breaks out, he joins the combat as a soldier and proves talented with military strategy. When we first see him in the final film installment, he's planning strategy for a sneak bomb attack against the Capitol—one that Katniss notes would have a very high civilian casualty rate. Gale accepts this, believing effectively that all's fair in war. Here, we see his philosophy diverge from Katniss's in an important way—a point to which I shall return.

Conversely, Peeta is not a fighter or a rebel. In fact, he is by traditional masculine standards emasculated in many ways, rendered weak and dependent. He is the son of bakers who have little faith in him and treat him poorly. In the first film, we see his mother hitting him on the head for burning bread as he looks sad and cowed. After the reaping, he tells Katniss that his parents said District 12 may have its first champion, and they didn't mean him. He may have enough physical strength to throw a 100-pound sack of flour, but his approach to fighting is often to hide and stay back, using his cake decorating skills to camouflage himself to blend into the background. Instead of having the chance to join the rebellion and fight as a soldier, he is taken captive by the Capitol and brainwashed and needs to be rescued. When Katniss sees him after the rescue for the first time at the end of the third movie, he is emaciated and broken. There is little evidence of traditional masculinity in his slight appearance or frightened demeanor. He is clearly a victim. Peeta is also primarily defined by his kindness, his dedication to her, his love of her strength and confidence (he was initially attracted to her in school, when Katniss was the first to raise her hand in class to show off her singing skills). If anything, he thinks she is more capable than he, and he touts her skills often in the first two films. For example, in the first installment, he brags about her ability to kill squirrels, getting an arrow right in the eye each time (a most humane way to kill).

One of the main differences between Peeta and Gale stems not only from Peeta's general lack of violence but also from his refusal to lose his humanity. He shares this hope with Katniss the night before they enter the first Hunger Games, saying he doesn't want to be changed by the games, that he wants to show that they don't "own" him. For Katniss, who struggles to do the same, he offers a positive influence that ultimately allows her to fight with compassion, not give in to her desire for revenge or to place innocent people in danger. It's why she goes to such great lengths to save Peeta over and over. Katniss never has to save Gale—she has nothing she can really offer him the way she can offer her strength and support to Peeta. Peeta is a partner in love and life. Gale is a partner in battle. He eventually loses his humanity to the violence and, as the last film implies, leads to the death of Katniss' sister Prim, as Coin uses the strategy Gale came up with at the beginning of the film to win the rebellion. Hundreds of children lost their lives—a loss that Katniss could never approve of, even if it hadn't also led to her sister's death.

Of course, like all fantasies, there is a flaw. Peeta seems to force the relationship based on his own feelings. In the first movie, he publicizes his crush for her on-screen without telling her in person first. He makes up the story of their impending wedding and baby in the second film. However, there is a real benefit to this, one that could be seen as part of his strategy. Katniss is rightly upset when she learns about his feelings from the television, but for the wrong reasons. She thinks his proclamation makes her "look weak." However, Hamish (Woody Harrelson)—the mentor assigned to Katniss and Peeta to prepare them for the games—realizes it's a good strategy because it makes her "look desirable."

As problematic as this claim is in terms of typical expectations of female desirability—as defined by men—it also highlights how Peeta was trying to make Katniss appear more human, more likable because she needed the favor of the people to get sponsors. It's a turnaround in the world of heroes. The female love interest for the male hero is usually the one who humanizes him, but this time, it's the opposite. Thus, it's possible to read Peeta's move as that of a savvy navigator of human emotions, skilled in manipulating the people, which also aligns him with the kind of male emotional intelligence we saw happening in the love-buddy narratives in Chapter Two. Also, one could read his behavior as an attempt to win the Hunger Games through love. By creating a love story, he made it possible for the Gamemaker to change the rules that would allow two victors instead of one. Love is the one thing he does fight for—not for the rebels, not to save Panem, but to save Katniss. Also, at the end of the last film, he wants her to decide whether she wants to be with him, and he does so by asking whether or not the love she portrays is "real or not real?" By having Katniss choose Peeta, the story makes a statement about desirable masculinity as behaviors that not only support women's strength and independence but also defy masculine privilege and dominant power.

All in all, the postfeminist fantasy exemplified by *The Hunger Games* films is that women can and should become leaders and practice compassionate justice, but they must still negotiate the struggles between the idea that they can be both empowered and oppressed at the same time. It coheres with the fraught fighting female fantasy of the survivor as an empowered position that navigates the dualities that women today face from expectations of strength and independence in an American culture still struggling to imagine female identity outside of the constraints of rigid and traditional notions of femininity. Looking at mass media attempts to navigate this divide is particularly relevant in a period when ideas about female identity are changing, in which increasing awareness of women's authority and ideals regarding women's autonomy are being cultivated by the kind of heroic characters fighting females in general represent. These questions also reflect existential struggles that real women face in coming to terms with experiences that defy their authority and autonomy and with experiences that may remind them of their weaknesses but also demand their strength to overcome those struggles.

A character like the young woman leader Katniss represents can certainly be seen to contribute to the belief that young women can wield power—after all, she helps lead a revolution. Still, she does so within limited circumstances, again, like the fraught fighting female, with one important difference. The fraught fighting female narratives addressed sexism and gender-based violence against women, creating a very distinct sense of the *woman* in dual positions of victim and agent. As demonstrated, the fantasy of overcoming sex oppression might hold more appeal for certain older female audiences aligned with feminist-friendly views because they can remember a time when sexism was much starker and easier to identify. The young woman leader fantasy redirects toward a more "universal" experience with oppression and shows the majority of men and women dealing with the victim/agent position. This fantasy could be more appealing for an audience seeking more of a postfeminist fantasy of empowerment, one that doesn't align with the hero's sex or gender. The story makes it possible to see Katniss as a hero, not necessarily as a woman hero. Thus, the female hero's experience facing institutionalized obstacles (in this case, class inequalities) reflects a problem to which many of today's young women *and* men can relate, and the basis of the fantasy's appeal is in eradicating those obstacles without making it about women in general.

The romance narrative maintained throughout *The Hunger Games* also makes an interesting statement about the function of hetero-romance in the young woman leader's life. First, the romance exists on the margins of the hero's journey—her primary goal is to survive, to take care of herself, and to follow her path—which, in this case, is to be an inspiration to rebellion and a soldier against oppression. Romance is often the last thing on Katniss' mind and rightfully so. She has a rebellion to inspire and people to save. These attributes speak to a progressive trend toward the ability to imagine an idealized form of leadership that doesn't just appeal to but relies upon female participation and revolutionary aims.

At the same time, the romance is central to her journey and helps her become a better leader, and it's intertwined with her quest to save Peeta. The story thus exemplifies one expression of what the fantasy of having it all can mean for young women today (in the end, we even see Katniss as a mother with two children). The fantasy is "we saved each other," the statement Katniss makes to correct Peeta's claim at the end of the first movie that Katniss saved him. Peeta plays an equal to Katniss—one who must often be saved, but who can save her in other meaningful ways. It means that men and women are in the fight together to free other women and men who are oppressed. It reworks the ideal of partnership in love as a partnership in liberation.

He for She: Men Stepping Up

Only a few years before Katniss led *The Hunger Games* into record-breaking returns, in 2008, Hillary Clinton earned the honor of being the first woman to win a presidential primary. Standing at her side was her husband and longtime political and personal ally, Bill Clinton. That same year, Beyoncé and Jay-Z married and began their now billion-dollar empire, and while Jay-Z has more net worth, Beyoncé earns the higher annual income. Neither of these romances would be considered ideal, as both men have had very public battles staying monogamous, and these men are both much older than the men in the young fighting female fantasies. However, these very public power relationships do reflect two interrelated, burgeoning trends that help us understand the culture that nurtures and sustains the fantasy of female leaders that Katniss and other new, young fighting females promote.

First, this reflects the trend of the powerful woman with enough political or popular cred to "run the world," to use Beyoncé's optimistic claim. While far from being equal in power and access, there are more women leaders than ever before. The second trend is that of the strong man standing with his woman or even taking a back seat to her. By no means is this the leading trend in America—a land in which women still experience a significant wage gap, in which the "feminization of poverty" recognized by sociologists across all racial and ethnic groups continues, and in which article after article warns women of the struggles women face should they outearn their men. For example, studies have found that even when a woman has a slightly higher income than her husband, the rates for divorce and for the husband to cheat increase, as does the amount of housework the wife does. Despite numerous remaining obstacles, women's gaining in the workplace and in leadership is a trend, if a slow-moving one, as data expert Mona Chalabi reported in 2015: 38 percent of women were earning more than their husbands, as compared with 18 percent in 1987 ("What Happens").

The problems these two public power couples face also remind us of an implicit concern about the possibility of success for any hetero-romance or intimacy for the strong, independent woman: what will it take of men to make things better for women? It seems the "how do I find romance as a strong, independent woman?" question has been supplemented in some circles by the "how can I do more, have more, or earn more than a man and find a man who can handle it?" question. The answer to both of these questions lies firmly in the man's hands and reminds us that, at some level, the struggle the strong, independent woman has faced has always been one of men not trying to assert themselves, not being able to step up to meet her, or not stepping out of her way as she progresses and remaining behind to support. Men have to take charge of themselves and reckon with the way they are responsible for their part in maintaining inequity. Men have to learn how to be better partners, to be what a 2014 UN campaign refers to as "he for she." This is the name of what the UN refers to as a "solidarity movement for gender equality," and it gained a lot of notoriety during a speech Emma Watson gave to launch the campaign.

While critics have rightly noted the problematic gender binary the name reinforces—thus excluding other gender identities—the campaign, and Watson's support, garnered a lot of interest from young women who had felt alienated by feminism because of their mistaken belief that feminist equated with man-hating. The "he for she" campaign also makes it clear that men must participate in efforts to improve women's equality. "He for she" calls for men and women to work together, just like the fantasy that emerges from Katniss's story, only the fantasy also includes a version of maleness that is not so thwarted by the woman's role that the love or connection fails.

This stand-by-your-woman version of the hetero-romance fantasy has gained a solid toe-hold in popular culture in the last few years and has been portrayed in other recent films featuring young fighting female leaders, in which the hetero-relations also exhibit a range of possibilities. Tris Prior's story is probably the closest to the Katniss narrative. Like Katniss, Tris is the one who will lead her city's people into the future. Like Katniss, Tris has a reliable and enlightened male character, Four/Tobias (Theo James), who will stand by her until the end. Tobias presents a character who combines the best of both Gale—his fighting capability and overall strength—and Peeta—his whole-hearted support of and respect for Tris's strength and independence, and his belief in her as a leader of the rebellion. Unfortunately, because of production problems and the poor returns of the final Divergent film release, *Allegiance*, moviegoers who don't read the books will not learn the ending of Tris's story. In the movie, Tris sacrifices herself to save her city and unite the people by taking the death serum. She makes a choice as a leader on her own, and as much as she loves Tobias, the possibility of a future in love is not as important to her as a future for her people. Because of her strength at a genetic level (her divergence means that she has not been genetically damaged by the scientists who were experimenting on the people of her city), as well as on emotional and mental levels, she doesn't die, at least not from the serum (she gets shot). The book ends with Tobias mourning her more than two years after her death. He is the one tasked with keeping the memory of her heroism alive at the end of the story.

This willingness to sacrifice oneself and face terrible odds to do what's right is a common theme for many of the fighting females addressed in this book—specifically those who dedicate themselves to justice, like the cops, detectives, and spies, and the reluctant revolutionaries Katniss and Tris. Other recent fantasies of female power make this willingness to take up the sword a goal for young women of the future, the women who would lead the world to a better place. Additionally, these fantasies all include some form of enlightened male support for the female protagonists. Before *The Hunger Games* hit the big screen, the famed Alice earned fighting female cred and a position as a young leader for the people of Underland, thanks in part to a steadfast group of supporters, both male and female. First, she had the faith of her father, who supported her imagination as a child (which brought her to the "Wonderland" Underland in the first place). When she returns to Underland, she has the support of many friends, but most importantly, she has the loyalty and friendship of the Mad Hatter (Johnny Depp), who becomes her best ally. Theirs is an example of an alternative hetero-relationship that is intimate but entirely platonic. The Mad Hatter is not there to save Alice or to teach her how to fight. He is completely vulnerable and gentle (and, well, "mad")—even more so than Peeta. His part in the story is to remind Alice of her own "muchness," the strength within her heart and the belief that she can make anything possible—including, as we learn later in the film, standing up to a patriarchal society that would deny her "muchness" by encouraging her to marry a man she doesn't love and to give up her dreams. After she slays the Jabberwocky to save Underland, she returns home to captain her own ship and live a life of adventure. There is no hint of romance between Alice and the Mad Hatter, only deep friendship, trust, and love. This friendship continues into the sequel *Alice Through the Looking Glass* when Alice must return to save the Mad Hatter by saving his family.

Another telling example of expanding representations of hetero-intimacies for fighting females occurs in the rebooted Snow White story, *Snow White and the Huntsman*. The seven dwarves eventually become the young woman's comrades in arms, and the Huntsman, Eric (Chris Hemsworth), helps her face Queen Ravenna (Charlize Theron) and break the witch's final curse. While there are those who mistakenly read a romance between Snow White and Eric at the end of the film, theirs is a unique platonic relationship that builds through shared hardships and shared fighting throughout the film. It's understandable that people would misread their relationship as romantic because Eric is the one who awakens Snow White with a kiss. However, the narrative had already established William (Sam Claflin), the son of Duke Hammond, as Snow White's romantic interest. Their romance could be easy to overlook because she denied following through with her romantic impulses for him through most of the story. After all, she had bigger concerns—like saving her kingdom. However, she and William exchange numerous longing glances throughout the film in a way she never does with Eric. Snow White also kisses William. Even though it ends up being Ravenna in disguise, Snow White's action confirms her feelings for him. When the real William then finds her poisoned, lying on the ground, he kisses her tenderly, believing she's gone. At the beginning of the sequel, *The Huntsman: Winter's War* (2016), we learn that William and Snow White married, which offers final confirmation of their romance.

Also, the kiss that the Huntsman gives Snow White does not have to be read as romantic simply because it's between a man and woman. Granted, before Eric kisses her, he gives a monologue about how similar Snow White is to his deceased wife, the wife he couldn't save from Ravenna's forces. But what's similar is their "heart" and their "spirit," not his feelings of romantic love. His wife saved him once. Snow White saved him the next time. He feels that he failed both, and he kisses her sadly, mourning the loss of a person who gave him a chance. Certainly, his kiss could be seen as confounding, considering that he showed no romantic interest in her for the entire movie (and even tells Snow White early on not to "flatter yourself" when he has to rip her dress to make it easier for her to maneuver). Thus, it's easy to assume the kiss reflects a forced romance that "plays to the adolescent female fantasy of romantic desirability" (Brown 192).

However, considering the other factors, it should be just as easy to assume that the kiss reflects a platonic love. The reason it's not easy to assume this is the long-standing set of expectations of the romantic script for female characters of all kinds. The fact that Eric doesn't even seem to like Snow White, in the beginning, wouldn't necessarily preclude any romantic possibility. As this analysis has previously shown, having one or the other (or both) of the main characters in a film or television show dislike each other—or even sometimes despise each other—is often the basis for a love that emerges later. Neither would it be unusual that Snow White would end up with an older man, as that tends to be the case in many romance narratives. So, the fact that Eric isn't obviously attracted to her at the beginning can be read as normal. *Snow White and the Huntsman* doesn't seem to play on this trope consciously; the more likely explanation is that audience expectations of the trope informed misinterpretations of the kiss because it's so unusual for a film to deny a romance between co-stars. But that's exactly what the film does by not having Snow White's kiss of "true love" be a romantic one but a platonic one.

In a way, the kiss from Eric is more like the spell-breaking kiss Maleficent gives Aurora at the end of the Sleeping Beauty reboot *Maleficent*. Despite the witch's change of heart about Aurora over the course of the film, the young girl still succumbs to the curse Maleficent had placed upon her as an infant, a curse meant to make her fall into a sleep from which she can awaken only after receiving "true love's kiss." When the curse comes to pass, and Aurora is the Sleeping Beauty, Maleficent finds Prince Phillip, the young man with whom Aurora had fallen in love earlier in the movie, to kiss her. Only, as with William in *Snow White and the Huntsman*, the kiss doesn't work. It's only when Maleficent kisses the young girl on her forehead that she awakens—a kiss, like Eric's, that comes from sorrow and regret and loss felt with another kind of love, one of kinship. The understandable misreadings of Snow White's hetero-relations is proof that one of the difficulties women audiences face is not only the fact that there are still plenty of traditionally normative hetero-romance scripts that do reflect and replicate conservative gender divisions but also that even progressive scripts that rewrite hetero-relations in subtle ways still tend to hold, for many, negative associations simply because it's a romance storyline. These assumptions deny the importance of such storylines for many male and female viewers who need to see a new kind of love that keeps the promise of what intimacy between the sexes can be—an opportunity for community, caring, support, and acceptance that can make new norms for hetero-relations as an experience of cooperation rather than competition, partnership rather than opposition, and reassurance rather than fear of loss. It is an opportunity that demands men meet challenging women where they are and do not try to keep them down.

Love should not have to make women choose between their dreams and their desires for intimate connections and romance, and women should be able to stand up for and find the kind of love that suits their personal goals without thinking that choosing independence means choosing to remain uncommitted against their wishes. And of course, love is not and should not be the only story told about women's lives. Still, the love is important, not because romantic love and intimacy are purely an "adolescent female fantasy of romantic desirability" (Brown 192) but because they are key experiences of human connection that encourage people even to want to try to work together for something better.

Many of the new relationship fantasies on-screen are more progressive and provide models of egalitarian intimacies that have long been missing from popular culture. Models that may still reflect more wishful thinking than the reality for today's strong, independent women, but they are important models nonetheless. There are still lingering problems in terms of female representational parity in the mass media: while more of the women on screen have female allies as well as male, the women on screen still tend to be outnumbered. Traditional heteronormativity abounds, as does a lack of racial diversity and class divides that affect what women's stories and experiences are told. Objectification and overt sexualization of female characters remain rampant problems, even in a large number of the progressive narratives included in this book. And television programs and films could certainly do with more women characters who have the skills and who mentor men.

However, some avenues in popular culture are headed there. Look at what both of these fairy tale do-overs leave audiences: princesses who are heroes. Snow White inspires armies to fight with her, and she fearlessly faces a powerful witch to win back the kingdom. Aurora, who isn't a fighting female but becomes a leader thanks to a fighting female, stands with Maleficent to end a dangerous feud between the kingdoms and to help right the wrong Aurora's father, King Stefan (Sharlto Copley), perpetrated on Maleficent by stealing her wings and betraying their friendship. These fantasies offer something different than what *The Hunger Game* and *Divergent* stories provide, fantasies that can appeal to those who remain skeptical about the potential of romance in a narrative to enhance, rather than diminish, the strength and independence of the female heroes because they marginalize but don't exclude the romance. At the end of both *Snow White and the Huntsman* and *Maleficent*, the princesses are crowned queens, and neither of them has a man standing with her. All the men, as allies or lovers, watch from the sidelines as the women take on their roles as leaders. Both of these young women are empowered—they get to be strong, independent, and in love, and they live in worlds where empowering male allies fight alongside them. All of the fighting female romance fantasies have, in some way, contributed to re-imagining masculinity in ways that can give women room to protect and take to control. Out of the strong, independent woman role emerges a strong, supporting male role, an image of a man who does not abandon, betray, or otherwise punish his partner for her abilities, even when those abilities make her a leader. That's the fantasy of the future, a world where "he for she" becomes the reality.

Interdependence and Intimacy: Future Alliances

As this project has progressed over the last few years, I have had more opportunity to consider the struggle that women continue to face in conflicts between their personal and professional agendas, between the lives they live for others and the lives they live for themselves. The more I see women struggle, the more I am surprised that more women don't consider themselves feminists or see feminism as a way to help them navigate the confusion they face when their ideas about being strong and independent conflict with their desires for heterosexual relationships. In Chapter One, I mentioned a post from blogger Sara Dobie Bauer in which she aligned feminism with an all-in version of female strength that she felt didn't apply to her because she isn't an activist and because she likes the idea of being saved by men. If I could share what I have learned through this project with Sara, and the many other women who share her misapprehensions, I would tell her this:

> Enjoying strong men, not being tough at times, and wanting to be saved sometimes totally fits with being a feminist. There are so many kinds of feminists out there! You don't identify yourself as a feminist, and that's fine. I wouldn't presume to tell you your identity because that's your place. But I would like to share a perspective about feminism that broadens the term and helps undermine pernicious misapprehensions about what a feminist identity is that encourage others to be anti-feminist. Feminism is, in part, about questioning oversimplified thinking about identity, about introducing nuance into our understanding of the ways people live and love. In terms of strength, no person is ever always strong. We can't be; we're all only human. The reason many feminists promote the inclusion of more images of strong women, strong in ways that extend beyond the limited mama bear, overbearing corporate ladies, or violent femme types, is to recognize and celebrate the reality of diverse ways of being women.
>
> In keeping with that, many feminists celebrate versions of men who don't always have to be strong to be the fantasy, or who can be strong in more nurturing ways. When we consistently have narratives in which men save women, we do two things. First, we limit our understanding of women's abilities to save themselves and others. Second, the narratives reinforce an idea of masculinity that is just as static and underdeveloped as the damsel theme often is. It's overwhelming to be part of a sex that has been tasked as the protector for, let's face it, most of history. In essence, that's the real problem many feminists have who dislike the male/hero and female/victim story. It's not only overdone, but it's done without nuance, without giving either character something more. Sure, some feminists might entirely discount any sign of female weakness and subscribe to the women-don't-need-men thing. But that's only one interpretation

of feminism and not one that's likely to unite people to work together toward liberation.

Your version of male/female romance, one in which women get tired of taking care of themselves and like the idea of partners to share the responsibility—to be gentle, loving, supportive, in whatever way you need—aligns well with feminism and is actually a logical perspective. I mean, we live in a society with men. Many women love a man or men, whether romantically, platonically, or in a familial way. It only makes sense that we find ways to allow ourselves to be imperfect and to rely on them and to allow them the same courtesy. Being dependent on someone doesn't have to degrade our independence and vice versa. And feminism isn't about always being on the front lines of the fight or about being on at all times. It's about acting to do what you can in the ways that you can to foster equality. It's also about surrounding yourself, whenever possible with allies and collaborators who can help you do more because equality is a social goal. What better ally than the person you love? Who better to help you succeed? To support your strength? To encourage a healthy interdependence?

That's what so many of the fighting female romance narratives I've addressed attempt to do. Some do it better than others. Yet, they all highlight how influential intimate relations are to women's success, and achieving success with male allies doesn't have to be degrading or weaken a woman's power. Katniss made that assumption about Peeta's confession of love: that it would make her appear weak. But in the end, that love, and the love she felt for her family and for the oppressed civilians of Panem, was a source of strength.

When I was sitting at the theater watching the last installment of *The Hunger Games,* I remember thinking how amazing it would be to be a young person sitting in that very same audience watching Katniss loom large and powerful on the screen. I believe that had Katniss been alone at the end of the film, instead of surrounded by her new family with Peeta, the impact would have been equally as powerful, only different, because it would still be an image of a triumphant woman who helped lead a revolution. I can't imagine what's in store for young people growing up as female-identified in the 21st century. They're growing up in a time of female empowerment *and* a war against women—the world remains an imperfect place, a place that threatens women constantly as well as men in very different ways. Yet, I can imagine that young people growing up knowing that the world needs to be fixed and believing that no matter their gender identity, they have the strength to do it—and also knowing that they don't have to do it alone. In addition to the support of like-minded women, that child can count on more like-minded men to fight, as allies and as intimates, whether the intimacy is romantic or not. There is a whole other kind of strength in that.

Conclusion

"Surely it must be possible for a man and a woman to have a beautiful love-life and yet be devoted to a great cause"
—(Goldman *Living My Life* 154)

The "strong, independent woman" archetype offers evidence of gender blending that undermines two common American cultural assumptions about women as a whole: first, the idealized traditional conceptions of femininity that assume women are incapable of or lacking in the skills, personality, and desires necessary to be autonomous and powerful, which necessitates male protection and support; second, that women portraying strength and independence are man-hating, unstable, and a threat to social order, which necessitates regulation and/or punishment. Successful iterations of the archetype thus enlarge possible subject positions for female characters on-screen—positions that promote less stereotypical demonstrations of heterosexuality and that reject a one-woman-fits-all conception of womanhood or female identity. As a result, female characters, whether fighters or not, are being developed in more humanizing and complex ways on television and in film, in part simply because they are participating in new narrative options because of access to previously unavailable roles, particularly within action genres and storylines. The humanizing rejection or at least complication of stereotypes engenders the most feminist-friendly fantasies that influence audience perceptions in relation to their own lives and offer a way for them to compare and contrast their own experiences as they navigate their relationship desires and identities.

Increasing Diversity

The danger behind representations of the "strong, independent woman" archetype in romance narratives, whether the character is a fighting female or not, has been "the danger of a single story," as Chimamanda Ngozi Adichie refers to it. In this case, the single story is where love is the only form of success by which women have been and are ultimately defined. Through this study, I have attempted to expand the thinking about this single story using feminist analysis in an effort to reform thinking within and about the romance paradigm so deeply entrenched in people's daily lives. This is not to say that the majority of romance narratives, whether or not they include a fighting female, are changing the paradigms of male/female intimacies. I also want to be clear that audiences, and the way they view gender, will most certainly benefit from more exposure to queer romances and alternative examples of hetero-intimacies. Seeing other ways of being from diverse groups and cultures that have an entirely different set of norms, principles, and standards is definitely the most effective way to release women and men from the tyranny of narrowly defined parameters of success, romance, and gender expression. It is also the most effective way to encourage people to question and change the status quo when it denies the presence and validity of such diversity when those ways of being fail to be inclusive or equitable. Radical diversity breeds radical inclusion, and this inclusion is the way forward for any 21st-century feminist-friendly fantasy, romantic or not. Future media will be truly feminist only when it depicts an intersectional standpoint that is deliberately diverse and inclusive, rejects or critiques all stereotypes, and both reflects and interrogates the complex interplay of privilege and disadvantage or access and marginalization that emerge from each individual's identities.

Two promising examples of feminist-friendly on-screen relationships that reflect increasing diversity are on television, thanks to The CW Network. They not only provide diverse examples of hetero-intimacy but also do so by including both women of color and queer women in *Supergirl* (2015–present)[1] and *Black Lightning* (2018–present). *Supergirl* is the story of Kara Zor-El (Melissa Benoist), Superman's cousin. She is sent to the Earth to be his protector when he is evacuated from Krypton as an infant. However, her pod gets lost in space for many years, and by the time she hits Earth, Superman has grown into an adult, and she is still a young girl. Kara is adopted by the Danvers family and grows up hiding her powers until one day, she has to save a plane from crashing—a plane on which her adopted sister Alex Danvers (Chyler Leigh) is a passenger. That's the day the world meets Supergirl. Shortly after, Supergirl begins to work for the Department of Extranormal Operations (DEO), helping save the city from aliens and meta-humans with powers. Her alter ego, Kara, is also a reporter for CatCo magazine and quickly rises through the ranks to become one of their top reporters. *Supergirl* features the first female comics superhero to headline a television series since the short-lived *Birds of Prey* from the WB Television Network in 2002—preceding the Netflix production *Jessica Jones* by one month. When Supergirl's adopted sister Alex Danvers came out as a lesbian in season two, the show became one of the first to portray an openly queer fighting female character as a co-lead on television since Willow Rosenberg (Alyson Hannigan) came out in season four of *Buffy the Vampire Slayer* (1997–2003).[2]

While Alex Danvers is no superhero, she's definitely a Renaissance woman in badassery who is not only a doctor and scientist but also ends up becoming the director of the DEO. She often fights side by side with her super sister with an ensemble cast of liberal-minded and social-justice-oriented colleagues who seek to protect alien rights and Earth's safety. Supergirl enjoys her own relationship dramas in seasons one and two; Alex's romances get equal time if not more focus during seasons two through four. She becomes engaged at the end of season two to Detective Maggie Sawyer (Floriana Lima), though they break up right before the wedding in season three when Alex learns Maggie doesn't want kids. In season four, Alex finds her second love relationship with Kelly Olsen (Azie Tesfai) after they bond over Alex's first attempt to adopt a child (which fell through because the mother decided she didn't want to give the baby up). Kelly's characters will join the regular cast in the upcoming season five.

What's interesting about the dynamic between Alex and her romantic partners is that there is little to distinguish them from an enlightened hetero-romance in which the conflicts emerge not because of gender differences but simply because of differences in priorities. Alex spends a lot of time in the fourth season in particular reckoning with her own desires to have a family, which she rarely if ever questions as possible, even though she spends so much time at the DEO fighting to keep the world safe from aliens who harm and those who would harm aliens. As of season four, Alex also loses her token queer fighting female character status when Nia Nal joins the cast as a transgender woman, played by transgender actress Nicole Maines. Nia not only ends up enjoying a flirtation with one of the DEO agents, an alien from the future called Brainiac 5, or "Brainy" (Jesse Ruth), but she also turns out to have her own superpowers. She becomes Dreamer as the season progresses, making Nicole Maines the first transgender superhero to be featured on screen.

In addition to portraying enlightened LGBTQIA+ politics and having a cast with some racial diversity, *Supergirl* complicates romantic heteronorms and also includes intimate hetero-relations that are platonic and cooperative. The romantic relationships Kara enjoys are not subject to the struggles of her work/life balance. She doesn't worry about making the relationship fit with her work commitments (for the DEO or CatCo). The problems her relationships encounter include timing, finding the right person, moving on, and finding ways to stay friends with past paramours in order to fight together as partners. In fact, she ends up platonic partners with her two big romance interests. Her first love on the show is James Olsen (Mehcad Brooks)—better known as Jimmy Olsen of *Superman* fame. Except this James is a black man who moves to National City after the traumas inflicted by being continually kidnapped and tortured for being Superman's best friend. He works for CatCo as a photojournalist and art director before eventually becoming the CEO of CatCo. Kara's second love, Mon-El/Lar Gand (Chris Wood), is also an alien and has to flee Earth to avoid dying. He leaves Supergirl just when their romantic relationship is developing, but not before she teaches him how to be a hero. He returns in a later season, married, and Supergirl must work together with Mon-El and his wife to fight another alien foe. Supergirl not only becomes friends and partners with her exes, but she maintains very close personal relationships with her male colleagues and friends, like J'onn J'onzz/Martian Manhunter (David Harewood) and "Brainy."

Supergirl's fantasy reflects a few of the feminist-friendly hetero-romance themes I have touched upon: the colleagues-as-family theme I address in Chapter Two where they are always together—for missions, holidays, celebrations, mournings, and pro-alien activism. The male characters all portray a redemptive parallel in which their own victimizations orient them on a more level ideological playing field, struggling often as survivors—especially James Olsen, who must resolve his struggles with PTSD and the fact that he has chosen to fight as The Guardian (a Batman-like character who uses gadgets and fight training to make up for his lack of superpowers). All of the show's male protagonists are also comfortable under female leadership, whether at CatCo or at the DEO.

It also includes queer characters and relationships that subvert certain heteronorms and show women following other paths to romance. In fact, *Supergirl* has proven to have staying power through the iffy first seasons—including a network change—because of its diversity with regard to the queer relationships, as fans across the internet have noted and celebrated. A small-scale study of fan perceptions of both *Supergirl* and *The Flash* completed by Alan Carroll, an undergraduate completing his B.A. at Dundalk Institute of Technology, noted that the second favorite storyline cited by Reddit fans who discuss the shows was the burgeoning relationship between Alexa and Maggie in season two.[3] It's important to note that many of the fans who responded also felt that "independence is the aspect that most respondents looked for in a female character" (Carroll 25), whether it be independence from men or romance, but what felt so compelling about Alex and Maggie was the chemistry, a point noted as necessary to offset the feeling that the love relationship was forced. Ultimately, all of the show's characters engage in relationships that promote trust, cooperation, and shared autonomy as the foundation of functional interdependency that allows them to negotiate their personal and professional lives.

Black Lightning is another CW ensemble cast DC superhero show that debuted just as *Luke Cage* (2016–18)—the only other program featuring a superhero of color as the lead—wrapped up its second and final season on Netflix. *Black Lightning* offers the first live-action superhero family drama since the one-season ABC program *No Ordinary Family* (2010–11) as well as the first crime-fighting black couple on film or television since NBC's *The Undercovers* (2010), which was canceled after only eleven episodes. The program takes place in fictional Freeland, Georgia. It features the Pierce family: Jefferson (Cress Williams), a high school principal, his brilliant neuroscientist wife, Lynn (Christine Adams), and their two daughters, Anissa (Nafessa Williams)—a medical student and part-time health teacher at the high school—and Jennifer (China Anne McClain), an independent-minded high school senior.

At the beginning of the story, we learn that Jefferson is a meta-human (a human who gains superpowers) who goes by *Black Lightning*. He fought violent crime in Freeland for many years but retired nine years before the pilot begins. He quit because he thought he had killed the nefarious Tobias Whale (Marvin "Krondon" Jones III) but also because his crime-fighting exploits had torn his marriage and family apart. He and Lynn are divorced and sharing custody of their daughters, but he harbors hopes for a reconciliation. When Jefferson learns that Tobias is still alive and has returned to Freeland, Jefferson takes up his Black Lightning mantle again. As the first season progresses, we learn that both of his daughters are also meta-humans with their own powers, both to some extent stronger than he is. Anissa is Thunder, and Jennifer eventually becomes Lightning.

As much as the show focuses on the usual struggles of good against evil, it focuses equally on each individual's struggles to deal with the responsibility of protecting and saving others and the resultant dangers each must face while doing this—balanced with their desires for romance and intimacy and a stable family life. Jefferson and Lynn slowly come back together as the story progresses, but there is a definite tension about the longevity of their reconciliation as crime-fighting duties continually threaten everyone's safety—a will-they-won't-they-stay-together arc. Jefferson also struggles to deal with his daughters' growing up, their demands for autonomy and a fair voice, and the violence they face on a daily basis. Both women are defiant and capable and generally follow their own instincts more often than his advice. He must also learn to respect Lynn's choices and the fact that she will do what she thinks is best, even if he disagrees. He strives to reduce his paternalistic impulses and learns to be a partner with all three.

Now, the show may be called *Black Lighting*, but it doesn't center only on Jefferson, and the stories of the three women in the family are just as central to the overall narrative. Once again, there is no question of the strength and independence of any of the female characters, all of whom participate in the fight against evil in one way or another. Lynn has to learn to reconcile her concern for her husband and family's welfare with the necessary role her husband and daughters play in fighting against the corruption and violence Tobias and his gang inflict on the community. Additionally, she has to find her own role in the fight, first with her intellectual abilities, by working to keep "Green Light Babies" alive and able to live with their new powers. She is the only one with the knowledge and skill to subvert the work of a rogue American government agency that has been experimenting on the citizens of Freeland for the last thirty years trying to find a serum that would render the members of the community (who are primarily black or Latinx) more docile. All they ended up creating is a new drug called Green Light, described as a cross between PCP and crack, and it turns some of the users into meta-humans by triggering dormant genes. Lynn also dons the role of a protector during the season one finale, when she picks up a gun and kills an agent threatening a (male) family friend—and again in season two, when she physically fights and takes down the corrupt psychopath Dr. Helga Jace (Jennifer Riker)—the one responsible for creating the "vaccine" that turned out to be Green Light.

Lynn's youngest daughter Jennifer does not quickly or easily embrace her powers and wants to simply enjoy her teen years and grow up and have a family—until she experiences the thrill of protecting and saving others who are in danger. She also has a complicated relationship with her ex-boyfriend, Khalil. His spine is severed by a bullet, but he is healed with special technology, thanks to Tobias, who then brings him into his gang and requires him to be an enforcer. In fact, it's when Jennifer is on the run with an injured Khalil that she learns the benefits of her abilities and begins to embrace them most fully.

Anissa easily accepts her powers and eagerly embraces her new role, reveling in her ability to take down drug dealers, sex traffickers, and any criminal who threatens the community. In fact, she's so into heroism that she creates a second hero identity—unbeknownst to her father—as Blackbird, a vigilante who steals from criminals to give to projects like the new community health clinic. Yet, she struggles to find a place for love, which her sister constantly reminds her is out there. To be more specific, she struggles to decide if she even wants to find a place for love in her life. Anissa is a bit of a player who is also a lesbian. She likes her lifestyle and is less concerned with finding love than having fun. However, she does recognize the need to have more of a personal life so that she is not living to work, so to speak—though it's hard to imagine that going to medical school and teaching part-time would leave her much time for anything including dating, much less a side career as a superhero. As of the end of season two, she decides she wants to try a real relationship with Grace Choi (Chantal Thuy), a bisexual bartender who seems to have some secret superpowers of her own.

It's useful to note that the show is very nonchalant about introducing the first on-screen queer, black superhero. Anissa is openly gay at the beginning of the series, so there's no brief "coming out" as with Alex in *Supergirl*, but like Alex, there are no conflicts revolving around the character's sexuality, only in Anissa's work/life balance. Additionally, Anissa's casual dismissal of monogamy and desire to enjoy different partners offers its own challenge to romance expectations based on monogamous heteronorms.

Overall, both programs paint rosy pictures of casual and untroubled acceptance of attractive, young LGBTQIA+ individuals right next to bleak portraits of the state of individual freedoms in political climate threatened by authoritarianism and intolerance. In other words, we see fantasy worlds featuring an America rife with anxieties about identity politics, even as the characters on *Supergirl* and *Black Lightning* are themselves outside the "norms" as well as wholly accepting of others who are. Both narratives imply that queer identity is no big deal, offering a welcome boon in terms of representing diverse sexual orientations that also avoids stereotypes and gives queer women characters co-lead roles. Taken in conjunction, we see different expressions of queer romance, ranging from Alex Danvers's initial desires for a more "traditional" path to monogamy—fall in love, marry, have kids—to Anissa's more haphazardly defined relationships. This inclusion plays a part in how they offer better forms of feminist-friendly viewing for the fighting female romance fan, and it's just the beginning of a trend that is spreading fast, from basic cable to streaming content. The CW is slated to launch the first lesbian superhero lead during the 2019–20 season: *Batwoman*, with Ruby Rose playing the title character. She made her debut in the *Arrow* crossover[4] episode "Elseworlds" (07.09), in which she enjoyed a surprising flirtation with Supergirl as they fought together.

While the fighting female protagonists in *Supergirl* are primarily white and read as upper-middle-class professionals, which very much orients their portrayals of strength and independence in constructing their whiteness, their experiences aren't very far off from the experiences of the fighting females in *Black Lightning* who are also upper-middle class professionals. So, we are not seeing relationships between women and men who are struggling for economic survival, the toll that takes on the relationship, and the ways that stereotypical gender roles tend to emerge out of those efforts—the story that would be told by the working class. What we do see are relationships between men and women who struggle to survive against the criminals they face and the toll that sharing a responsibility for protection and fostering change requires, which makes room in the narrative for less traditional gender performances: economic privilege tends to open space for more transgressive expressions. Probably more than any narrative I've discussed in the course of this study with the exception of *The Hunger Games*, economic hardships in the community undergird many of the injustices against which the heroes fight. A number of the characters the Pierce family protects are working class and from an economically struggling community.

Of course, race is central to the narrative in *Black Lightning* and the very existence of Freeland—so named by the show's creator Salim Akil because of the determination of Black Lightning to free the people of the city from crime and corruption. Themes throughout the show emphasize elements of some black cultures that are easily recognized: the role of the church in people's lives and communal activism; references throughout, including quotes, from important black historical figures like Fannie Lou Hamer, Coretta Scott King, and Harriet Tubman, whose ideas clearly inform the actions of the characters (also, Jennifer's nickname for her sister Anissa is Harriet); the conflict between the politics of respectability and the politics of revolution; and the tension between calls for violent and non-violent protest. Moreover, there are themes that emphasize the institutional racism orienting the characters' lives: the problems white saviors and white paternalism cause for black communities; governmental experimentation on people of color; over-policing and punishing black men and women and the related over-incarceration rates; violent gang culture; a lack of available medical clinics and effective care; and a struggling education system that promotes rule-following more than student agency and development.

One noteworthy way the show demonstrates gendered constructions of race that are central to *Black Lightning's* feminist-friendly romance fantasy is that rather than work relationships creating the family, the family is where the work originates. And the family's work is in protecting the people within the community, fighting villains who are not superpowered aliens but merely diabolical humans pushed by greed and a desire for power that exploits and endangers the community, whether that villain is the mercenary local gang leader or a the leader of a twisted American government agency. Through the roles that the fighting females play, *Black Lightning* highlights what bell hooks refers to as the "significant and valuable" contribution black women make that defines their place in the community and that differentiates male/female relationships between black people from those within white hetero-relations (70). In part, this is because of shared "sufferings and hardships" that show black women that "they have more in common with men of their race and/or class group than with bourgeois white women" (70). In this way, *Black Lightning* asserts its own egalitarian version of hetero-relations like the romaction *Mr. and Mrs. Smith*, through an implication of gender-blended similarity between the male and female protagonists. Yet there is an additional redemptive parallel in which they all share the basis of adversity and suffering because of the institutional racism they face.

The community-based values, relationships, and activism that make shared oppression meaningful as a basis for partnership and support is equally important in *Black Panther*, which was released one month after *Black Lightning* debuted. The two storylines portray evidence of the women's strength and independence very differently. The comparison helps us understand one of the unique aspects of racial stereotypes and their impact on gender performances and what would be considered transgressive of norms and stereotypes when race informs performances of hetero-relations.

Black Panther focuses on the title character and tells the story of T'Challa (Chadwick Boseman), the Black Panther, coming to terms with his new role as the king of Wakanda following his father's death. T'Challa is surrounded by some brilliant, brave, loyal, and fierce women, including his tech-genius sister Shuri (Letitia Wright), his mother the queen Ramonda (Angela Bassett), his ex-lover and spy ally Nakia (Lupita Nyong'o), and his cadre of women warriors led by General Okoye (Danai Gurira). These women are strong and independent, to say the least. However, they do not have their own stories, and they are very much sidelined to Black Panther's quest. Their biggest role is to support him in his fight to protect his people and his position as their king. We see an example of this reliance on female input from Black Panther's women when they stand on the sidelines and cheer or yell encouragement for him to win: when he fights M'Baku (Winston Duke) for the throne and wins when he fights the movie's villain Erik Killmonger (Michael B. Jordan) for the throne and loses. When he is lying near death, the women chant around him to awaken him to live to fight again. The movie continually positions the women, even Nakia, as more supportive than autonomous.

At the beginning of the film, Nakia is on a mission to find and take down a group of rebels who have abducted women and forced young boys to become soldiers. T'Challa chooses both to interrupt and to complete this mission because he wants to share news of her father's death and have her with him when he becomes king. Of course, she wants to be there to support him when she learns why, and the country's traditions are very important to her. However, I did find myself questioning what makes his ceremony and loss more important than finding the insurgent camp and releasing all of the women and child soldiers and not just the recent batch being transported. Ultimately, the crowning is essential to his story, and that what makes it important to her.

Throughout most of the film, T'Challa chooses his own path despite the women's counsel, but in the end, he shows that he listens when he does finally follow Nakia's advice for Wakanda's future. Throughout the movie, she tries to convince him to share Wakanda's resources with the world and no longer hide their technology and knowledge. Still, he is very much the king and in charge; he is in the dominant position and has the most autonomy, and it's a position that none of the women have. Granted, when it comes time to allow challengers to Black Panther's ascension to the throne during the first part of the film—when anyone from one of the Wakanda tribes can choose to battle him to the death or surrender and become the ruler—we learn that it is his sister's prerogative to challenge if she so desires. But while Shuri is fearless and more than capable with big guns when the time comes to fight, it's obvious that she would be no match for her brother's might and fighting skills, and it becomes a moot allowance. Also, Queen Ramonda gives Nakia the opportunity to take the special herb that grants Black Panther his strength, so she can save T'Challa when he is gravely injured by Killmonger. But Nakia dismisses this chance, saying, "I'm a spy with no army. I wouldn't stand a chance."

However, the same circumstances also limit T'Challa, once he regains his Black Panther power. He has no army. He only has the women in his life. Even his loyal general has chosen to maintain her loyalty to the throne and not to one particular king, and she only changes her mind when Black Panther leads the fight against Killmonger, which he also started with no army. When the showdown against Killmonger occurs, Black Panther is alone, and he triumphs alone before returning to his family and loyal subjects.

In addition to a story that somewhat sidelines even the most important female characters to his personal journey, *Black Panther* falls in line with narratives that overemphasize the fighting female's abilities by creating a sense of her as an indestructible protector, which I discussed in Chapter Four. Does this mean that the film is not a feminist-friendly triumph? Definitely not. After all, one of my new favorite characters is Captain Marvel—the most indestructible fighting female in the Marvel universe—and my own obsession with the strong, independent woman began with just such a portrayal of Wonder Woman. Also, Nakia's preference for following her own journey over marrying T'Challa, as well as Okoye's willingness to kill her lover to save Wakanda, should it come to that, are commendable expressions of strength and independence. They offer the pleasures of alternative constructions of female experience that sideline romance, even if we only get a partial sense of them as people from a lack of character development. However, a narrative in which black women exist easily reveling in their strength and their roles in the community as protectors is in some ways as limiting as the damsel in distress. It may be just as racially constructed because it is a stereotypical story that relies on assumptions about an emasculating and already masculinized "strong black woman" identity. The "strong, independent woman" ideal emerges in contrast to a longstanding positioning of women, in particular white women, as less capable protectors and providers. The "strong black woman" stereotype (or what Chanequa Walker-Barnes calls "the StrongBlackWoman") emerges in contrast to longstanding expectations of black women's ability to face crushing hostility and daily obstacles.

So, where the "strong, independent woman" archetype rejects and expands traditional conceptions of femininity by incorporating previously forbidden performances of strength, the "strong black woman" embraces the stereotype to hide behind as a kind of mask, to use Tamara Beauboeuf-Lafontant's analogy. As she notes, "The defining quality of Black womanhood is strength. As a reference to tireless, deeply caring, and seemingly invulnerable women, the claim of strength forwards a compelling story of perseverance" (1) that is distinctly racially marked. The problem with this mask is that it functions "to defend and maintain a stratified social order by obscuring Black women's suffering, acts of desperation, and anger" (2)—in other words, it presumes that the black woman can take as much misery as society can give, and she'll never crack or buckle under the pressure. This puts an extreme amount of pressure on black women that encourages "radical self-sufficiency" (Walker-Barnes 160) and discourages self-care or seeking help for depression and other forms of mental illness as well as medical conditions, as both Beauboeuf-Lafontant and Walker-Barnes warn. In a way, it's similar to the position of the "survivor" identity that emerges from watching female characters negotiate experiences of victimization and agency, and the warnings about the "strong black woman" begin to align with the problem of the "superwoman" who is supposed to do it all on her own. Of course, when we look at the women of *Black Panther*, their strength is worn as a mantle of triumph and with the comfort and assurance of a millennium of power for their people—something that other black people in the movie who aren't from Wakanda and in the American mass media, in general, don't have. Still, it's a fantasy, one that presents insight into the "dilemma of strength" that portraying a strong black woman character evokes (Beauboeuf-Lafontant 5).

If we contrast the valiant Wakandan woman warriors with the fighting females Lynn, Anissa, and Jennifer from *Black Lightning*, we can see what a less stereotypical portrayal of black female strength might look like, and it's because of the intimate relationships they have with each other as family and in their romances with the women and men in their lives. Lynn often stands up for herself and is explicit about her needs with Jefferson: when she decides to pursue her work to save the "Green Light Babies," she says, "I don't need your support, but it would be nice to have it" (02.01). She also says they will get through this with the family intact. Jennifer struggles with the "gift" of her powers and the forced responsibility that her new strength requires, including the need to learn to control her strength, and she does so with the full support of her family as they help her face her fears helping her learn that "it's okay to be strong and scared at the same time," as Lynn tells her (01.11). Beginning in episode three of the first season, Jennifer also takes advantage of "therapy" sessions with another meta-human to work through emotional problems that are causing her stress and anxiety and, as a result, making her powers dangerous and harder to control. Anissa has to learn to be more than simply a protector putting herself out there to save others all the time and to have a life and some fun. They all regularly share the pain and confusion and difficulties they face, as does Jefferson.

These women get to express "desires to be assisted and nurtured," they get to "share what is going on 'deep down inside' and retain the esteem of those around" them, they get to "take care of others and expect reciprocation" (5), and they get to express "emotions of doubt, anger, and frustration" (6)—all of which are expectations and experiences that assumptions of black female strength discourage, according to Beauboeuf-Lafontant. All of these counter the stereotypical pitfalls of overemphasizing the expressions of their strength and resilience, contributing to an overall feminist-friendly fantasy that assures us of their complex humanity and the role that love—whether inter-racial, intra-racial, familial, queer, or heterosexual—plays in the expression of that humanity. The result is a reassurance of what Patricia Hill Collins describes as the way that "[f]or African Americans, the mark of humanity (and, by implication, for everyone else) may be the ability to love fully, or see other people for who they are as fully human beings, to love within the context of oppression, and to bend or break the rules" that reduce people to stereotypes and that oppression relies upon to structure hetero-relations (277). Breaking the rules governing the "strong black woman" image thus becomes part of enlarging the number of strong black women's stories out there and rejecting over-emphasizing strength, which can become its own burden on anyone, especially when one is expected to bear it alone.

Comparing the two storylines to determine which is the most feminist-friendly is pointless. They both clearly embrace and champion the female characters in ways that are relatively appropriate for the specific stories being recounted. It's also unrealistic to imagine that a movie would have as much character development as a television show, even though it's still important to note the primary story being told and whether it challenges the majority of other stories being related. It's more useful instead to highlight that there is still diversity within the constructions of the female identities that offer multiple subject positions for black women in relationships with men. The impact of having stories with black lead characters—and audiences' excitement over these stories—can't be emphasized enough. What is even more important, however, is that both narratives are clearly critical of the racist people and institutions that create obstacles for black people, and they were still successes with both critics and fans.

Doing Romance Better

I have imagined this study as a starting point for other investigations into the "strong, independent woman" archetype and the romances that reflect, reject, or complicate the new norms of female identity related to or emerging from this ideal. The fighting female seems primed only to evolve as a character because the number of narratives that feature her as a lead or co-lead who is neither white nor heterosexual has increased in the past few years, thanks in large part to the slowly increasing diversity behind the scenes. More people whose own identities have been historically marginalized or ignored are now writers, directors, producers, and creators of the stories they wanted to see. As the available examples accumulate and offer more numerous and developed queer female characters and female characters of color who take the lead, they show how issues of race and sexual orientation bring their own complicated cultural gender dynamics to romance narratives in ways that deserve further comprehensive investigation.

While it may have been the case previously when there were far fewer representations of the fighting female version of the "strong, independent woman" archetype on-screen, it is no longer so easy to claim that all heterosexual relationship depictions reduce the fantasy of either the female character's strength or independence or that they reinscribe a limited or limiting form of femininity that is opposed to strength and independence. Rethinking the same old ways of being from new angles of perception and using many of the new fighting females who have proliferated in the last twenty years is a way of encouraging viewers to take steps toward recognizing diverse possibilities within their own lives. This study is, in part, a call for better portrayals of relationships between women and men in our fantasies because they are so often inextricably linked with how we define our realities. Certainly, romance shouldn't be the primary story told about women, but when romance is part of the story, it needs to be better. It needs to reflect multiple possibilities for intimacy in women's lives without necessarily privileging romance, where romance becomes one potential intimacy; it also needs to reject the scripts that promote power struggles between those in love; and it needs to feature a variety of female identities and versions of strength and independence without relying on flat, reductive stereotypes.

People are going to continue living and working together in a society where women and men continue to connect romantically, and this connection continues to be weighed down by the hierarchical traditional gender divide that privileges men and female dependence on men, so we have to learn how to reimagine that relationship. For many, that kind of reimagining process is hard to do without first seeing examples of it—a lot of examples, enough examples to counteract the pervasive storylines that rehash the same old stereotypes of men and women and their relationships. Some of the popular films and television programs I've analyzed offer the first examples to promote *both* the gender-blending strong, independent woman ideal *and* new standards of heterosexual relationship behavior that counter the pervasive traditional heteronorm (even if the examples still promote a heteronorm). They provide evidence for an intimate relationship that promotes egalitarian autonomy and interdependence as well as the pitfalls that still exist and need to be looked out for as the boundaries of gender continue to expand. They make some relevant and useful claims about what it takes to achieve what Emma Goldman sought for herself and all women in the fight for social justice, a "dream of love and true companionship" (*Living My Life* 151): Women and men who want an equitable relationship require an combine equitable marketplace and professional and domestic spheres to facilitate it. Emotional intelligence is necessary for men and women to have successful relationships in which they can relate to each other as partners, through trust and collaboration, not competition. Protection is a form of caring that coincides neatly with nurturing and is important in all families—no one sex or gender is more obligated and/or capable of it. The very notion of family is ever-expanding and reflects the necessary primacy of close relationships in our lives, and professional institutions need to make room for everyone's family. Oppression and victimhood do not render women or men helpless, and interdependence doesn't either. And we will not change the world for anyone until women and men become collaborators in feminist social justice.

Epilogue:
Evolving Pleasures

I have been fortunate enough to have grown up with fighting female icons that became more prevalent and multi-faceted as characters at the same time I became more complicated and engaged as a human being. There was always a kick-ass woman who would inspire or empower me, one whom I could seek out for fantasies or validation of my frustrations. In those free and easy years as a young media watcher, those characters brought me immense pleasure. But as I grew older, I became a more critical viewer, as I started to learn about texts as ideological constructions, about discourse and power, about culture, and about nature versus nurture. All of my fighting females became tools of an oppressive and sexist system.

As a viewer, I had swung from unadulterated pleasure to constant critique. I felt engulfed by oppressively sexist ideology every time I entered a movie theater or switched on the TV—insipid plots and gender stereotypes. And don't get me started on objectification. I became one of those jaded people who wrinkled my nose when others would discuss their favorite sitcoms, who would only rent independent films that still had plenty to critique but seemed somehow more acceptable. I had hopped on the high art train. It was as if I were trying to run away from "influence"—as if being critical and deriding pleasure would help me achieve some state of ideology-free nirvana—even though I knew there could be no escape.

Oddly enough, my continued study helped me rediscover the pleasure of popular media. Not because I was being introduced to more nuanced studies about media and culture that explored the notion that pleasure and critique might not be mutually exclusive, though that was certainly happening. Rather, the more advanced my studies—my coursework, the level of scholarship, the density of complex reading—the more I found myself needing some kind of mindless escape. I gorged myself on explosions, gratuitous fight scenes, one-liners, and cheesy puns. The more I watched, the more I questioned my rejection of pop culture, and the more my own scholarship turned toward understanding the transgressive potential in pleasure, toward understanding that popular media is more complex than I had realized and that scholarship aimed toward media analysis and providing insights into the most prevalent aspect of the average Western person's life is extremely beneficial and necessary.

Eventually, my path led me back to the fighting female, who now inspires and excites me both because of the many varied aspects of her representations and because she is frankly a very difficult construct to interpret: for every skimpy costume, there's a respectable talent; for every perky breast, a devastating mind. Knowing the pleasures she's brought me over the years gives this project meaning to me. Moreover, since my project arouses a good deal of excitement and interest whenever I mention it to women *and* men—inspiring them to wax nostalgic over beloved female characters, propose new fighting female narratives, or chime in with their own frustrations regarding depictions of strong, independent women—I hope this work will have as much meaning for other readers.

Chapter Notes

Introduction

1. For overviews on Asian fighting females, see Ric Meyers' chapter "Women Wushu Warriors" in *Films of Fury: The Kung Fu Movie Book,* and for a brief feminist analysis of Asian fighting females, see Wendy Arons' "'If Her Stunning Beauty Doesn't Bring You to Your Knees, Her Deadly Drop Kick Will'" in *Reel Knockouts.* Jeffrey A. Brown's book *Beyond Bombshells* has two excellent chapters that address issues of race and ethnicity in contemporary action heroines on-screen and in comic books.

2. This list is obviously incomplete and doesn't include a number of genres or character types. For example: rape-revenge and final girl characters who emerged in the late 1970s; cartoon fighting females like the *Powerpuff Girls* (1998–2005 / rebooted 2016–present) or the ladies of *Archer* (2009–present); witches using magical violence like those in *Charmed* (the original from 1998–2006 or the 2018 CW reboot) or *The Chilling Adventures of Sabrina* (2018); or criminals—whether forced or intentional ones—who are fighting females, like the characters in *Set It Off* (2002) or *Widows* (2018). The possible entries for this list only continue to grow, exponentially, especially with the ever-increasing contributions from the SyFy Network and The CW.

3. *The Incredibles* came out with a sequel in 2018.

4. See also Stevi Jackson, who addresses the interplay of complicity and resistance in heterosexual love in *Heterosexuality in Question* 114.

5. For an extensive overview of the uses and applications of the term postfeminist (or postfeminism), see Gamble or Genz and Brabon.

6. Like many fans of action drama, I am ready and excited for the changes I see in this arena and amassing research for a more in-depth approach into hetero-alternative representations of on-screen relationships that explores the gender dynamics that race, queer sexualities, non-binary identities, and ability demand, which fall outside the scope of this analysis.

Chapter One

1. See also Friedman as well as Joanne Hollows' chapter on "Women's Genres" for another overview of different feminist views on love and romance.

2. Designated as such in the book of the same name, written by Arlie Hochschild.

3. This phrase was coined in a 1990 *Newsweek* article entitled "Mommy vs. Mommy."

4. Addressed in Anthony Gidden's work on intimacy.

5. See also the collection *Feminism and Community,* edited by Weiss and Friedman.

6. Chapters Two and Three address romance-based partnerships in more detail.

7. Later, Lady Gaga admitted to being "kind of a feminist." For a list of celebrity women who reject feminism, see "I'm Not a Feminist, But…" on *Salon.com.*

8. For further discussions about alternative romance arrangements that fall outside of heteronorms and offer potentially liberating experiences, see Bell & Binnie as well as Berlant.

Chapter Two

1. Critics have made the Nick and Nora association for all of these shows except *Chuck*.

2. Using the term "buddies" is a play on the "buddy cop" terminology used to describe the genre that pairs two male characters, like the *Lethal Weapon* movies, though instead of the pairing leading to love, it led to friendship and camaraderie. Brown identifies and analyzes the implications behind this connection in Chapter Two of *Beyond Bombshells*, where he calls the male-female pairing "buddy-partners."

3. The series began in Britain in 1961 but was only broadcast in the U.S. between 1965 and 1969. Even after the series was syndicated, it included mainly the episodes after 1965.

4. The 1976–77 final season became *McMillan* after the wife was written off in a plane crash.

5. This theme was central to another popular television show in the 1980s featuring fighting females, *Cagney and Lacey*; I deal with it in more detail in Chapter Four.

6. Susan Douglas refers to this change as a "media compromise with feminism" rather than an incorporation (*Where the Girls Are* 218).

7. Up from 37.7 in 1960 ("Women in the Labor Force").

8. Only Alexis Carrington from *Dynasty* (1981–1989), Julia Sugarbaker from *Designing Women* (1986–1993), and Angela Bower from *Who's the Boss* (1984–1992) come to mind. Other women on television, fighting female or not, were employees, usually of male-run or -dominated offices.

9. *Working Girl* (1988) reflected a similar interrogation of women in corporate business from which women had long been excluded, like crime-fighting professions. The film's primary tension was whether Tess McGill (Melanie Griffith) would prove herself worthy of business success. See Tasker's *Working Girls*.

10. In *Moonlighting*, David refers to "the movement" and "the rights women dropped their mops for" in an argument with Maddie, but this is the closest reference that happens in the series.

11. I was not yet a teenager when this "statistic" emerged and still remember the shock and fear it caused. Twenty years later, on June 4, 2006, *Newsweek* printed a follow-up story entitled "Marriage by the Numbers" to retract their findings and report that marriage opportunities for women are more optimistic than they thought. They also claim the terrorist analogy was never meant seriously. Pamela Abramson, the author of the line that was actually first written in a memo, said, "It's true—I am responsible for the single most irresponsible line in the history of journalism, all meant in jest." In New York, writer Eloise Salholz inserted the line into the story. Editors thought it was clear the comparison was hyperbole. "It was never intended to be taken literally," says Salholz. Most readers missed the joke, probably because it was easy to believe when taken in context with all of the similarly dismal reports out there.

12. See Adams.

13. The producers and actors of *Remington Steele* and *Moonlighting* (as well as critics writing about them) explicitly noted how the shows were essentially reboots of just these sorts of screwball comedies so popular in the 1930s and 1940s.

14. For example, in "Vintage Steele" (01.19), we meet the ex with whom she lived for some time, and he describes Laura as "[i]mpulsive. Uninhibited. Absurdly passionate," and he says to Remington, "It must get trying for you at times, keeping her in check?"

15. *TVTropes.org* notes how the trope commonly happens amongst a squabbling male and female pair before they are a couple. Also, the blog *Megapegs Land* provides a list of other examples of this trope, ranging from the film *Father Goose* (1964) to *Cheers* and *Indiana Jones* to *Buffy the Vampire Slayer* and *Gossip Girl*.

16. They rushed to a church to get a priest to marry them, but he wouldn't do it.

17. Kate Beckett said this to Rick Castle (*Castle* 03.14).

18. For example, *How to Get Away with Murder* (2014–20), *Scandal* (2012–8), *Grey's Anatomy* (2005–present), *The Closer* (2005–2012), *The Good Wife* (2009–16), *Parks and Recreation* (2009–2015), *Damages* (2007–2012), *Dexter* (2006–2013), and *Body of Proof* (2011–2013) are all programs with women in positions of power and/or management that have run at the same time.

19. The media scrutiny referred to here is *not* in terms of backlash tactics meant to

undermine feminist social gains by concluding that women don't need or shouldn't have it all—tactics meant to privilege a return to traditional gender roles and the heterosexual contract. This statement refers to media scrutiny from feminists who don't question the validity of having a career, romance, and a family, if so desired, but rather question what stands in the way of its happening or how the concept can even be a backlash tool.

20. I would argue that since 2010, and especially with the rapid development of streaming options since 2015, this white-centrism has been challenged by a new diverse stories and perspectives being shared on all of the available services—even with the limitations the filter bubbles that also accompanied this technological advancement encourage. Also, the highly publicized relationship between Michelle and Barack Obama provided a refreshing model of modern love that impacted many audiences, so much so that their relationship was dramatized in the 2016 movie *Southside with You*.

21. See Szalai.

22. The *Castle* wiki took the joke seriously and actually added up the total number of saves (though it's unclear how many seasons this includes), with Beckett saving Castle only seven times and Castle saving Beckett eleven—though his saves tend to be more happenstance and less violent than hers. Castle saves other characters three times, and Beckett saves others four times ("Who Has Saved Whom?").

23. See also Douglas *Where the Girls Are*.

Chapter Three

1. See Pappas; Mindy et al.; and Griffin.
2. See Mulligan; Morello and Keating.
3. See Friedman.
4. Turner's next most violent female role, Barbara Rose in *War of the Roses* (1989) also died for her violence, but then, so did her husband.
5. This honor even extends to the small screen, where Sydney Vaughn (Jennifer Garner) on *Alias* is probably the first excessively violent woman in love to stay in love by the series' end, but the series finale portraying this happy ending doesn't occur until 2006.
6. *Mr. and Mrs. Smith* DVD insert.
7. The recent movie *Game Night* (2018)

does something similar, with a normal married couple fighting against international smugglers. It's an exciting addition to action film that doesn't include any marital problems and has them working as amateur partners from the start to the finish.

8. Despite the "bromances" that have cropped up over the last ten years, like *The 40-Year-Old Virgin* (2005), *Wedding Crashers* (2005), *Zoolander* (2009), and *The Hangover* franchise.

9. She even made use of her good right hook in the rom-com *The Holiday*, punching a cheating boyfriend, and her fighting cred as the voice of Fiona in the *Shrek* movies—Fiona who proves to be quite a fighter.

Chapter Four

1. The term *detective* here includes cops and FBI agents. The primary role of the fighting female hero is to both discover and apprehend the enemy. Spy heroes differ from the detectives in that they spend less time identifying the criminal and more time organizing and executing the offender's defeat.

2. The book was *From Reverence to Rape* by Molly Haskell, published in 1974.

3. Rosenzweig has since been very vocal supporter of the show, even today, and insists on its influence on all female-driven cop shows to follow.

4. See also D'Acci.

5. Some of these controversial responses to *Thelma and Louise* are mentioned in the previous chapter. Tasker's chapter on "Action Heroines in the 1980s" also provides a useful analysis of the different critical responses to *Thelma and Louise* and *Terminator 2* (*Spectacular*).

6. The influence of the Hill testimony has been well-documented by feminist critics, though not in relation to the victim/agent popular media construction of female identity.

7. The same increase happened after Dr. Blasey Ford's testimony, and *USA Today* reported that "The National Sexual Assault Hotline saw a 57 percent increase in calls compared with an average weekend after Ford went public" (Groppe). RAINN (Rape, Abuse & Incest National Network) manages this hotline.

8. See Sifferlin or Marcotte.

9. See O'Neill or Cain Miller.

10. See "40% of Managers" or "Toronto Woman."
11. See Steiger.
12. See Cooney for a list of the 122 public figures who have been accused of sexual misconduct since the Harvey Weinstein allegations.
13. O'Keefe's article "TV's Renaissance for Strong Women" from *The Atlantic* addresses the increase in varied female character types in recent television.
14. Christine Cagney was played by three different actresses: Loretta Swit in the original TV movie in 1981; Meg Foster for the first televised season in 1982; Sharon Gless for the remainder of the series from 1982–1988 and in the five made-for-TV movies in the 1990s.
15. Both the British version (1991–2006) and its brief U.S. version (2011–12). This chapter only includes an analysis of the former in detail; Chapter Five addresses the reboot.
16. There's some speculation regarding the influence of *Cagney & Lacey* had for creator La Plante. Sharon Gless reported in an interview in 2011 that La Plante wrote *Prime Suspect* as an "homage to us" (Williams), but other writers have noted that La Plante specifically attempted to avoid the melodrama of *Cagney & Lacey* (Cavender and Jurik).
17. See also Hageland.
18. Noomi Rapace portrays this character in the three Swedish versions of the Girl films from 2009 and by Rooney Mara in the 2011 American version of *The Girl with the Dragon Tattoo*.
19. Claire Foy plays Salander in the the film, with Daniel Craig continuing his role as Mikael Blomkvist.
20. Played by Michael Nyqvist and Daniel Craig in the Swedish and American versions, respectively.
21. See Brown, *Beyond Bombshells*, Chapter One for a more in-depth exploration of the action heroine and rape-revenge in the Larsson trilogy.
22. The novel's inception has its own basis in female trauma, inspired as it was by Larsson's experience as a teenager watching a young girl named Lisbeth being gang-raped by three boys—an experience that haunted him thereafter.
23. Not all critics of the show would agree with this, as many felt that after either replacing Meg Foster with Sharon Gless for the Cagney character or the distinct change in styles on the show in season four, the feminist-friendly potential was severely restricted (D'Acci).
24. For some convincing comparisons, see Branch and Doux.
25. Hagelin uses this description in her reading of the movie *GI Jane* (1997).
26. See also Brown's discussion of Blomqvist's character in the Larsson trilogy in Chapter One of *Beyond Bombshells*.
27. Even within feminist circles, assertions of female victimization are not always clear-cut or readily agreed upon. See Wolf and Sommers regarding the rejection of the term or position of victim. See Cole and Lamb for explorations of the effects of rejecting victimhood.
28. See also Genz's work on the "postfeminist woman" and Bell's work on the "Desiring Woman" psychological ideal.
29. There are other platonic examples of nurturing hetero-intimacies throughout the FFFs that have been discussed that go beyond the scope of this chapter's focus.

Chapter Five

1. In 1992, a film version of *BTVS* debuted, but it was not particularly well received.

Conclusion

1. *Supergirl*'s first season was on CBS, and The CW picked it up for its second and subsequent seasons.
2. Another CW show, *The Legends of Tomorrow*, debuted in 2016 and includes an ensemble cast with a bisexual co-lead: Sara Lance, who is also the superhero White Canary (Caity Lotz). One could also argue that the characters Root (Amy Acker) and Sameen Shaw (Sarah Shahi) and their smoldering flirtations on *Person of Interest* were the first co-leads after BTVS, seeing as how they joined the cast in 2013 for the third and remaining seasons, but they were generally supporting characters, not co-leads.
3. The number one storyline is the fight against the primary antagonist.
4. The "crossover" specials are an annual event in which the characters from *Arrow*, *The Flash*, and *Supergirl* come together to

fight new threats emerging from the multiverse. Each program features one crossover episode in varied orders. So, for example, the first crossover episode for "Elseworlds" was on *The Flash* (05.09) on December 9, 2018; the second episode (which introduced Batwoman) was on *Arrow* on December 10, 2018; the third and final crossover episode was on *Supergirl* (04.09) December 11, 2018.

Bibliography

Abele, Elizabeth. *Homefront Heroes: The Rise of a New Hollywood Archetype, 1988–1999.* Jefferson, NC: McFarland, 2014.
Abrams, J.J., creator. *Alias.* Disney-ABC Domestic Television, *Netflix*, 2001.
Adams, Rebecca. "If You Feel Bad about Being Single, It's Not Because You're Single." *Huffpost Women.* TheHuffingtonPost.com. 29 May 2014.
Akil, Salim, creator. *Black Lightning.* Warner Brothers Television, *Netflix*, 2018.
Anne, Libby. "That Just Means He Likes You." *Patheos.* 26 Mar. 2013.
Arons, Wendy. "'If Her Stunning Beauty Doesn't Bring You to Your Knees, Her Deadly Drop Kick Will.'" *Reel Knockouts: Violent Women in the Movies.* Eds. Martha McCaughey and Neal King. Austin: University of Texas Press, 2001. 27–43.
Associated Press. "More Women Postponing Marriage." *The New York Times.* 10 Dec. 1986.
Avedon, Barbara, and Barbara Corday, creators. *Cagney and Lacey.* 20th Century Fox Home Entertainment, CBS, 1981.
Aymar, Jean Christian. "Is the Bechdel Test Overlooking Feminist Films?" *Televisual.* 30 Aug. 2010.
Beauboeuf-Lafontant, Tamara. *Behind the Mask of the Strong, Black Woman: Voice and the Embodiment of a Costly Performance.* Philadelphia: Temple University Press, 2009.
Bell, Leslie C. *Hard to Get: Twenty-Something Women and the Paradox of Sexual Freedom.* Berkeley: University of California Press, 2013.
Berlanti, Greg, Andrew Kreisberg and Ali Adler, creators. *Supergirl.* Warner Brothers Television, CW, 2015.
Berman, Jillian. "Xerox CEO Ursula Burns' Advice for Young Women: Marry Someone Twenty Years Older." *Huffpost Business.* TheHuffingtonPost.com. 20 Mar. 2013.
Black Panther. Dir. Ryan Coogler. Buena Vista Home Entertainment, 2018.
Blue Steel. Dir. Kathryn Bigelow. Lightning Pictures, 1990.
Box Office Mojo. "The Hunger Games: Mockingjay, Part 2." IMDB.com, Inc. N.d.
_____. "Mr. and Mrs. Smith." IMDB.com, Inc. N.d.
Braden, Maria. *Women Politicians and the Media.* Lexington: University Press of Kentucky, 1996.
Branch, Chester Elijah. "Nikita vs. Alias." *Parables Today.* N.p. 5 Aug. 2013.
Brown, Jeffrey A. *Beyond Bombshells: The New Action Heroine in Popular Culture.* Jackson: University Press of Mississippi, 2015.
Butler, Robert, and Michael Gleason, creators. *Remington Steele.* 20th-Century Television, NBC, 1982.
Cain Miller, Claire. "Millennial Dads Aren't the Dads They Thought They'd Be." *The New York Times.* 30 Jul. 2015.

Campion, Jane, and Gerard Lee, creators. *Top of the Lake*. BBC Worldwide, Sundance Channel, 2013.

Caron, Glenn Gordon, creator. *Moonlighting*. Disney-ABC Domestic Television, 1985.

Carroll, Alan. *A Bird, a Plane, a Woman: An Analysis of Factors Influencing Audience Perceptions of Female Characters in DC Comics TV Shows*. 2017. Dundalk Institute of Technology, BA thesis. *Researchgate*.

Cavender, Gray, and Nancy Jurik. *Justice Provocateur: Jane Tennison and Policing in* Prime Suspect. Urbana: University of Illinois Press, 2012.

Clarey, Aaron. "Why You Should Not Go See '*Mad Max*: Feminist Road.'" *Return of Kings*. Kings Media. 11 May 2015.

Clark, Danae. "*Cagney & Lacey*: Feminist Strategies of Detection." *Television & Women's Culture: The Politics of the Popular*. Ed. Mary Ellen Brown. London: Sage, 1990. 117–133.

Clover, Carol. *Men, Women, and Chainsaws: Gender in the Modern Horror Film*. Princeton, NJ: Princeton University Press, 1992.

Cooney, Samantha. "Here Are All the Public Figures Who've Been Accused of Sexual Misconduct After Harvey Weinstein." *Time*. 26 Jan. 2018.

D'Acci, Julie. *Defining Women: Television and the Case of* Cagney & Lacey. Chapel Hill: University of North Carolina Press, 1994.

Date Night. Dir. Shawn Levy. 20th Century Fox, 2010. DVD.

de Beauvoir, Simone. *The Second Sex*. 1952. London: Vintage, 1989.

Depares, Ramona. "*Mad Max: Fury Road*—10 Reasons It Isn't Actually Feminist." *What Culture*. 29 May 2015.

DiBattista, Maria. *Fast-Talking Dames*. New Haven, CT: Yale University Press, 2001.

Dobie Bauer, Sara. "Stephanie Meyer's New *Twilight* Book Infuriates Me." *She Knows*. 6 Oct. 2015.

Dockterman, Eliana. "Shailene Woodley on Why She's Not a Feminist." *Time*. 5 May 2014.

Donalson, Melvin. *Masculinity in the Interracial Buddy Film*. Jefferson, NC: McFarland, 2005.

Douglas, Susan. *Enlightened Sexism: The Seductive Message that Feminism's Work Is Done*. New York: Times Books, 2010.

_____. *Where the Girls Are: Growing Up Female with the Mass Media*. New York: Random House, 1994.

Doux, Billie. "*Alias* Versus *La Femme Nikita*." *Doux Reviews*. N.d.

Dresner, Lisa. *The Female Investigator in Literature, Film, and Popular Culture*. Jefferson, NC: McFarland, 2007.

Duff, James, Michael M. Robin, and Greer Shephard, creators. *The Closer*. Warner Brothers Television Distribution, TNT. 2005.

Dunn, Stephane. *"Baad Bitches" and Sassy Supermamas: Black Power Action Films*. Urbana: University of Illinois Press, 2008.

Ebert, Roger. "Romancing the Stone." RogerEbert.com. Ebert Digital, LLC. 1 Jan. 1984.

"Facts on Working Women." *Women's Bureau*. U.S. Department of Labor. No. 89. 5 Dec. 1989.

Fake TV Critic. "Pilot Review: *Prime Suspect*." Blogspot. 25 Sep. 2011.

Faludi, Susan. *Backlash: The Undeclared War Against American Women*. New York: Three Rivers, 1991.

Ferguson, Kevin J. "Yuppie Devil: Villainy in Kathryn Bigelow's *Blue Steel*." *Jumpcut: A Review of Contemporary Media*. Eds. John Hess, Chuck Kleinhans, and Julia Lesage. 50. Spring 2008.

Fishman, Steve. "The Liman Identity." *New York Magazine*. 13 Jan. 2008.

"40% of Managers Avoid Hiring Younger Women to Get Around Maternity Leave." *The Guardian*. 11 Aug. 2014.

Friedman, Marilyn. *Autonomy, Gender, and Politics*. London: Oxford University Press, 2003.
Gamble, Sarah, ed. *The Routledge Companion to Feminism and Postfeminism*. New York: Routledge, 2001.
Garber, Megan. "Call It 'The Bechdel-Wallace Test.'" *The Atlantic*. 25 Aug. 2015.
Gates, Philippa. *Detecting Women: Gender and the Hollywood Detective Film*. Albany: State University of New York Press, 2011.
Genz, Stephanie. "Singled Out: Postfeminism's 'New Woman' and the Dilemma of Having It All." *The Journal of Popular Culture*. Vol. 43, no.1, 2010, pp. 97–119.
Genz, Stéphanie, and Benjamin A. Brabon. *Postfeminism: Cultural Texts and Theories*. Edinburgh: Edinburgh University Press, 2009.
Gerson, Kathleen. *The Unfinished Revolution: How a New Generation Is Reshaping Family, Work, and Gender in America*. New York: Oxford University Press, 2010.
Girl with the Dragon Tattoo. Dir. by David Fincher, Columbia Pictures, 2011.
_____. Dir. Niels Arden Oplev, Yellow Bird, 2009.
Goldin, Claudia. "The Quiet Revolution That Transformed Women's Employment, Education, and Family." *American Economic Review*. 96.2 (2006): 1–21. JStor.
Goldman, Emma. *Living My Life: Volume I*. Newburyport: Dover, 1970.
_____. *Nowhere at Home: Letters from Exile of Emma Goldman and Alexander Berkman*. Eds. Richard Drinnon and Anna Drinnon. New York: Schocken Books, 1975.
Goodwill, Joe. *New Female Action Hero: An Analysis of Female Masculinity in the New Female Action Hero in Recent Films and Television Shows*. New York: Brave New World, 2011.
Green, Philip. *Cracks in the Pedestal: Ideology and Gender in Hollywood*. Amherst: University of Massachusetts Press, 1998.
Green, Susan. "Violence Against Black Women—Many Types, Far-reaching Effects." *Institute for Women's Policy and Research*.13 Jul. 2017
Greer, William R. "The Changing Women's Marriage Market: Later May Mean Never, Study Says." *The New York Times*. 22 Feb. 1986.
Griffin, Neil. "Losing Your Masculinity: The 'Mancession' and Men's Health." *A Canadian Naturalist*. 18 Nov. 2012.
Grimes, William. "Detective Tennison Develops a Swagger." *The New York Times*. 2 Feb. 1993.
Groppe, Maureen. "Kavanaugh Confirmation: Abuse Allegations Spark Rise in Calls to Sexual Abuse Hotline." *USA Today*. 26 Sep. 2018.
Gross, Jane. "Single Women: Coping with a Void." *The New York Times*. 28 Apr. 1987.
Grossi, Renata. "Romantic Love: A Feminist Conundrum." *The Feminist Wire*. 2 Sep. 2013.
Hagelin, Sarah. *Reel Vulnerability: Power, Pain, and Gender in Contemporary American Film and Television*. New Brunswick, NJ: Rutgers University Press, 2013.
Haglund, David. "Your Favorite Show Is Too Long: Why the Miniseries Is the Ideal Form for Television." *Slate*. 18 Mar. 2013.
Haimoff, Michelle. "Salt!" *Feministing*. Accessed 23 Jul. 2019.
Halberstam, Judith. "Imagined Violence/Queer Violence: Representations of Rage and Resistance." *Reel Knockouts: Violent Women in the Movies*. Eds. Martha McCaughey and Neal King. Austin: University of Texas Press, 2001. 244–66.
Hale, Mike. "A Series Romance Comes Full Circle." *The New York Times*. 10 Aug. 2012.
Han, Angie. "'The Hunger Games' Becomes First Female-Led #1 Film Since 'The Exorcist.'" *Film: Blogging the Reel World*. 10 Jan. 2014.
Hanson, Hart, creator. *Bones*. 20th Century Fox Television. Hulu, 2005.
Hess, Amanda. "Steubenville Gets the Lifetime Treatment (And Cheerleader Erupts into Flames)." *Slate*. The Slate Group. 19. Sep. 2014.

Hill Collins, Patricia. *Black Sexual Politics: African Americans, Gender, and the New Racism.* New York: Routledge, 2004.
Holmes, Brenda. "Stephanie Zimbalist Fan Page." *Facebook.* 12 Nov. 2013.
Holston, Noel. "Sexual Tension Teases Stars and Viewers." *Chicago Tribune.* 9 Feb. 1986.
hooks, bell. *Feminist Theory: From Margin to Center.* Cambridge, MA: Southend Press, 2000.
Hopkins, Susan. *Girl Heroes: The New Force in Popular Culture.* Annandale, NSW: Pluto Press, 2002.
Hornaday, Ann. "Hit-hungry Hollywood Gambles on Litany of 'Romaction' Flicks." *The Washington Post.* 6 Jun. 2010.
Horwitz, Jane. "Undercover Blues." *The Washington Post.* 10 Sep. 1993. Web. Accessed 1 Oct. 2012.
The Hunger Games. Dir. Gary Ross. Lionsgate, 2012.
The Hunger Games: Catching Fire. Dir. Francis Lawrence. Lionsgate, 2013.
The Hunger Games: Mockingjay, Part 1. Dir. Francis Lawrence. Lionsgate, 2014.
The Hunger Games: Mockingjay, Part 2. Dir. Francis Lawrence. Lionsgate, 2015.
Illouz, Eva. *Why Love Hurts: A Sociological Explanation.* Cambridge: Polity, 2012.
Inness, Sherrie A. *Tough Girls: Women Warriors and Wonder Women in Popular Culture.* Philadelphia: University of Pennsylvania Press, 1999.
Jackson, Stevi. *Heterosexuality in Question.* London: Sage, 1999.
Jermyn, Deborah. *Prime Suspect.* British Film Institute, 2010.
Jowett, Lorna. *Sex and the Slayer: A Gender Studies Primer for the Buffy Fan.* Middletown, CT: Wesleyan University Press, 2005.
Kang, Indoo. "What Happened After Swedish Theaters Introduced a Bechdel Rating for Its Movies?" *IndieWire.* Penske Business Media, LLC. 17 Feb. 2016.
Kantor, Jodi, and Megan Twohey. "Harvey Weinstein Paid Off Sexual Harassment Accusers for Decades." *The New York Times.* 5 Oct. 2017.
Kessler-Harris, Alice. "Working Women: Myths and Realities." *The New York Times.* 18 Aug. 1982.
Khomami, Nadia. "#MeToo: how a hashtag became a rallying cry against sexual harassment." *The Guardian.* 20 Oct. 2017.
Killers. Dir. Robert Kuketic. Katalyst Media, 2010.
Kinberg, Simon. "On the Film Program: Simon Kinberg." Columbia University School of the Arts. N.d.
Klauss, Cindy, and Diane Hopkins. "Maddie Hayes." *DavidandMaddie.com: Moonlighting.* CYber SYtes, Inc., 2003.
Knight and Day. Dir. James Mangold. Regency Enterprises, 2010.
La Femme Nikita. Dir. Luc Besson. Gaumont, 1990.
Landay, Lori. *Madcaps, Screwballs, and Con Women: The Female Trickster in American Culture.* Philadelphia: University of Pennsylvania Press, 1998.
Langford, Wendy. *Revolutions of the Heart: Gender, Power, and the Delusions of Love.* London: Routledge, 1999.
La Plante, Lynda, creator. *Prime Suspect.* NBC Universal Televison Distribution, 2011.
_____. *Prime Suspect.* ITV Studios, PBS, 1991.
Lethal Weapon 3. Dir. Richard Donner. Silver Pictures, 1992.
Levy, Emanuel. "Thelma & Louise—Impact of Controversial Movie." Emanuel Levy Cinema 24/7. N.p. 29 Jan. 2011.
Linard, Laura. "Enterprising Women—A History." *Working Knowledge: The Thinking that Leads.* Harvard Business School. 18 Nov. 2002.
Lynch, KC. "*Moonlighting*: Gender in the Reagan Era." *Good, Dirty, or Else.* 5 Apr. 2014. Web. Accessed 15 Apr. 2014.
Marchetti, Gina. "Action-Adventure as Ideology." *Cultural Politics in Contemporary America.* Eds. Ian Angus and Sut Jhally. New York: Routledge, 1989.

Marcotte, Amanda. "Even When They Don't Have Jobs, Men Do Less Work Than Women." *XX Factor: What Women Really Think*. The Slate Group. 6 Jan. 2015.
Marcus, Sara. *Girls to the Front: The True Story of the Riot Grrrl Revolution*. New York: Harper, 2010.
Marlow, Andrew W., creator. *Castle*. Walt Disney Television, ABC, 2009.
Martin, Courtney E. "Confront the Superwoman Mystique." *The New York Times Opinion Pages*. 4 Sep. 2013.
McCaughey, Martha, and Neal King. "What's a Mean Woman like You Doing in a Movie like This?" *Reel Knockouts: Violent Women in the Movies*. Austin: University of Texas Press, 2001. 1–24.
McKenzie, Gracie. "Michelle Obama Says Books Are Better than Boys" *Amy Poehler's Smart Girls*. N.p. 12 Oct. 2015.
Mellencamp, Patricia. *A Fine Romance: Five Ages of Film Feminism*. Philadelphia: Temple University Press, 1995.
Meyers, Ric. *Films of Fury: The Kung Fu Movie Book*. New York: Eirini, 2011.
Mindy, Ronald, Monique Jethwani, and Serena Klempin. "What the Recession Did to American Fathers." *The Atlantic*. 1 Oct. 2012.
Mr. and Mrs. Smith. Dir. Doug Liman. Regency Enterprises, 2005.
Mizejewski, Linda. *Hardboiled and High Heeled: The Woman Detective in Popular Culture*. New York: Routledge, 2004.
_____. "Picturing the Female Dick: *The Silence of the Lambs* and *Blue Steel*." *Journal of Film and Video* 45.2/3 (1993) 6–23.
Morello, Carol and Dan Keating. "More U.S. Women Pull Down Big Bucks." *The Washington Post*. 7 Oct. 2010.
MSN. "Michelle Obama: Books before Boys, Girls." *News*. 30 Sep. 2015.
Mulligan, Casey B. "A Milestone for Working Women?" *The New York Times*. 14 Jan. 2009.
Murder by Numbers. Dir. Barbet Schroeder. Castle Rock Entertainment, 2002.
"NBC Prime Suspect Is Primed for Cancellation." *TV By the Numbers*. Tribune Broadcasting Website. 18 Oct. 2011.
Neroni, Hilary. *The Violent Woman: Femininity, Narrative, and Violence in Contemporary American Cinema*. Albany: State University of New York Press, 2005.
Ng, Philiana. "*Person of Interest* Bosses Talk Major Death, Team Fallout, and Reese Unhinged." *The Hollywood Reporter*. 20 Nov. 2013.
NormStansfiel. "Is This the Fedora that Will Doom NBC's *Prime Suspect*?" *TV.com*. CBS Interactive Inc. 3 Aug. 2011.
Noveck, Jocelyn. "Anita Hill in Spotlight Again as New Film Opens." *The Washington Times*. The Washington Times LLC. 21 Mar. 2014.
O'Keefe, Kevin. "TV's Renaissance for Strong Women." *The Atlantic*. 9 Oct. 2014.
O'Neill, Jennifer. "Why Men Become Sexist After Birth of Their First Baby." *Yahoo! News*. N.p. 28 Jul. 2015.
Orenstein, Peggy. "The Empowerment Mystique." *The New York Times Magazine*. 24 Sept. 2010.
Pappas, Stephanie. "'Mancession' Shifts Gender Roles." *Live Science*. 23 Aug. 2011.
"Percentage of Women Who Are Managers." *Women in the Workforce*. United States Census Bureau. Census.gov.
Perry, Linda A. M. "Difference, Dominance, and Dialectics: A Call for Change" in *Differences that Make a Difference: Examining the Assumptions in Gender Research*. Eds. Lynn H. Turner and Helen M. Sterk. Bergin & Garvey, 1994.
Phillips, Lynne M. *Flirting with Danger: Young Women's Reflections on Sexuality and Domination*. Albany: New York University Press, 2000.
Point of No Return. Dir. John Badham. Warner Bros., 1993.
"Prevalence Rates." *End Rape on Campus*. Accessed 23 Jun. 2019.

Prizzi's Honor. Dir. John Huston. ABC Motion Pictures, 1985.
Rampell, Catherine. "Mancession to He-covery." *The New York Times: Economix.* 6 Jul. 2011.
_____. "The Mancession." *The New York Times: Economix.* 10 Aug. 2009.
Read, Jacinda. *The New Avengers: Feminism, Femininity, and the Rape-Revenge Cycle.* Manchester: Manchester University Press, 2000.
Rosenberg, Melissa, creator. *Jessica Jones. Netflix,* 2015.
Roy, Jessica. "'Michelle Obama urges girls to forget boys and focus on education." *The Cut.* 1 Oct. 2015.
Rubinfeld, Mark D. *Bound to Bond: Gender, Genre, and the Hollywood Romantic Comedy.* Westport, CT: Praeger, 2001.
Rubinstein, Laura. "Can Strong Independent Women Find Love?" *Your Tango.* 7 Jan. 2015.
Rudman, Laurie A., and Peter Glick. *The Social Psychology of Gender: How Power and Intimacy Shape Gender Relations.* London: Guilford, 2008.
Salam, Maya. "A Record 117 Women Won Office, Reshaping America's Leadership." *The New York Times.* 7 Nov. 2018
Salholz, Eloise. "Marriage Crunch: If You're a Single Woman, Here are Your Chances of Getting Married." *Newsweek.* 2 Jun. 1986.
Salt. Dir. Phillip Noyce. Sony Pictures, 2010.
Sama, James Michael. "Power Couples: 10 Traits Men Need to Handle Strong, Independent Women." *Gulf Elite.* Gulfelitemag.com. N.d.
Schoenewolf, Gerald. *The Couples Guide to Erotic Games.* Citadel, 2006.
Schubart, Rikki. *Super Bitches and Action Babes: The Female Hero in Popular Cinema, 1970–2006.* Jefferson, NC: McFarland, 2007.
Schwartz, Josh, and Chris Fedak, creators. *Chuck.* Warner Home Video, NBC Universal Television Distribution, *Netflix,* 2007.
Scott, Joan. *Gender and the Politics of History.* New York: Columbia University Press, 1999.
"Sexual Assault and the LGBTQ Community." *Human Rights Commission.* Accessed 23 Jun. 2019.
Siede, Caroline. "Hollywood's Come a Long Way Baby—But It's Definitely Not a Meritocracy." *Quartz.* N.p. 21 Sep. 2015.
sieglinde. "Prime Suspect: Pilot 9/22/11." *Now Playing: TV Talk Show.* Jelsoft Enterprises Ltd. 23 Sep. 2011.
Sifferlin, Alexandria. "Women Are Still Doing Most of the Housework." *Time.* Time Inc. 18 Jun 2014.
Silverstein, Melissa. "The Sad Death of *Prime Suspect.*" *Women and Hollywood.* Indiewire.com. 29 Nov. 2011.
Sims, Yvonne. *Women of Blaxploitation: How the Black Action Film Heroine Changed American Popular Culture.* Jefferson, NC: McFarland, 2006.
Singer, Ben. "Female Power in the Serial-Queen Melodrama: The Etiology of an Anomaly." *Camera Obscura.* 8.22 (1990) 90–129.
"Softening and Sexualizing Lisbeth Salander." *Oh No They Didn't!* LiveJournal. 30 Dec. 2011.
Spar, Debora L. *Women: Sex, Power, and the Quest for Perfection.* New York: Sarah Crichton Books, 2013.
Stanley, Alessandra. "Female Detectives Revived: One Tough, Others Stylish." *The New York Times Television.* 21 Sep. 2011.
Stasi, Linda. "Jane on Top." *New York Post Entertainment.* 22 Sep. 2011.
Steiger, Kay. "Ted Cruz Just Laid Out the Most Anti-Woman Agenda Yet." *ThinkProgress.* Center for American Progress Action Fund. 23 Mar. 2015.

Stuller, Jennifer K. *Ink Stained Amazons and Cinematic Warriors: Superwomen in Modern Mythology*. London: I.B. Tauris, 2010.
Surnow, Joel, creator. *La Femme Nikita*. Warner Brothers Television. 1997.
_____. *Nikita*. Warner Brothers Television, CW. 2010.
Szalai, Jennifer. "The Complicated Origins of 'Having It All.'" *The New York Times Magazine*. The New York Times Company. 2 Jan. 2015.
Taking Lives. Dir. D. J. Caruso. Warner Brothers Pictures, 2004.
Tasker, Yvonne. *Spectacular Bodies: Gender, Genre, and the Action Cinema*. New York: Routledge, 1993.
"10 Celebrities Who Say They Aren't Feminists." *Huffpost Celebrity*. TheHuffingtonPost.com. 17 Dec. 2013.
Thorne, Barrie. *Gender Play: Girls and Boys in School*. New Brunswick, NJ: Rutgers University Press, 1994.
"Toronto Woman Lyndsay Kirkham Live Tweets Alleged Sexist Conversation of IBM Execs." *Huffpost Living Canada*. TheHuffingtonPost.com. 23 Jul. 2014.
True Lies. Dir. James Cameron. 20th Century Fox, 1994.
Tung, Charlene. "Embodying an Image: Gender, Race, and Sexuality in *La Femme Nikita*." *Action Chicks: New Images of Tough Women in Popular Culture*. Ed. Sherrie A. Inness. London: Palgrave, 2004. 95–121.
Undercover Blues. Dir. Herbert Ross. MGM, 1993.
"Useful Notes: The Bechdel Test." *TV Tropes*. N.p. N.d.
Vares, Tiina. "Action Heroines and Female Viewers: What Women Have to Say." *Reel Knockouts: Violent Women in the Movies*. Eds. Martha McCaughey and Neal King. Austin: University of Texas Press, 2001. 219–43.
Waletzko, Anna. "Why the Bechdel Test Fails Feminism." *Huffpost College*. TheHuffingtonPost.com. 27 Apr. 2015.
Walker, Rebecca. "Being Real: An Introduction." *To Be Real: Telling the Truth and Changing the Face of Feminism*. Ed. Rebecca Walker. New York: Anchor, 1995. XXIX–XL.
Walker-Barnes, Chanequa. *Too Heavy a Yoke: Black Women and the Burden of Strength*. Eugene, OR: Cascade, 2014.
Walsh, David J. "Small Change: An Empirical Analysis of the Effect of Supreme Court Precedents on Federal Appeals Court Decisions in Sexual Harassment Cases, 1993–2005." *Berkeley Journal of Employment & Labor Law* 30.2 (2009) 461–525. *JStor*.
Watson, Amy. "Favorite Film Genres in the U.S. 2018, by Gender." *Statista*. 7 Jul. 2019.
Webb Mitovich, Matt. "Exclusive *Bones* Finale Sneak Peek: Is Booth Above the Law? Is Brennan Slinging a Shotgun?" *TV Line*. TV Line Media, LLC. 15 May 2014.
Weiss, Penny A., and Marilyn Friedman. *Feminism and Community*. Philadelphia: Temple University Press, 1995.
Wexman, Virginia Wright. *Creating the Couple: Love, Marriage, and Hollywood Performance*. Princeton, NJ: Princeton University Press, 1993.
"What Are Women's Favorite Movie Genres to Watch on TV?" *Marketing Charts*. 12 Oct. 2017.
"What Happens When Wives Earn More Than Husbands." *NPR*. 8 Feb. 2015.
"Who Has Saved Whom?" *Castle Wiki*. Wikia. N.d.
Williams, Andrew. "Sharon Gless: *Cagney & Lacey* Has Given Me Lots of Opportunities." *Metro*. Associated Newspapers Limited. 20 Oct. 2011.
Witt, Linda, Karen M. Paget, and Glenna Matthews. *Running as a Woman: Gender and Power in American Politics*. New York: The Free Press, 1994.
Wittig, Monique. *The Straight Mind and Other Essays*. Boston: Beacon, 1992.
Wittmer, Carrie. "The Top Movie Genre Women Love Is 'Action'—and Only 9% Prefer 'Romance' or 'Romantic Comedy.'" *Business Insider*. 8 Mar. 2018.

Woerner, Meredith. "How Angelina Jolie Fought to Keep Salt from Becoming 'Pretty.'" *Gizmodo.* 19 Jul. 2019.
"Women in the Labor Force." *Women's Bureau.* U.S. Department of Labor. N.d.
Zutter, Natalie. "What Rape Apologists Need to Learn From Jessica Jones." *TOR.* Macmillan, 1 Dec. 2015.

Index

The A-Team 57
Abele, Elizabeth 9, 10, 88, 114, 182
accompanying man 176
activism 5, 13, 135–6, 189, 205, 209
Adams Rib 48, 182
Adichie, Chimamanda Ngozi 202
agency 6, 14, 16, 17, 30, 45, 71, 85, 124–6, 128, 130, 136, 139,149, 151, 155, 170–3, 207, 209, 212
Agent Carter 7, 183
Agents of S.H.I.E.L.D. 7, 183
Akil, Salim 209
Alias 8, 18, 69, 128, 152–4, 158–9, 166–7, 168, 175, 183, 220ch3n5, 222n24
Alice 35
Alice in Wonderland 18, 187
Alice Through the Looking Glass 18, 187
Alien 3, 4
ambiguity 38, 54, 60, 77, 78, 161–2, 165, 168, 173
Ang, Ien 30, 66
Anne, Libby 120
anti-feminism 129
Archer 219intron2
Arrow 7, 183, 208, 222–3concn4
Atomic Blonde 7
authority 2, 33, 34, 35, 38, 40–44, 47–8, 53, 55–6, 71, 77, 78, 82, 83, 107, 108, 115, 125, 126, 139, 140–1, 143, 151, 152, 154–6, 158, 160, 179, 180, 189, 193
autonomy 2, 12, 22, 36, 41, 56–7, 65, 81, 83, 85, 97, 103, 104, 139, 152, 154, 175, 189–91, 193, 204, 206, 210, 215
Avedon, Barbara 129
The Avengers (1961) 7, 34, 36, 126, 169
Avengers: Endgame 7
Aymar, Jean Christian 25

Baby Boom 3, 63
backlash 43, 45, 111, 131, 133, 135, 220–221n19
Batwoman 208, 223n4
Beauboeuf-Lafontant, Tamara 212–3
Bechdel-Wallace Test 24–6, 78
Bell, Leslie C. 171–3
Beyoncé 194

Bionic Woman 4, 7, 36, 169, 182
Black Lightning 7, 203, 205–10, 212–3
Black Panther 7, 210–2
Blasey Ford, Christine 132, 137, 221ch4n7
Blaxploitation 6, 8, 36, 169
Blindspot 80
Blue Steel 140, 142, 145–6, 161, 163
Body of Proof 220n18
Bond, James 2, 7, 163
Bones 17, 27, 32, 58–9, 67–8, 75, 175, 179, 183
Brave 187
Breaking Bad 163
Brown, Jeffrey A. 12, 27–8, 30, 145, 151, 160, 188, 189, 219intron1, 220n2, 222n21
"buddy cop" 220n2
Buffy the Vampire Slayer 7, 131, 184, 185, 186, 204, 220n15
Bullock, Sandra 27, 146
Burn Notice 27, 80
Burns, Ursula 75, 180
Butler, Robert 53

Cagney and Lacey 8, 18, 26, 66, 127, 129–30, 13, 136, 138–40, 143–5, 150, 162, 163, 164, 165–6, 180, 220n5, 222n14
Captain Marvel 1, 7, 169, 211
Carroll, Alan 205
Castle 8, 17, 27, 32, 58–9, 60, 61, 62, 67, 68, 69, 71–5, 175, 182, 183, 220n17, 221n22
Charlie's Angels 4, 7, 36, 75, 115
Charmed 219intron2
chauvinism 40, 43, 44, 47, 139, 143
Cheers 62, 220n15
Cherry 2000 87
The Chilling Adventures of Sabrina 219intron2
ChiPs 57
choice 4, 43, 44, 56, 71, 73, 104, 115, 130, 139, 142, 144, 152, 154, 155, 162, 185, 190, 196, 206
Chuck 17, 32, 58, 59–62, 67, 68–9, 70, 71–75
Civil Rights Act of 1991 132
Clinton, Bill 194
Clinton, Hillary 184, 194
The Closer 18, 123, 140, 148, 165–6, 178–81, 182, 183, 220n18

233

Clover, Carol 127, 160
cognitive dissonance 170–2
co-lead 8, 15, 17, 18, 48, 82, 86, 90, 91, 92, 111, 115, 118, 124, 176, 183, 204, 208, 214, 222*concn*2
Colette 5
Columbo 57
Come Drink with Me 7
competition 2, 3, 16, 48, 49, 52, 52, 84, 118, 198, 215
Continuum 7, 183
contradiction 5, 12, 53, 84, 174
Coon, David R. 66–7, 69
cooperation 190, 198, 205
Corday, Barbara 129
Cosby, Bill 135, 137
The Cosby Show 46, 63
Covert Affairs 80, 183
Crazyhead 7
Crouching Tiger, Hidden Dragon 7

Daly, Mary 23
Damages 220*n*18
damsel in distress 16, 211
Date Night 18, 81, 91, 105–09, 110, 111, 112, 116
Day O'Connor, Sandra 40
DC comics 1, 7, 205
Deadpool 2 24
de Beauvoir, Simone 5
"democratization of intimacy" 23
Depares, Ramona 28
Designing Women 220*n*8
Dexter 220*n*18
Diaz, Cameron 105, 114, 115
DiBattista, Maria 2
Die Hard 9, 88
Dirty Harry 164
Divergent franchise 8, 18, 111, 187, 196, 199
diversity 14, 15, 16, 26, 199, 202–5, 213, 214
Dobie Bauer, Sara 29, 200
domestic sphere 34, 48, 65, 82, 84, 88, 102, 115, 215
domination 6, 18, 25, 34, 64, 125–8, 130, 147, 149, 151, 153, 155, 160, 161, 168, 172, 175
Donalson, Melvin 117
Douglas, Susan 75, 77, 79, 127, 129, 133, 160, 168, 173, 178, 185, 220*n*6, 221*n*23
Dresner, Lisa 26, 27
Dunn, Stephane 6
Dworkin, Andrea 23
Dynasty 44, 47, 220*n*8

Ebert, Roger 10
Elementary 79, 183
emotional work 82, 107, 109, 110, 115, 116, 181
emotional intelligence 70, 73–6, 192, 215
enlightened men 56, 120, 142
Enough 7
Erdrich, Louise. 5
The Exorcist 188

Falcon Crest 44

Faludi, Susan 43, 45
Family Ties 63
fans 10, 32, 45, 77, 79, 153, 186, 205, 213, 219*intron*6
Fargo 91
Fatal Attraction 57, 87, 144
Father Goose 220*n*15
femininity 11, 12, 14, 16, 27, 36, 57, 59, 78, 91, 128, 136, 141, 145, 160, 168, 169, 173, 175, 179, 181, 185, 193, 202, 212, 214
femme-fatale 6, 87
La Femme Nikita (1990) 128, 151–2, 153, 168
La Femme Nikita (1997) 128, 151–3, 154, 157, 159, 161
Ferguson, Kevin J. 145
Ferraro, Geraldine 40–1
Fey, Tina 105, 112, 114
The 5th Wave 7
"final girl" 8, 114, 127, 150, 151
Firestone, Shulamith 22, 102
The Flash 7, 183, 205, 222–3*concn*4
The 40-Year-Old Virgin 221*ch*3*n*8
14 Amazons 7
French Kiss 3
Friedan, Betty 102
Friedman, Marilyn 56, 219*ch*1*n*1
Fringe 7, 58

Game Night 221*ch*3*n*7
Game of Thrones 7
Gates, Phillipa 2, 6, 12, 27, 48, 164
gender 11, 51, 59, 63, 84, 94, 95, 102, 115, 159, 168, 188, 202, 209, 214
Generation X 5
Genz, Stéphanie 173, 219*intron*5, 222*n*28
Gerson, Kathleen 81, 85
Get Smart 34, 169
G.I. Jane 7, 131
G.I. Joe 2
Ginsburg, Ruth Bader 184
The Girl in the Spider's Web 146
The Girl with the Dragon Tattoo 18, 127, 146, 150–1, 161, 162 163, 164, 222*n*18
Gleason, Michael 53
Goldin, Claudia. 36–7
Goldman, Emma 5, 22, 202, 215
The Good Wife 220*n*18
Goodwill, Joe 159
Gossip Girl 220*n*15
Green, Philip 9
Green, Susan 136
Greer, Germaine 22, 94
Grey's Anatomy 67, 220*n*18
Grimes, William 177
Grimm 183
Grossi, Renata 18, 23
Guardians of the Galaxy 7
Gurley Brown, Helen 63

Hagelin, Sarah 126, 131, 156, 168, 222*n*25
Hale, Mike 141

Index

Hamer, Fanny Lou 209
Hamilton, Linda 4, 60, 131
Hamm, Mia 184
The Hangover 221*ch*3*n*8
Harrington, Penny 41
Hart to Hart 34, 169, 182, 185
have it all 3, 62–6, 71, 75, 79, 89, 90, 98, 105, 121, 134, 137–8, 162, 164, 173, 177, 194, 221*n*19
Having It All (1982) 63
"he for she" 194–5, 200
The Heat 8, 164
"hecovery" 84
Heigl, Katherine 105, 112, 114
hetero-intimacy 11, 12, 52, 54, 55, 59, 80, 81, 82, 83, 87, 91, 116, 117, 126, 161, 164, 174, 203
heteronorms 6, 12, 15, 16, 23, 24, 27, 54, 120, 122, 137, 164, 174, 199, 204, 205, 208, 215, 219*intron*6
hetero-romance 13, 16, 21, 28, 50, 54, 57, 78, 80, 82, 88, 90, 116, 117, 118, 162, 168, 194, 195, 198, 204, 205
heterosexual contract 33–5, 38, 48, 50, 55, 69, 76–7, 78, 221*n*19
Hill, Anita 132–3, 137, 178, 221*ch*4*n*6
Hill Collins, Patricia 64, 213
Hochschild, Arlie 23, 65, 108, 219*ch*1*n*2
Hoff Summers, Christina 185
The Holiday 221*ch*3*n*9
Hollywood 6, 9, 83, 90, 113, 116, 133, 135
Holmes, Brenda 45, 79
Holston, Noel 62
hooks, bell 64, 209
Hopkins, Susan 95
Hornaday, Ann 83, 86, 90, 114, 116
How to Get Away with Murder 220*n*18
The Hunger Games 8, 18, 111, 187–94, 196, 201, 208
Hurston, Zora Neale 5

Illouz, Eva 22
"imagined violence" 169
In Plain Sight 80
The Incredibles 9, 219*intron*3
Indiana Jones 87
Inness, Sherri A. 12, 25, 26, 27, 29, 87, 110, 160, 164
intersectional standpoint 203
iZombie 7

Jackson, Stevi 22–3, 29, 219*intron*4
Jay-Z 194
Jem 2
Jermyn, Deborah 148, 149, 161
Jessica Jones 7, 127, 147, 151, 159, 161, 162, 163, 167, 168, 183, 203
Jewel of the Nile 2, 86
Jolie, Angelina 92, 94, 112, 114, 135, 146, 154, 157, 187
Jones, Grace 2
Jong, Erica 5
Jowett, Lorna 13, 19, 36

Kavanaugh, Brett 132
Kerrigan, Nancy 184
Kessler-Harris, Alice 37
Kill Bill 7
Killers 18, 81, 105, 109–11, 112
Kinberg, Simon 112–13
King, Neale 11
Knight and Day 81, 91, 105, 114–5, 119

LA Law 47
Lady Gaga 29, 136, 219*ch*1*n*7
Landay, Lori 2
Langford, Wendy 17, 22, 25
La Plante, Lynda 140, 177, 222*n*16
The Last Ship 7
leadership 14, 40, 41, 42, 134, 176, 191, 194, 195, 205
Legends of Tomorrow 7, 222*concn*2
Lethal Weapon 88–9, 90, 220*n*2
LGBTQA+ 137, 204, 208
liberated romance 182
Lifetime Network 136
lone-wolf 8, 9, 17, 23, 29, 91, 109, 163–4, 182
The Long Kiss Goodnight 91
Lynch, KC 45

Mad Max: Fury Road 10–1, 28, 147
Mad Men 133
Magnum P.I. 57
Major Crimes 183
Maleficent 187, 198, 199
man-hating 6, 80, 118, 161, 168, 195, 202
"mancession" 84
Marchetti, Gina 83, 85
Marvel 1, 147
The Mary Tyler Moore Show 35
masculinity 10, 14, 26, 95–6, 145, 168, 170, 171, 174, 175, 179, 181, 182–3, 191, 193, 199, 200
matrix of domination 64
Maude 35
McCaughey, Martha 11
McMillan & Wife 34, 169, 182, 220*n*4
#MeToo 134, 135, 186
Mellencamp, Patricia 160
"men's rights advocates" 135
Meyer, Russ 6
Milk Money 4
Mill, John Stuart 5
Millett, Kate 23
misogyny 96, 118, 148, 150, 161, 177, 178, 182, 96, 150, 161, 177, 178, 182
Miss Congeniality 2: Armed and Fabulous 27
Mission Impossible 157
Mr. and Mrs. Smith 18, 81, 88, 91–105, 108, 112–4, 116–7, 118, 119, 121, 124, 157, 175, 179, 209, 221*ch*3*n*6
Mizejewski, Linda 26, 56
"mommy wars" 23
monogamy 19, 208
Moonlighting 26, 32, 37, 39, 43, 45, 47, 50, 51, 54, 55, 56–7, 62, 87, 220*n*10

Mulan 184
Murder by Numbers 18, 140, 142, 146, 161, 163, 169
"musculinity" 8
The Mysteries of Laura 183

Natural Born Killers 91
Neroni, Hilary 8, 12, 26–7, 91, 94, 103
Netflix 127
Nikita 151, 153, 158, 166, 167, 168, 183, 222n24
Nin, Anaïs 5
No Ordinary Family 206
Norsemen 7
Noveck, Jocelyn 132
NYPD Blue 67

Obama, Michelle 21, 30, 31, 184, 221n20
objectification 11, 44, 50, 126, 139, 160, 199, 216
Once Upon a Time 187
oppression 17, 19, 22, 64, 66, 125, 126, 135, 137, 160, 173, 185, 186, 189, 193, 194, 210, 213, 215
Orange Is the New Black 24
Orenstein, Peggy 172
Orphan Black 7, 183

Paglia, Camille 185
Parks and Recreation 220n18
partner betrayals 126, 151, 158
partnership orientation 78
paternalism 18, 151, 155, 156, 209
Pearce, Lynne 30
Perry, Linda A. M. 103–4
Person of Interest 222concn2
Phillips, Lynne M. 170, 171–2, 174
Pitt, Brad 92, 112, 113
Point of No Return 128, 151, 161
Police Academy 57
Policewoman 36
polyamory 66
postfeminism 19, 23, 85, 125, 219intron5
"postfeminist sensibility" 23
Powerpuff Girls 219intron2
prejudice 40, 125, 139, 141, 142, 143, 150
Pretty Woman 3
Prime Suspect (American) 18, 150, 176, 178, 179, 182, 184
Prime Suspect (British) 18, 33, 34, 65, 67, 69, 70, 81, 117, 123, 127, 140, 142, 148, 149, 177, 178, 179, 184
Prizzi's Honor 87, 88
The Proposal 4
proto-romaction 88, 90, 92, 97, 114
"pseudo-tough" 29, 110
public sphere 33, 34, 65, 67, 68, 69, 70, 81, 85, 108, 117
Pygmalion 4

Quantico 183
"quiet revolution" 36

race 14, 15, 16, 26, 65, 137, 209–10, 214, 219intron1
Radway, Janice 30
Rambo 163–4
Rampell, Catherine 84
rape-revenge 8, 151, 219intron2, 222n21
Rapinoe, Megan 184
Read, Jacinda 151
recession 84–5
Red Sonja 7, 88
Red Sparrow 7
redemptive parallel 167–8, 176, 205, 209
Remington Steele 8, 17, 26, 32, 36, 37, 38, 41–2, 43, 44–5, 47, 49–50, 52–3, 55–7, 62, 87, 139, 182, 220n13
Resident Evil 4
Rice, Condoleeza 184
Rich, Adrienne 5, 23
Riot Grrrl 161
Rizzoli & Isles 8, 164, 183
Romancing the Stone 2, 10, 86
Rubin, Gayle 23
Rubinfeld, Mark D. 97
Rudman, Laurie A. 121

Salam, Maya 136
Salt 8, 18, 128, 152, 154, 157, 158, 161, 162, 163
Sandberg, Sheryl 75, 180
Santa Clarita Diet 8
Scandal 220n18
Schoenewolf, Gerald 119
Scott King, Coretta 209
Schubart, Rikki 12, 160
Scott, Joan 121
"second shift" 23, 65, 108, 133
Set It Off 219intron2
sexism 4, 10, 16, 18, 30, 40, 77, 123, 126, 138–40, 142–3, 149–50, 159, 160, 169, 176, 177–9, 184, 185, 193
sexual assault 18, 135, 136, 137, 138, 140, 143–51, 160, 163, 170, 172, 193, 221ch4n7
sexual harassment 129, 132, 134, 135, 139, 143, 178
sexual orientation 14, 15, 25, 26, 137, 164, 208, 214
She-Ra 2
Shepherd, Cybill 26, 32, 37, 54, 79
Shrek 221ch3n9
Silence of the Lambs 4, 131, 140, 142, 149, 161, 164
Silverstein, Melissa 150
Sims, Yvonne 6, 36
Singer, Ben 2
"slap-slap kiss" 51–2
Sleeping with the Enemy 7
Sleepy Hollow 80, 183
Snow White and the Huntsman 187, 197–9
social justice 3, 70, 215
Solo: A Star Wars Story 24
Southside with You 221n20
Spar, Deborah L. 65, 134

Spice Girls 184
Spy (2015) 8
Spy Kids 9
Stacey, Jackie 30
Stanley, Alessandra 178
Star Wars franchise 7
Stasi, Linda 177
Steubenville 136
Strahovski, Yvonne 33, 58
Strange Days 91
"strong black woman" 211–3
Stuller, Jennifer K. 23
subordination 6, 16, 22–3, 25, 29, 35, 189
Supergirl 7, 169, 203–5, 208, 222*concn*1, 222–3*concn*4
superhero 1, 7, 15, 95, 96, 169, 203, 204, 205–6, 207–8, 222*concn*2
Superman 1, 203, 205
"superwoman" 65, 79, 93, 107, 212
survivor 18, 123, 128, 129–31, 134, 135, 136–7, 142, 147, 151, 166, 169–70, 172, 173, 175, 176, 193, 205, 212
Swopes, Sheryl 184

Taking Lives 140, 142, 146, 161, 163, 169
Taming of the Shrew 4
Tasker, Yvonne 2, 8, 12, 128, 220*n*9, 221*ch*4*n*5
Ten Things I Hate About You 4
Terminator 2 4, 131, 132 221*ch*4*n*5
Thatcher, Margaret 40
Thelma & Louise 4, 8, 131, 221*ch*4*n*5
The Thin Man 32–3
Thor: Ragnarok 7
Thorne, Barrie 121
Le Tigre 161
Top of the Lake 140, 142, 145, 163
transgender 137, 204
trauma 27, 91, 124, 127, 146, 147, 150, 162, 168, 170, 173, 205, 222*n*22
True Lies 89–90, 110
Tubman, Harriet 209
Tung, Charlene 11
Turner, Kathleen 86, 87, 90, 114

Undercover Blues 90–1
The Undercovers 206
Untraceable 27

Van Helsing 7
Vares, Tiina 8

Veronica Mars 80, 184
victim 8, 9, 10, 18, 31, 38, 64, 73, 74, 86, 126–9, 133, 134, 135–8, 144–51, 159, 165, 166, 168, 169–74, 179, 185, 192, 193, 200, 205, 212, 215, 221*ch*4*n*6, 222*n*27
"victim feminism" 185
Vikings 7
Violet & Daisy 7

Walker, Alice 5
Walker, Rebecca 5
Walker-Barnes, Chanequa 211, 212
Walsh, Andrea 27
war between the sexes 4, 16, 83, 116, 119, 120, 121
War of the Roses 221*ch*3*n*4
"war on women" 134
Warehouse 13 80
The Watchmen 147
Watson, Emma 195
The Wedding Crashers 221*ch*3*n*8
Weinstein, Harvey 135, 222*n*12
Wexman, Virginia Wright 100
When Harry Met Sally 3
Whiskey Cavalier 80
Who's the Boss 220*n*8
Widows 221*intron*2
will-they-won't-they? 33, 37, 47, 50, 55, 57, 62, 78, 158, 206
Wittig, Monique 33
Wolf, Naomi 185
Wollstonecraft, Mary 5, 17, 22
Woman of the Year 48, 182
women's rights 12, 140
Wonder Woman 1, 4, 7, 36, 145, 169, 182, 211
Woodley, Shailene 29, 187
workforce 33, 35, 36–7, 39, 48–9, 64, 76, 77, 82, 85, 134
Working Girl 220*n*9
World War II 48
Wynonna Earp 7

The X-Files 7, 57
Xena: Warrior Princess 7, 25, 131, 184

"Year of the Woman" 133, 136
You've Got Mail 3

Zoolander 221*ch*3*n*8
Zutter, Natalie 147

www.ingramcontent.com/pod-product-compliance
Lightning Source LLC
Chambersburg PA
CBHW032038300426
44117CB00009B/1110